D1232105

The Mindscapes of Art

The Mindscapes of Art

*Dimensions of the Psyche
in Fiction, Drama, and Film*

Roy Huss

Rutherford • Madison • Teaneck
Fairleigh Dickinson University Press
London and Toronto: Associated University Presses

© 1986 by Associated University Presses, Inc.

Associated University Presses, Inc.
440 Forsgate Drive
Cranbury, N.J. 08512

Associated University Presses Ltd
25 Sicilian Avenue
London WC1A 2QH, England

Associated University Presses
2133 Royal Windsor Drive
Unit 1
Mississauga, Ontario, Canada L5J 1K5

The paper used in this publication meets the minimum requirements of the American National Standard for Permanence of Paper for Printed Library Materials Z39.48-1984.

Library of Congress Cataloging in Publication Data

Huss, Roy, 1927-
  The mindscapes of art.

  Bibliography: p.
  Includes index.
  1. Literature—Psychology. 2. Moving-pictures—
  Psychological aspects. I. Title.
  PN56.P93H87   1985 6801'.92   82-49280
  ISBN 0-8386-3182-7 (alk. paper)

Printed in the United States of America

For
Jim Allen
and
Ted and Rhoda Ross

Publisher's Note

In January 1983 Roy Huss was reported missing while traveling in Sumatra. Subsequent investigation led to the conclusion that he had been murdered in the course of a robbery. Proofreading and preparation of the index was done by Rhoda H. Ross.

Contents

Acknowledgments

Some of the material in this book has appeared in different form in various journals. For permission to transcribe passages from my own articles I wish to thank the editors of *The Psychoanalytic Review, The International Review of Psycho-Analysis, Literature/ Film Quarterly*, and *Modern Drama*. I am also grateful to the individuals and organizations listed below for permission to reproduce four stills used as illustrations for the text:

Ms. Eve Adamson, artistic director of the Jean Cocteau Repertory, for permission to use a still from her production of *Kirche, Kutchen, und Kinder* in 1979–1980.

Euro International SPA and Paramount Pictures for permission to use a still from *Brother Sun, Sister Moon*, copyright 1972.

Franklin Media and John Springer Associates for permission to use a still from *Each Other*, copyright 1979.

Paramount Pictures for permission to use a still from *A Separate Peace*, copyright 1972.

Among the people to whom I owe special thanks are Murray Sherman, former editor of *The Psychoanalytic Review*, for encouraging my work in applied psychoanalysis as a staff member of his journal, and Alan Roland for encouraging me to train as a psychoanalyst and for demonstrating in his clinical work and writings the value of a background in the arts. To Linda Heinz, who was my collaborator on the original version of the article on *A Separate Peace*, I wish to express my gratitude not only for her permission to restate some of our shared insights but for the kind of inspiration that only an enthusiastic student can provide.

Introduction

A few years ago the *New York Times*, looking for colorful high-lights in the gray welter of scholarly papers at the Modern Language Association convention in New York, chose to print one participant's vitriolic remarks about the value of psychoanalytic criticism. "Without exception I find it to be absurd, irrelevant, and damaging to literature," the speaker declared. In 1960 a critic writing about the impact of John Osborne's *Look Back in Anger* upon contemporary theater both here and abroad forewarned that psychoanalytic critics would soon be "sniffing at the bed pans" of the play's social realism.[1] Similarly, we find anti-psychoanalytic critics throughout the decades bewailing interpreters who might be concerning themselves with "such things as Hamlet's toilet train-ing."

Leaving aside any speculation on why such critics feel compelled to draw their metaphors from the excretory functions to express their aversion for psychoanalytic interpreters, let us briefly examine the standard objections to approaching a work of art psy-choanalytically:

> *Objection No. 1*—A fictional character is not a person with a past or future beyond the text, and therefore cannot be sub-jected to an analysis of his psychosexual development, childhood traumas, etc.

As against this objection, however, it may be allowed that readers and audiences are interested in the representational arts because characters empathized with as human are involved in recognizably human conflicts. Even "straight" literary critics speak of motivation, dénouement, climax, and catharsis—all of them emotional qualities. And Aristotle spoke of drama as the movement of the protagonist's "psyche," which of course encompassed feelings as well as mind and soul. Psychoanalysis can, within the framework of the given text, make submerged patterns or obscure relationships come into focus. The early

psychoanalytic critics, particularly those of Freud's circle in
Vienna, were unfortunately predisposed to deforming criticism
and interpretation by treating fictional characters as case studies
detached from the text and context in which they are presented.
But modern critics need not do so.

The answer to the objection, therefore, is to admit at once the
absurdity of speculating on the details of Hamlet's toilet training
but to insist on the value of citing his Oedipal reasons for not killing Claudius, as reflected and confirmed, of course, by as many
aspects of character, conflict, imagery, and language as can be
cited. In general, any interpretation—whether psychological, biographical, cultural, linguistic, or archetypal—that leads us away
from a comprehensive view of the text has little validity. Similarly,
any critical framework that throws light on the unity and effect of
the whole work seems worth considering.

Objection No. 2—Psychoanalytic criticism is usually reductive,
    that is, reduces a rich tapestry of feeling and personal rela-
    tionships to a simplistic causal statement.

For some odd reason *reductivism* is usually the first word
uttered by anti-psychoanalytic critics, whereas these same critics
never use that term to describe other approaches that, like all
strategies, are to some degree limited or unsatisfactory.* The truth
is that any interpretation that does not account for every aspect of
a work, either in its quantitative or in its qualitative parts, is
"reductive." Insofar as psychoanalysis itself becomes less
obsessionally concerned with tracing the phylogenetic and
ontogenetic roots of personality and more involved with
uncovering the dynamics of relationships, it can be seen to be
holistic rather than reductive. And it can be valid whether it
concentrates on the *intra*psychic sphere of a character's conflicted
desires and motives or on the *inter*psychic opposing claims of
different characters or of characters and their cultural milieus.

Objection No. 3—Psychoanalytic criticism can elucidate the
    dynamics of a work of art but does not provide any touch-
    stones for distinguishing good works from those which are
    mediocre of trash.

*For instance, in the plethora of papers with which literary journals are inundated, entitled
"Form and Structure in the Novels of _____," the emotional complexity of a character
is often lost in the desire to point out his paradigmatic function, and the historical or social
relevance of the text may be ignored entirely.

Suzanne Langer most prominently raised this issue in the 1940s in her classic work *Philosophy in a New Key*, and several critics have since echoed her complaint.

Frankly, I do not think any school of criticism, plan of attack, or individual reviewer can definitively tell us whether a work of art is good or bad, or even aesthetically pleasing. Or at least they cannot go much beyond the faith we have in their system of reference or our own liking for an individual critic. The late F. R. Leavis frequently used the word *mature* to exalt the works he admired, but *mature* is a slippery term that we accept from Leavis mainly because of his self-possessed tone and scholarly reputation. The emotional impact of a work of course precedes the job of interpretation, which of course may recolor the first impression before it leads to a set judgment or evaluation. Critics like Leavis try to establish laws for the more cerebral part of this process, which may relate to such externals as "social relevance," but they can only either entirely suppress or convey somewhat impressionistically their initial emotional responses.

The best that can be said of psychoanalytic interpretation—I insist on the word *interpretation* (elucidation) rather than *criticism* (normative judgment)—is that it can reveal more than the tips of icebergs, the heretofore impalpable parts of a work. The reader/viewer can then be shown by the psychoanalytic interpreter whether these parts cohere, belong, as it were, in the same sea of feeling and meaning—in other words, whether there is real connectedness among apparently disparate parts.

Although the discovery that a work is indeed a "well-wrought urn" is usually pleasant, a competently constructed work is, nevertheless, not necessarily a great work of art. It may in fact be quite dull, like, for example, the architectonically perfect symphonies of Spohr. What animates the work and its audience will always be an elusive "dystax," a disorderly rather than a connected system. Taste here, as always, must be the final arbiter. Any critical approach ultimately does not have an aesthetic reference beyond itself.*

Objection No. 4—Psychoanalytic criticism assumes that art stems from the pathological condition of an artist or of his

---

*In chapter 1, in which I compare and contrast the ways Freud and latter-day depth psychologists view artistic form, I raise the question of to what extent psychoanalysis can actually throw light on form as opposed to content alone, and then question whether such attempts, even when successful, really provide a clear means for distinguishing between "good" and "bad" art.

age—what Joyce Carol Oates calls the "art out of neurosis theory of culture."[2]

Since the dramatic impact of works of representational fiction always stems from a disruption of humdrum everyday activity, there is a sense in which our interest in literature, drama, and film must always focus on the "abnormality" of a character's life condition. However, the recent emergence of a psychology of normal development, including both cognitive psychology (e.g., that of Piaget) and the psychology of early object relations (e.g., that of Winnicott, Klein, Mahler, et al.), allows us to look at the more universal aspects of a character's *vicissitudes*, which is a better word to use than *conflict* when we think of stages of maturation. The newer ego-psychologies that stress the integrative as well as the defensive functions of the ego and the still more recent formulation of a "self-psychology" that focuses on the cohesiveness of the self promise a greater emphasis on emotional growth than on the pathology of repression, regression, perversion, and fixation in dealing with fictional characters. This is consistent with our old-fashioned desire to find life-enhancing insights, cathartic releases of tension, and *universal* conditions of suffering and joy in comedies, tragedies, and romances.

Therefore psychological critics heretofore predisposed to seeing a work or a character in a work as merely a symptom, sign of defense, or even sublimation of the author's neurosis, have, because of these recent theoretical and clinical developments, been given a new slant on the communicative aspect of art. Now psychological criticism can draw upon the concept of an integrative and synthesizing force in the ego and in the self—which indeed may encompass *conflict* in the sense of a set of opposing forces held in dynamic balance—rather than counting on merely defensive maneuvers being at work. Gilbert Rose, for instance, sees the power of artistic form as growing out of the artist's ability to fluctuate comfortably between the pleasures of symbiosis, characteristic of neonatal life, and the more conflict-ridden process of individuation of later development.[3]

When we look at the whole question of art-as-communication from a psychological point of view, we gain still another perspective. Critics have for a long time been tied to Freud's notion that art transmits under repression the artist's taboo drives, wishes, and impulses and that the work's form is both a disguise and a "forepleasure" for the forbidden desires lurking in the unconscious and preconscious underlayer of the psyche. Later, Norman Holland looked more at the receiver than at the sender of the communication. In his milestone work *The Dynamics of Literary Response* he emphasized the aspects of the work of art that allowed the reader to manage and defend against certain consciously unacceptable fantasies, particularly ones of oral eroticism and aggression that are stimulated by the very act of reading, which is itself a gesture of "oral" incorporation.

More recently, however, Holland has been exploring the matter of audience response a bit differently, and I think more fruitfully because he emphasizes the integrative function of art—to which I just referred—rather than its defensive nature. This is his notion of an "identity theme" that readers bring to a work in the hope of finding a confirmation of a solid and continuous self. The ingredients here would be not only the problems of their own emotional development (such as symptoms, traumas, and complexes) but their ego-ideals, past identifications, and their joy from a sense of autonomy in the unconflicted areas of their egos. Since one's "identity" is constructed not only from all of these but out of influences from the culture and the environment as well, interpreting a work of art in terms of one's own identity theme can become an act of empirical richness.[4]

Another virtue of Holland's most recent reader-oriented approach to literature is that it threatens the too-complacent neo-Aristotelian tendency in art criticism to postulate for a work a universal audience (e.g., Aristotle's "a tragedy is the story of a man better than *we* are"). It also indirectly attacks the wish of the so-called new critics to see the work of art solely as a "well-wrought urn," its meaning remaining independent of the matrix of its creation or the world of its perceivers. The recent emergence of psychohistorical and psychobiographical criticism has of course offered the same kind of salutary threats.

ii

How a work can be plumbed for ever deeper feelings and meanings when we apply our accumulated knowledge of depth psychology can be illustrated in brief by looking at D. H. Lawrence's short story "The Prussian Officer." Here as elsewhere in his fiction Lawrence self-consciously wrote from a psychoanalytic perspective, frequently using words like *consciousness, the subconscious*, and *repression*. In this tale few readers could miss his rather manifest point that the officer's sadistic treatment of his orderly is an attempt to deny his homosexual attraction to him. Traditional Freudians are tempted to regard the officer's horror and fascination with the orderly's scarred thumb as fear of retaliatory castration for his barely repressed wishes, and his over-reaction to the spilled wine as fear of arousal to ejaculation. This is of course true, but it accounts for a very small part of the tale, for the story really focuses more on the feelings and behavior of the young orderly, detailing the steps of his emotional and physical breakdown under the pressure of the officer's persecution. Our empathy for this part of the narrative is deepened by recent clinical descriptions of the process of psychotic decompensation, beginning with the depersonalization of self that the orderly practices as his main defense against the officer's cruel intrusions. Also, we can hardly read these passages without thinking of such Laingian phrases as "divided self" and "ontological loneliness."[5]

Finally, we can better understand the nature of the orderly's semi-delirious wanderings after he kills the officer as a regression to and reenactment of earlier stages of identification and separation, the whole relationship between the orderly and the captain having evolved before the murder into a parody of a defective symbiosis between infant and mother. What at first appears to be solely a denial of sexual attraction reveals itself, both for the orderly and the officer, to be a denial of symbiotic fusion, which is shown in a number of ways: by the way in which the two shadow each other, by their sensitivity to each other's eyes (the essential communication of mother and child during nursing), and by their counterbalancing increase and depletion of energy. In regard to this last phenomenon, recent observations of mother-infant behavior have shown that a happy symbiosis between mother and child engenders a mutual surge of energy and well-being; a defective one imbued with frustration and anger causes one member of the pair to feel obliterated when the other tries to assert his independent wishes. Lawrence makes it clear at several points that this ebb and flow of energy between a feeling of nullity and one of soaring excitement constantly passes back and forth between the two men.

The dryness in the orderly's mouth caused by the officer's constant railing and intense scrutiny amounts to a deprivation of the maternal breast for this symbiotically involved young man, exacerbated by the mutual aversion of eye contact. Understandably, the action that provokes the orderly to kill the officer is the latter's vampiric reversal of the infant-mother role of feeder-nourisher when he gulps down the tankard of beer. By breaking that thin guzzling neck (with which he has suddenly become obsessed) and thus cutting off oral gratification (as well as life itself), the orderly masochistically reestablishes an identification with, and thus a symbiotic tie to, the officer.

A negative symbiotic bonding, in which healthy separation is impossible, thus seems to be revealed in the final hours of the orderly's life. Our understanding of this makes some of his hypersensitive reactions and hallucinations seem less arbitrary. The woman in the fields, who might have quenched his thirst had he asked her for water, he projects as the bad mother who would look without seeing him. This seeming denial of the contact that he longs for and that he once had from his very maternal peasant girl friend, evolves into the nightmare of the squirrel's eyes monstrously exaggerated in size, the eyes of the nursing mother becoming those of a Brobdingnagian giantess. That the woman in the field "would make a noise of words that would confuse him" is more an indication of his regression to the preverbal state of infancy (for he too "had no language with which to speak to her") than a real indication of hostile action on her part.

The anxiety-provoking aspects of the sadism in the symbiosis with the officer have clearly caused a splitting into multiple ego states and a feeling of emptiness and remoteness. Lawrence's picture of this psychological condition almost amounts to an impressionistic case study of the schizoid personality:

> He [the orderly] lay still, in a kind of dream of anguish. His thirst seemed to have separated itself from him, and to stand apart, a single demand. Then the pain he felt was another single self. Then there was the clog of his body, another separate thing. He was divided among all kinds of separate beings. There was some strange, agonized connection between them, but they were drawing further apart. Then they would all split.[6]

We now understand the orderly's refusal to seek water to be a masochistic collusion with the determination of the mother/officer not to nourish him. Thus the spilled wine takes on another meaning, as does the distant mountain lake (now internalized as unattainable mother).

Indeed, deeper psychological penetration into the tale prevents us from dismissing Lawrence's magnificent descriptions of nature as merely decorative. One might say many things about them, but the psychoanalyst would see that they reflect the personality structures of the protagonists and resonate with the projections of their inner needs. The sunlit-checkered fields that are like the variegated patterns of diurnal life are placed in contrast to the cool blue mountain, which, with its peaks like "gentle blue folds" and gleaming snow and lakes (later described as "cool and tender"), suggests throughout the story the ideal nourishing maternal body that can never be reached. These images embody the same paradoxes of change and timelessness, of discontinuousness and harmony that characterize the fluctuating merging and individuating propensities that are held in balance in all of us and that Gilbert Rose sees as the magnetic power of form in great art.[7]

Here Lawrence's intuition and artistry go beyond his self-conscious Freudianisms, for he anticipates later object-relations theorists who have only recently been able to formulate how relationships begin in original undifferentiated experience, in which the mother is not separated from the self-image, fantasies, and wishes of the child, a state that is blissful when the mother is loving and at ease, but frightening and seemingly annihilating when otherwise. Thus succeeding developments in psychological theory and clinical practice add broader and deeper unity to our aesthetic responses and intellectual understanding of Lawrence's story.

iii

Obviously, as long as we guard against the reductivistic dangers enumerated earlier, our increase in psychological knowledge and awareness continues to validate the practice of dealing psychoanalytically with characters that appear in representational art. As Norman Friedman has pointed out, "we need not . . . be concerned with psychoanalyzing writers, or regard art as a neurotic symptom, or assume that fictional characters are 'real,' and so on, in order to make profitable use of psychology," for "if we regard it as a way of enlarging and deepening—conceptualizing, if you will—our already considerable knowledge of human emotions and motivations, then we will appreciate the possibilities of combining psychology and criticism in a unified approach."[8]

It is the intention of this study to redirect attention to the psychological interpretation of the *characters* of fiction, drama, and film, and to do so in such a way as to allow a whole new spectrum of psychological approaches to demonstrate their value. It will be apparent throughout, I think, that the particular psychological framework (or frameworks) chosen to illuminate a specific work is partly by invitation, so to speak, of the work itself. That is, just as some patients in therapy seem to dream Jungian dreams instead of Freudian ones, so also do some works seem to reveal more of their "inner dimensions" to one conceptual approach than to another, although in some instances a pluralistic view will be seen to be of even greater value in getting most of the facets of a work to shine forth. Thus this book is designed to demonstrate from a variety of depth psychologies the richness and flexibility of the psychological interpretations of the fictional arts.

By beginning with a reevaluation of traditional Freudian views of character and form in art and then moving rapidly to the approaches of both Freudian dissidents and later neo-Freudian elaborators, I have in a rough way made the arrangement of my psychological interpretations of literature, drama, and film parallel the historical development of psychological theory and clinical practice, although I do not claim any completeness on that score.

The particular works of fiction, drama, and film selected for interpretation were chosen for significant contrasts that go beyond those of nationality, period, and genre. As the reader will discover, the chapters advance in significant groupings, each containing a common ground against which marked differences appear. Both the Grimms' tale and the Sophocles play are close to the primitiveness of folklore and ritual, and therefore seem to be a fitting starting place for psychoanalytic investigation. Fairy tales and the Oedipus plays have traditionally invited Freudian (id-defended) and Jungian (archetypal) analysis. In fact, since *Oedipus Tyrannus* helped Freud give voice to one of his earliest and most crucial discoveries—that of the Oedipus Complex—one thinks of it as the literary matrix for psychoanalysis itself. Probably for this reason, psychoanalytic interpretation of the play has seldom gone beyond elaborations of its oedipal theme.

But both the Oedipus myth and Sophocles' Oedipus plays can be shown by further psychological investigation to reflect the larger world of society. Unlike the more instinct-ridden fairy tale, they provide an excellent opportunity to jolt the reader into a different kind of perception of them—the psycho*social* perspective of Adler, for example—so that I might begin to demonstrate my thesis that works of art stand ever ready to yield fresh pleasures and insights from new and diverse systems of approach.

The works covered in the next three chapters also form a unity that contains significant contrasts. They deal primarily with adolescents and therefore offer the best opportunity to introduce the value of object-relations theory in artistic interpretation. As a highly charged half-way house between infancy and adulthood, adolescence dramatically highlights the saga of human development both by its intensity and by its being a process of emergence of the self. But within this framework of similarity the works dealt with in these three chapters exhibit exciting differences. In "The Pupil" Henry James chooses to treat the young Morgan Moreen almost clinically, insisting on uncovering the family dynamics that form his character. However, Larry Peerce, following John Knowles, whose novel he adapted for the screen, entirely divorces both Gene and Finny from a parental matrix and focuses exclusively on the outward defenses of their personalities in their problems of peer identification. The Perrys' *David and Lisa*, though placed squarely in the clinical setting of an institution, and Matsuyama's *Happiness of Us Alone*, though built upon the psychological consequences of deaf-mutism, paradoxically find their emotional center not so much in a clinical situation as in an optimistic reliance on the resilience of the ego to ultimately adapt.

The special problem that the film medium faces in presenting the complex internals of feeling as photographable events is also discussed within the span of these three chapters in order to contrast with it the fiction writer's ability to omnisciently report and directly analyze what is going on in the minds and emotions of his characters. The presentation of complex psychodynamics poses a special problem for the filmmaker, for the lyric poet and the dramatist traditionally rely on the self-revelatory power of words (monologue and dialogue) to reveal inner states, while the filmmaker, as Erwin Panofsky has so convincingly argued, must do this primarily through the dynamic portrayal of objects moving in space if he is not to produce a static work. Readers who wish to pursue the technical aspects of this problem are referred to my discussion of Tennessee Williams's *Kirche, Kutchen, und Kinder* and Akira Kurosawa's *Throne of Blood* in Appendix A.

The next two chapters contrast a popular play, in which a social class theme is a subterfuge that masks a neurotic underpinning, with two classic short stories, in which the hidden psychic element is either a repressed or an unexpressed feeling whose derivatives in action and imagery actually give them the beauty and coherence of their artistic form and the comic pathos of their effect. Hence the question raised here is: to what extent is a hidden element in a work of art shown by psychology to be a truly dynamic enhancement of the work's aesthetic effect, and to what extent might it be shown to be an impurity or a disruptive part?

The last chapter traces seven treatments of the Prodigal Son parable that have appeared in fiction, drama, and film. Within this section there is also contrast and development—contrast not only of the artistic forms and genres in which the tale is embodied but contrasts in the psychological and psychosocial assumptions upon which different artists draw. The thematic movement in the chapter is away from the tightly circumscribed patriarchal ideal in the biblical version, in which the nuclear family conflicts are enmeshed, toward the complete breakdown of patriarchy, with ensuing problems in identification and identity, these latter seeming to require a greater reliance on pre-oedipally oriented object-relations theory for their understanding.

In the second appendix I have briefly examined the whole question of the relationship between art and psychology from the opposite end of the telescope—that is, I have shown the inspiration that psychology and psychoanalysis have derived from literature and art and their precursors in myth. This I hope will reinforce my argument that the arts and psychology are equally indebted to each other and mutually enriching.

It is probably best at this point to confess what my biases are as well as what my judgment has prompted me to exclude from this study. The work of such well-developed schools of depth psychology as those of Carl Jung, Karen Horney, Arthur Janov, and Fritz Perls is omitted merely because of lack of space, not because of personal animosity or apathy.* Alert and informed readers will in fact recognize the ideas of some of them incorporated in my various interpretations and will find passing references to others throughout the book.

Two recent developments in psychological theory and practice have been intentionally omitted as either unworkable or simply unappealing. Behaviorism, for example, seems to hold no promise for the interpretation of character, since its antihumanistic stance that behavior has no meaning beyond itself and what immediately stimulates it seems incapable of enriching the interpretation of a humanistically based text.

Second, I have found semiotics, structuralism, and psycholinguistics to be as coldly removed from human feelings as

---

*Elsewhere, in my capacity as an editor, I have tried to highlight the value of these theorist-clinicians in interpreting literary work. See, for example, the special issue of *Psychocultural Review* 2 (Spring 1978), entitled "New Directions in Psychoculture," which contains interpretations of literature from the viewpoints of Perls, Rank, Janov, and Horney. The first three issues of *Psychocultural Review* 1 (Winter 1977, Spring 1977, and Summer 1977) contain articles demonstrating the application of Jungian concepts to literature.

behaviorism, and therefore too enervating to work with. The same can be said of Roy Schafer's recent attempts to present psychoanalysis with a seemingly more scientific "language of action."[9] It was Schafer's plan to demetamorphose the rich, imaginative nature of psychoanalytic discourse that chiefly prompted me to write the second appendix to this book, in which, as I have said, I count the blessings bestowed by myth, literature, and folklore upon psychoanalytic expression and thought.

The Mindscapes of Art

1
Awakening to the Dream: A New Look at Freud's View of Literary Creativity

> Works of art...exercise a powerful effect on me, especially those of literature and sculpture, less often of painting.
>
> Freud, "The 'Moses' of Michelangelo"

i

It was inevitable that Freud, a sensitive, self-analyzed genius whose passion extended to his cultural milieu, should want to understand the feelings aroused in him by works of art and the minds that produced them. And it was inevitable that the image-making, symbol-forming, story-building, character-delineating aspects of fantasies and dreams, which he found so abundant in his clinical work, should remind him that these are also the province of the representational arts. That Freud's first published venture into the psychoanalytic interpretation of literature should come in 1900 in *The Interpretation of Dreams* (as a long footnote on Oedipus and Hamlet) is therefore not surprising. But eight years more were to pass before he was to set down, in the form of a short paper, what would become the first psychoanalytic *Ars Poetica*. "The Relation of the Poet to Daydreaming" (sometimes translated as "The Creative Writer and Daydreaming"),[1] became for him a kind of blueprint for gauging the artist's mind and that mind's impulse to create, for demystifying the nature of art itself and its effect upon an audience.

Despite its casual organization and style, Freud's little essay on literary creativity is a seminal work. Almost everything that Freud himself wrote both before and after on the subject of the artist and his art can be seen as elaborate footnotes upon it. Every daring foray he made into the world of literary and art criticism seems eventually to circle back to this work as its home base.

Artistic language itself provided Freud with the cue of where to begin. The dramatic production known as a "play" suggested to him the affinity of art to a child's game, which is also called "play," and it can in fact be seen that both fulfill the same basic human need. The child's play is a form of magic gesture in which he shifts about and embroiders upon identifiable objects and persons from the real world in order to create a world to his own liking. But he is always, unlike the psychotic but like the playwright and actor, able to keep the boundary between reality and illusion clear.

The daydream or fantasy is essentially an adult phenomenon that develops out of the necessity to both suppress the socially frowned-upon acting out of childish wish-fulfillments known as play and to hold onto the pleasure formerly afforded by the contrivance of such ego-aggrandizing images. Thus the overt activity in children's games, which is a concrete exercise of imagination, becomes for the adult a purely mental phenomenon, now withdrawn from real objects and cherished in secrecy. The wishes that his daydreams or fantasies fulfill are also different from the child's wishes for omnipotence. Either they are concerned with the achievements of social and professional ambition or they are preoccupied with the consummation of a sexual desire, or possibly a combination of both. Since society considers it immodest to be too openly ambitious and erects strong taboos against unbridled sex, the fantasies or daydreams that provide a vehicle for these feelings are kept secret, even though the kind of pleasure they fulfill is a derivative of those frankly exhibited pleasures in childhood games.

The triggering of daydreams—like the day-residue that helps to generate dreams—has its origin, according to Freud's essay, in a present event or experience, but like a dream it has roots in the past with hoped-for implications for the future. A situation or object in the present revives a half-buried pleasant memory or wish-fulfilled dream of childhood, which impels the construction of a pleasant illusion for the immediate future.

In showing how the works of poets and novelists are similar to wish-fulfilling games of childhood and the daydreams and fantasies of adulthood, Freud turns to popular writers of adventure and romance rather than to original literary geniuses or to authors working with mythic or traditional material. This is not because his literary tastes are lowbrow—his writings on Geothe, Shakespeare, and Dostoevski prove the opposite—but because this type of literature represents in the most transparent form both the child's wishes in play and the derivative of these wishes in the adult's daydream: the hero who has both superhuman strength and providence on his side (an infantile dream of omnipotence) and whom all women love (an adult fantasy of uninhibited eroticism).

As for the more sophisticated types of literature, Freud argues that they too are wish-fulfillment fantasies even though their form and expression may be more devious and disguised (just as dreams have different screen devices at their disposal). Thus he accounts for the author's identification with a "wish-fulfilled" hero, even in such complex forms of fiction as the so-called psychological novel, in which the author's ego is split among several characters, or is consigned to a choral or *ficelle* type of onlooker role (the "observing ego").

Even though universally shared, daydreams are held to be shameful by those who conjure them up. The notion of communicating them would therefore seem to be repellent. Their transmission to others is made palatable, and therefore possible, in Freud's view, by the technique, tricks, and disguises inherent in the poet's aesthetic form, and the communication is itself desirable because it frees deeper sensations and wishes without entailing shame.

Since a daydream or fantasy is usually the release, by a present event, of a storehouse of images created by wishes rooted in the experience of the past, Freud speculates that a work of art may also have its well-springs hidden in aspirations dating back to a far-removed past. This might explain, I suppose (though Freud does not say so), the suddenness and mysteriousness of poetic inspiration.

ii

Freud shared with Aristotle the feeling that the child's impulse to imitate reality in play contained a clue to artistic creativity. However, whereas Aristotle is content merely to observe that "imitation is natural to man from childhood" (*Poetics*, chap. 4), Freud defines the child's relation to reality as more tenuous and tentative, since it is governed by the more "unrealistic" demands of the pleasure principle—in this case the youngster's wish to be grown up and to have what he or she imagines to be the concomitant of being grown up: complete control of one's destiny.

If Freud had found that the value of a child's play and its derivatives in daydreams and art lay solely in the way in which the pleasure principle defeated the reality principle through self-induced illusion, he would have justified Plato's insistence on expelling the "insanity inducing" poets from his Republic. However, both Freud and Aristotle had the answer to Plato: neither the daydream nor the work of art lures the audience or spectator into madness, but on the contrary both have the value of a catharsis—of a release of tension which, if pent up, might cause madness, or at least neurosis.

Paradoxically, the therapeutic value of art, both for the artist creating it and for the audience witnessing it, is that it is seductive enough to allow emotional identification with its protagonist but remote enough so that the ego is not engulfed by the fiction.* This is not hard to understand if one remembers that the child at play enters totally into the spirit of his make-believe but never really loses account of what is real and what is imaginary.

Like Aristotle in his *Poetics*, Freud postpones his discussion of the cathartic effect of art until the end of his essay. However, while Aristotle concerns himself immediately with the formal arrangements of the artist's material, Freud pursues its psychological origins.

Since fantasies and daydreams are the results of wishes unfulfilled in reality, they are the products of essentially unhappy minds. Art, by analogy, is the product of a mind that is in some way unhappy, unfulfilled, perhaps neurotic. This implies that there would be no need for art in a utopia or paradise. We might recall that in Aldous Huxley's *Island*, where, among other accomplishments, the Oedipal complex had been diminished or obliterated by encouraging children to "adopt" a variety of surrogate parents, complex art forms did not exist. The public demand was only for bland, realistic, landscape paintings, their purpose being to bring into sight what was not immediately available to the eye, rather than to make accessible (as in Freud's "neurotic society") what is not readily available to the conscious ego. When Plato ostracized the poets, he was, according to Freud's assumptions, banishing a *symptom* of reality distortion, not a *cause* of it.

When Freud likens the male artist to the child at play and chooses as his example the romantic novelist whose hero both overcomes physical obstacles by feats of derring-do and wins the damsel in distress, he seems to imply that the artist's underlying

*This "margin of safety" of course narrows or completely disappears for the psychotic or nearly psychotic artist or audience. In this regard, see my discussion of Rilke in chapter 9.

wish is conscious or preconscious, since this is a fairly transparent wish in men and boys. However, since the artist also conveys daydream material that is regarded as "shameful," he must, as Freud says, use his aesthetic form and technique to disguise its nature to make it palatable.

Here I must raise an important question: is the material in both the daydream and the artwork merely moderately shameful, and thus held as a conscious secret, or is it repugnant enough to fall victim to repression, which is of course unconscious? Freud does not make it clear in this essay whether daydreams and fantasies of poets also harbor *unconscious* wishes. But judging from the comparisons he makes between daydreams and dreams, and his later studies of fantasies,[2] he must have felt that some of the wishes in fantasies and daydreams were unconscious because repressed. Therefore the imagery of the daydream and of the poem might have *screened* such wishes as much as *revealed* them.

This conclusion has important implications for Freud's aesthetics. If the artist, as daydreamer or fantasizer, is not merely consciously arranging his material to both reveal and disguise strong wishes but is also *unconsciously* revealing and screening them (as in a dream), then the form of his art is partly determined by his unconscious defenses. We would then have to ask if the "dynamics" of the work has the characteristics of a fixation (one sometimes speaks of a writer's recurring themes as an *idée fixe*), of a regression (one could point to the regressive anal sadism in Swift's scatological satires), or of sublimation (Freud's own study of Leonardo da Vinci's mastery of homosexual impulses by cathecting objects of art and science).

Unfortunately, Freud does not at this point throw any light on aesthetic theory by exploring how the *form* of a work might be determined by the form of the defense or screen for the unconscious wish-seeking expression. I shall return later to the question of whether Freud indeed uses psychoanalysis to illuminate the influence of psychodynamics on artistic form. At this stage he is concerned mostly with treating art as an embodiment of certain states of mind bound to the pleasure principle and as one of several clues to the emotional lives of its creators.

iii

Freud's use of psychobiography to further illuminate the creative impulse is demonstrated most ingeniously in his writings

about Shakespeare and Leonardo da Vinci. In both cases he is able
to utilize the aforementioned mechanism that he elucidated in
"The Relation of the Poet to Daydreaming": a contemporary
event creates a work of art by triggering a past wish that the artist
hopes will be fulfilled in the future. Freud is able to show that the
best work of both Leonardo and Shakespeare encompasses these
three coordinates in time and in addition represents an
unconscious wish.

The chief work of art that leads Freud back to the enigma of
Leonardo's mind is of course the famous *La Gioconda* (*The Mona
Lisa*) with its equally enigmatic smile. Freud's investigation of the
operation of Leonardo's psyche brings him through many mazes,
but his understanding of its analogy to the daydream (as developed
in the essay on poets and daydreaming) allows him to arrive at a
fairly simple solution to the mystery of La Gioconda's smile: the
(present) appearance of a female model having a mouth resembl-
ing that of da Vinci's mother sets off a childhood (past)
"memory" in which a large bird lashed its tail against his mouth as
he lay in his crib. This reinvoked "memory" broke up his mental
block against painting, and he produced *The Mona Lisa* as well as
other pictures containing figures wearing the famous mysterious
smile—a projection of the past into the future.

Leonardo's self-advertised "memory" was no doubt a screen
fantasy revealing the oral pleasure he got from his mother's breast
and concealing through symbolization the homosexual attempt at
fellatio as a "solution" for having been deprived of it later (the
phallic bird's tail against his mouth). But the discovery of the
mouth that in reality resembles his mother's brings the solution
back to a more primitive symbiotic level, dissolving the need for
the homosexual screen and for the compulsive "sexual" investiga-
tions enacted by his scientific interests. Here the work of art, *La
Gioconda*, and those that folowed, are a *sublimation*, not a
defense or screen, a function that had already been served by the
"memory" fantasy. As in a dream, the figure painted is a "condensed" personality: her "day-residue" nature is that she represents the real model, but her latent wish-fulfilled quality is,
through the symbolization of the smile, the beloved traits of both
the real doting mother, to whom he had exclusive access until
about age five, and the attentive stepmother of later childhood.

Freud read the psychobiographical implications of
Shakespeare's *Hamlet* somewhat differently, but he still saw the
play as an illustration of the mechanism of the daydream, dream,
and fantasy. In his often-quoted footnote in *The Interpretation of*

Dreams, Freud understands Hamlet's inability to kill Claudius as a projection of Shakespeare's own unresolved Oedipus complex. The basic mechanism outlined in "The Relation of the Poet to Daydreaming" is demonstrated here as well. Events in the present—the death of Shakespeare's own father and son—fulfilled part of an unconscious Oedipal wish ("I wanted my father dead, and now he is"), but the guilt and anxiety aroused by this partial wish fulfillment ("My wish may have killed my father, but it is wrong to kill him; and sleeping with my mother is still socially taboo even though my competitor has been removed") demand inhibition and self-punishment ("I, the offending son, must not only remain inactive, i.e., impotent, but must die").

Freud's shrewdest observation about the play is that what happens to the character Hamlet is not the dramatization of a wish fulfillment, as Oedipus's patricide and incestuous marriage can be seen to be a tribal wish fulfillment. The inaction and indecision of Hamlet are instead a dramatization of the *inhibitions* to wish fulfillments—the anxiety aspects of dreams rather than their blissful cathartic aspects, an operation of superego more than of id.

Freud, in dealing with the character Hamlet as a representation of inhibitory and repressive facets of the poet's mind—

> The distaste for sexuality expressed by Hamlet... [is] the same distaste which was destined to take possession of the poet's mind....
>
> It can of course only be the poet's own mind which confronts us in Hamlet[3]—

recognized that he was dealing with literature more complex and labyrinthine than the popular heroic romance in which wishes of ambition and eroticism were expressed more directly and consciously. In explaining Hamlet he was inferring that a poet projects not only his unconscious wishes but also the inhibitive forces against those wishes as well. A short while later, in 1906, Freud was to characterize as "psychopathic" the drama in which, as in the case of *Hamlet,* one of the elements of conflict is a repressed one, and as "neurotic" the audience that, like Shakespeare's appreciators, revels in the open demonstration of a repressed impulse.[4] However, despite this complication, Freud's assumption is still that the character created in drama, poetry, or fiction is the completed jig-saw puzzle of the poet's conflicts, whether or not it contains and dramatizes repressed material.

But suppose what the artist embodies in his work is neither a direct wish fulfillment nor a circuitous inhibited one but a *rigid* or highly elaborated defense against a desire or conflict, or even a secondary defense against the distastefulness of the primary defense? In that case a complete analysis of the work must include—as in the complete analysis of a dream image—an external contextual reference, an extraliterary or extra-artistic knowledge of the artist's mind. One might have to think of the work as merely a partial picture—an isolated evasion, screen, or defense—rather than as a completed picture of sublimation with imperfectly disguised rudiments of the initial wish.*

Two latter-day neo-Freudians have in fact taken Freud to task for seeing only the projected aspect of Leonardo's and Shakespeare's work and overlooking the defensive or screening aspect of it. In a recent article entitled "Freud, Leonardo and the Lamb,"[5] Durwood Markle argues that Freud's "sentimentality" prompted him to see the smiling Madonnas in da Vinci's "The Holy Family" (also called "St. Anne and Two Others") as sublimated wish fulfillments projects from the painter's childhood, that is, the experience of having been kindly dealt with by both his real and his foster mother. Although Freud recognized that in life Leonardo defended against anal-sadistic tendencies by a reaction formation of excessive kindness to animals, and even though Freud saw that the child Jesus in the painting was treating the lamb "a little unkindly," he did not understand, Markle charges, that the rather cruel handling of the animal was an unconscious protest against the ultimate desertion of him as a child by the smiling "mothers."

In like manner Edmund Bergler—although paying tribute to "Freud's analysis of Hamlet's superficial layer of unconscious defenses"[6]—points out that the then-undeveloped nature of psychoanalysis prevented him from seeing the deeper defensive layers in Shakespeare's own psyche, obscured by the more revelatory ones that delineated Hamlet:

The original analytic formulation on this subject [of creativity] ran as follows: The artist expresses in his work his *unconscious* fantasies. This was a great improvement on the one previously accepted by the world in general, which assumed that the work

---

*In *A Separate Peace*, discussed both in its novel and film versions in chapter 5, ego-defenses comprise the main text, the psychic picture being completed by the conscious and unconscious motives of the narrator-protagonist one year later, who may or may not be a precise replica of the author.

represented his conscious wishes and experiences in modified form. Despite this, our increased understanding of the artistic personality [as well as the work emanating from it] was only relative. We still failed to distinguish between the unconscious wish and the unconscious mechanism of defense against this wish.[7]

Picking up a hint by Ernest Jones that Shakespeare's presentation reveals a compromise between his own suppressed Oedipal wishes and his frustrated homosexual impulses, Bergler goes one step further and proclaims that the rather overt Oedipal wishes of Hamlet (material that normally undergoes repression) are made accessible to consciousness (insofar as Hamlet is Shakespeare) in order to screen a "deeper, repressed guilt"—homosexuality. He writes:

> It seems to me that Hamlet's crime of Oedipal fantasies, so brilliantly elucidated by Freud, is but a camouflage obscuring a deeper [oral] conflict which antedates the Oedipal one.... That Shakespeare himself saw male homosexuality only in terms of femininity is one of the poet's rationalizations (for example, the queen in *Hamlet* compares her son with a "female dove").[8]

Thus when a figure in an artistic creation stems from a strong secondary defense rather than becoming a direct projection of a wish fulfillment or a transparent defense against it in its author's mind, a thorough understanding of such a character must depend on accesses to the mind of its creator other than those offered by his work alone or even by a fairly detailed biography. Consequently, many of Freud's attempts at a definitive analysis of characters like Hamlet, Lady Macbeth, and Richard III were probably foredoomed by the paucity of external sources of knowledge about Shakespeare.

One further observation before I conclude with Freud's involvement in the biographical matrix out of which a work of art arises. In examining the wellsprings for creative genius, Freud seems to have stumbled upon a truth that was later to be confirmed by psychoanalytical investigation: both creativity and certain kinds of mental disturbances have their origin in an abundance of maternal affection in the early years of life. In the case of Goethe, the mother's attentiveness in his infancy, which subsequently gave so much force to his later sibling-rivalry memory of smashing the crockery, also gave Goethe "that victorious feeling, that confidence in ultimate success, which not seldom brings actual success with it.''[9] In the case of Leonardo, Freud shows in considerable detail not only how a great deal of maternal affection in infancy gave Leonardo this same success impetus, but how by also stimulating erotic feelings that the child was yet unable to understand or satisfy, his overindulgent mother prompted his flight first into narcissism and then into homosexuality.*

In the light of his view of the neurotic nature of art, Freud might very well have agreed with Theseus's statement in *A Midsummer Night's Dream* that "the lunatic, the lover, and the poet/Are of imagination all compact." If, like his disciples Bergler and Jones, he had seen art as a frequent representation of the unconscious defenses and secondary defenses of its creator, he would have had to agree that much poetic imagery and much iconography in the pictorial arts express "symptoms" as well as "symbols." Had he developed further the parallels he began to draw between artwork and dreamwork, he probably would even have arrived at an explicit statement of this view.

iv

Having traced the way in which Freud in his paper on "The Relation of the Poet to Daydeaming" illustrated first the writer's direct translation of wish fulfillment into popular romantic and heroic literature, and then the author's indirect revelation of secret and even unconscious wishes in a more complex kind of personal artistic statement, I must turn back to Freud's remarks on the type of artist who uses traditional, mythological, or legendary material as the basis for artistic expression. Freud defined myths, we may remember, as "distorted vestiges of the wish phantasies of whole nations—the age-long dreams of young humanity."[10] A rather involved question immediately springs to mind: is the writer or artist who deals with such material merely a transmitter of the racial wishes embedded in it; or does he reshape it to suit his own individual wishes, presenting a dual problem of unraveling for the psychoanalytic critic? The chances are that the latter is more often true than the former, and that the "distortions" Freud refers to are the necessary disguises, sublimations, and perhaps even unconscious defenses that both the culture and the individual spokesman

---

*Such observations of the pre-Oedipal mother-child relationship paved the way not only for later developments in object-relations theory but for the application of such a theory to art as well, one of the main concerns of this book.

contrive in order to make the work acceptable. (There is also, of course, the possibility that by "distortion" Freud merely meant what he later called the "laws of aesthetic form." But I shall deal with this problem later.)

Even though Freud was for the most part willing to leave the interpretation of mythic art and literature to such members of his circle as Otto Rank and Hanns Sachs, he did make a notable excursion into the field in 1913 in his rather charming analysis of "The Theme of the Three Caskets" in Shakespeare's *The Merchant of Venice*.[11] After dismissing a scholarly contention that the episode involving Bassanio's winning of Portia's hand is derived from an Esthonian astral folk epic, he sees the suitor's choice of the least ornamental box as more closely connected to the familiar stories of Cinderella, Psyche, and King Lear. All of these tales concern a man's preference for a mute daughter from among three. This silent and ultimately most desirable one-of-three is revealed by Freud to stand for the inevitability of death, although the originators of the legend *distort* her true identity in order to make her more palatable. Thus she appears disguised as love.

Significantly, Freud uses his clinical observations of the more unconscious levels of dreams rather than of the more conscious strata of fantasies and daydreams to locate symbolically the casket theme in the larger class of myths to which it belongs. First, caskets are traditional dream symbols for women; lead is, on the other hand, merely a conventional cliché for silence. Thus Portia, who is associated with the leaden casket, is the one woman out of three who is silent. Second, dumbness is a traditional dream-image for death. Finally, since men wish to avoid death, they often create in their dreams a reversal in which longed-for love is substituted.

One cannot help wondering if Freud's later discovery of the "death instinct" as part of primary desire would have made him soften his notion that a love-wish is necessarily a reversal/denial of a death-thought rather than a complement of it. He seems to flirt with such a notion when he points out that Shakespeare, as he comes to write *King Lear*, makes an aged and dying man the one who chooses Death, personified as Cordelia (really the mute third woman disguised as love-goddess). Thus, in Freud's words, Shakespeare in *Lear* gives a "regressive treatment" to the myth, "which was disguised by a reversal of the wish"; he "undistorts" it and moves us by Lear's acceptance of (and, I would add, even *yearning* for) death, which now becomes identical with love (for the *dead* Cordelia).

Although comparisons with the structure and meanings of
dreams obviously provided Freud with special insight into literature having a mythological basis, he discovered one element in it
that seemed to be diametrically opposite to dream manifestations.
I refer to the tendency of myth to "decompose" a heroic character
into several figures, whereas the dream tends to "condense"
several figures into one.[12] Not that these are mutually exclusive, of
course. One could easily agree with Jones's point that the original
Saxo Grammaticus legend upon which Shakespeare based *Hamlet*
had behind it an even more primitive myth in which the father
(Hamlet, Sr.) and the tyrant (Claudius) were one figure, but that
the unbearable hatred of tyranny in the father caused a decomposition or splitting of the father figure into two men in Saxo
Grammaticus—a "good" and a "bad" character. And finally,
one could argue that revulsion in Shakespeare's own mind caused
the father figure to be split further, that is, into three: the Ghost,
Claudius, *and* Polonius. However, in Shakespeare's *Hamlet* this
decomposition of the primal father does not prevent the character
Hamlet from identifying them with each other symbolically or, as
we say in psychoanalysis, transferentially (to the extent of envying
the father in Claudius and killing him in Polonius) and therefore
responding to all of them in basically the same way (with ironic
dark humor), as if they were the single condensed figure of a
dream.

The only use Freud makes of his awareness of "decomposition"
of characters in mythic or legendary literature is in his explanation
of why Lady Macbeth's attainment of her wish to be queen causes
her mental breakdown. After discounting her childlessness as a
cause (because the time-span represented is too short for childlessness to appear a certainty), Freud remarks rather casually that
Shakespeare may be pursuing a "technical trick" of splitting a
character into complementary parts—Macbeth and Lady Macbeth
as "two disunited parts of the mind of single individuality" or
"divided images of a single prototype."[13]* But Freud fails to
explore Jones's thought that this decomposition may be the result
of the defense of denial or repression, whether in Shakespeare's
mind or in the collective racial mind from which the legend
(recorded in Holinshed) evolved.

---

*We can see an ingenious embodiment of this idea in *Throne of Blood*, Akira Kurosawa's
film adaptation of *Macbeth*, which I discuss in Appendix A.

v

Just as Aristotle directs the whole last part of his poetics toward how the dramatist brings about a catharsis in his audience (in this case a purging of pity and terror), so also does Freud conclude his consideration of the writer's relation to daydreaming by pondering the nature and value of his emotional effect upon his audience.

According to Freud *all* men—the writer as well as his readers—share the same fantasies, but no one is able to communicate them *directly* to another because of their shameful, taboolike—often even repressed and therefore unconscious—nature. The artist or writer functions as a communications link between forbidden feelings in himself and in his viewers or audience. In Freud's view the aesthetic form of the work is a "disguise" or "bribe" with beauty to accept the normally disagreeable. However, since this socially and consciously unacceptable material really conceals a wish fulfillment, the work of art has the therapeutic, cathartic function of releasing deeply suppressed or repressed tensions[14] in an acceptable, even public (in the case of a performing art) manner. (He later discovered that the joke performed this same function.) Thus Freud regards the aesthetic beauty or formal arrangement of a work to be a "forepleasure" designed to release a deeper psychic pleasure.

We must go to Freud's article "Psychopathic Characters on the Stage" (1905-6) to learn more about what he thinks this deeper undamming of energy consists of. Beginning with Aristotle's notion that the business of tragedy is both to arouse and to "purge" the feelings of pity and terror, he quickly arrives at the conclusion that such catharsis has "an accompanying sexual excitation" because as a general law eroticism "appears as a by-product whenever an affect is aroused," and "gives people the sense, which they so much desire, of a raising of the potential of their psychical state."[15] This would be true even if the sexual pleasure were "masochistic," Freud says, as in tragedy, for the greatness of the tragic hero is insisted upon despite his defeat.[16] I would assume then that Freud is implying that of the two components—"ambition for success" and "eroticism"—that he found in the daydreams of poets, *ambition* is subsumed under *eroticism*, the more basic element. That is, the "raising of psychic potential" may result in seeking success in the real world (often stated in terms of the hero's rebellion against God, family, or state). But the feeling of "potency" that makes such ambition possible is sexual gratification. Would Freud have added—as a result of his later discovery that the aim of pleasure is the lowering of energy levels—that the tension-releasing aspect of art also satisfies that homeostasis ultimately identified with the "death wish"?

vi

Now that I have fully explored Freud's notions about the nature of the creative impulse, the wishes that it embodies in art, and the emotional effect that it has on an audience or viewer, I come finally to a consideration of his views on the nature of aesthetic form itself. What Freud regards the psychological *function* of form to be has been quite clear all along: it is a disguise of the true emotional (sometimes repressed) content, and thus serves as a kind of distancing to make this content communicable on a conscious level in a public setting. But does Freud throw any light on the way in which the formal arrangement itself—what he alternately calls the "necessities of art," the "laws of beauty," and the "requirements of aesthetic form"—is psychologically determined? It would seem that this lies beyond his interest, for as he tells us at the beginning of his paper on "The 'Moses' of Michelangelo,"

> I have often observed that the subject-matter of works of art has a stronger attraction for me than their formal and technical qualities, though to the artist their value lies first and foremost in the latter.[17]

In his paper on "The Interest of Psycho-Analysis from the Point of View of the Science of Aesthetics" (1913),[18] Freud refers to the "laws of beauty" as having value merely as a bribe to the onlooker "with a bonus of pleasure" rather than as having a direct correspondence to psychological laws. Does Freud (or do any of his followers for that matter) ever imply—or even consider—that any of the elements of formal, aesthetic arrangement—symmetry and asymmetry; harmony and discord; repetition of symbol, object, or technical device; proportion in physical shape or in time continuum; continuation or reversal of a line of development, and so on—have a correspondence to, or a determination in, the psychic structure? If a work of art could be regarded as a kind of "secondary revision" of a dream, does the *form* of the modification follow a certain pattern?

The evidence seems to be that Freud did not think of the formal aesthetic structure of a work of art as having any psychic configuration, although it both served and affected the psychic structure of its content. The form of art is for him something imposed from without by convention and tradition, just as the form of events in the day-residue of a dream have been externally determined. However, in a dream the pattern of this "outer" material helps determine the selection, shape, and intensity of the "inner" impulses to be released through it. Freud's comparison of poetic creation with dream work on the basis of the ways in which the manifest day-residue and the conventional requirements of rhyme similarly determine the manner of expression of libidinous impulses is especially illuminating:

> Any one thought [that is "dream thought," which implies a forbidden wish and feeling], whose form of expression may happen to be fixed for other reasons, will operate in a determinant and selective manner on the possible forms of expression allotted to the other thoughts, and it may do so, perhaps, from the very start—as is the case in writing a poem. If a poem is to be written in rhymes, the second line of a couplet is limited by two conditions: it must express an appropriate meaning [and feeling], and the expression of that meaning [and feeling] must rhyme with the first line. No doubt the best poem will be one in which we fail to notice the intention of finding a rhyme, and in which the two thoughts have, by mutual influence, chosen from the very start a verbal expression which will allow a rhyme to emerge with only a slight subsequent adjustment.[19]

If I read him correctly, Freud seems to be saying that an imposed form or logic provokes an internal system to select, choose, and rearrange the images and words that can provide the most efficient channel for the discharge of affect.

The enunciation of this principle seems to be as close as Freud comes to making aesthetic form a part of psychodynamics: form provides the special well-designed circuitry by which potentially chaotic feelings are discharged as acceptable "expression." Thus even when Freud takes pains to distinguish among the different genres of art—as, for example, he does in "Some Psychopathic Characters on the Stage," where he discusses lyric poetry, tragedy, comedy, heroic drama, epic, and modern psychological drama—it is always from the standpoint of how different levels of erotic feeling or defenses against them are evoked, or about what "terrain" of conflict in the psychic structure is chosen for depiction, or about the degree to which the form is able to distance the artist and the spectator from a too-direct view of exciting but

shameful material. Never does he seem to see aesthetic form as a
replica of the psychic structure itself.[20]

vii

One might well ask at this point if modern psychoanalytic
criticism has been able to deal any more subtly than Freud has with
the nuances of form and style in a work of art. Both Pinchas Noy[21]
and Gilbert Rose[22] are two recent critics who have used modern
ego-psychology and object-relations theory to confront aesthetic
form. They have independently arrived at similar conclusions that
are not really so different from what Freud had already implied in
his theory of form as "foreplay," namely that form and style in
art are important guarantees against some form of emotional
chaos. The difference is that the potential over-loosening is for
Freud unbridled id-wishes (instinctive drives of libido and aggression); for the object-relations theorists it is loss of ego- and self-
boundaries. As Noy puts it,

> There is no doubt that an enormous and constant inner
> organizational effort is needed in order to maintain the cohesion
> and integrity of the self against all the forces that pull it in
> various directions. . . .
> The reach for "perfect form" in art, including its elements of
> order, symmetry, harmony and balance, is a part of the organi-
> zational effort, and it reflects the activities of the ego in ordering
> the disparate parts of the self, in reconciling the opposites that
> may threaten to tear the self apart, and in enabling the
> maintenance of a stable image.[23]

Rose introduces a bipolar and hence more paradoxical dimension
to the mediating role of artistic form with relation to the integrity
of the self. He points to the bliss of oceanic chaos—whether we
define this as id-drive, primary process, symbiosis, or primary
narcissism—as well as to its dangers and taboos. Thus artistic form
flirts with the relaxation of control as well as the tightening of it,
with emotional release as well as with tension build-up, with the
classical insistence on traditional structure as well as with romantic
rebellion against it. Rose concludes,

> the structure of aesthetic form correlates primary with secon-
> dary processes—undifferentiated with differentiated percep-
> tion, emotional impulses toward action with intellectual thought,

and constancy with change. It thus offers an idealized model of how the mind works in at least two contradictory ways at once. Aesthetic form exploits plasticity to transform this dialectic into a dynamic unity which yet preserves the unique integrity of the contrasting elements within the person and his or her sense of space and time.[24]

Both Noy and Rose seem to agree that when form and content are most economically expressed and most seamlessly joined, the effect is most artful, for the order of form superimposed on the chaos of feeling is felt to be part of a perfectly balanced, but always dynamically changing self. But, as I have said, this notion was really adumbrated by Freud, when for instance he saw in the rhymed poem an emotion-laden "meaning" (parallel to the dream wish) achieving acceptable expression (liberation) via mutual adjustments and negotiations between its crude animating principle (primitive instinct) and the external requirements of the traditional rhyme scheme (civilized order and "beauty"). If the choice of the rhymed word seemed natural, then the contrary forces of disruption and harmony were being expressed simultaneously and, as in a "successful" nonanxious dream, unfolding with seeming effortlessness.

One might say that the poets themselves were intuitively ahead of all three—Freud, Noy, and Rose—in understanding this principle of form as both controlling and safely releasing the danger/bliss of internal chaos. Take, for instance, some of Wordsworth's statements about poetry in which he saw spontaneous feeling as a potential loss of ego-boundaries despite the pleasure it entailed, thus needing the balance and control of certain traditional elements of literary form:

The end of Poetry is to produce excitement in co-existence with an overbalance of pleasure; but, by the supposition, excitement is an unusual and irregular state of mind; ideas and feelings do not, in that state, succeed each other in accustomed order.[25]

Here Wordsworth seems to be describing a "primary process" form of thinking evoked in the reader. Although the liberating influence is basically pleasurable, there is a danger of excess and loss of control:

If the words [of the poem], however, by which this excitement is produced be in themselves powerful, or the images and feelings have an undue proportion of pain connected with them, there is some danger that the excitement may be carried beyond the proper bounds.[26]

This is where a formal element—in the shape of regular metrical patterns—enters the picture: to provide "secondary process" control, familiarity, and identifiable boundaries:

> Now the co-presence of something regular [meter], something to which the mind has been accustomed in various moods and in a less excited state, cannot but have great efficacy in tempering and restraining the passion by an intertexture of ordering feeling, and of feeling not strictly and necessarily connected with the passion.[27]

Like Rose, Wordsworth finds the power of literary form to be paradoxical in its ability both to tap the beautiful strangeness of the primary-process reality and to bring it under the discipline of the secondary process:

> though the opinion will at first appear paradoxical, from the tendency of metre to divest language, in a certain degree, of its reality, and thus to throw a sort of half-consciousness of unsubstantial existence over the whole composition, there can be little doubt but that more pathetic situations and sentiments, that is, those which have a greater proportion of pain connected with them may be endured in metrical composition, especially in rhyme, than in prose.[28]

Freud, who was always appreciative of the ways in which the artist—and particularly the imaginative writer—anticipated the discoveries of the psychoanalyst, would probably have reveled in these lines from Wordsworth's famous *apologia* for the romantic lyric, had he been aware of them.

Seeing artistic form as the careful regulating of potentially chaotic but vital energy can obviously lead to the meticulous analysis of form in individual works of art. Based on the artist's strategies in choosing and placing the devices that most effectively accomplish this fluctuation between differentiation and dedifferentiation, between time and timelessness, between ebullience and sobriety, between experiencing ego and observing ego, et cetera, one could attempt to judge his work successful or unsuccessful. This would apply to abstract art as well as to representational art, of course, for principles of harmony and dissonance, of tension and release, are inherent in it as well.*

But does this approach really provide an ironclad, fail-safe way for psychoanalysis to distinguish between good and bad art? The requirement and tolerance for tension and release, for needing a sense of integration and being willing to risk feelings of oceanic fusion varies with the art consumer's personality structure, previous experiences, present expectations, cultural acclimation, and the like. The Eiffel Tower may seem beautiful to some because its lines sweep gracefully heavenward like the tower of a Gothic cathedral. However, an engineer, aware of its having used a great deal more metal than necessary to support its structure, might see it as ponderously ugly. Western viewers might see the films of Yasujiro Ozu or of Satyajit Ray as too emotionally restrained and therefore sluggish and dull. To an Indian, Ray's slow-paced dramatic movement would be merely "stately," and to a Japanese a trivial gesture such as the opening of a fan or the raising of an eyebrow might be fraught with drama and dire social consequences.

viii

A final comparison of Freud with Aristotle will, I think, throw all of the above observations into a better perspective. Both Freud and Aristotle began by discussing art as an imitation of reality, and both praised its cathartic and therapeutic effects. However, whereas Freud went on to devote most of his energy to examining the dreamlike wish-fulfilling content of the imitation and substantially ignored its formal structure, Aristotle proceeded to devote most of the *Poetics* to analyzing the architectonics of form that produced the required effects. Part of Aristotle's justification for doing so, it seems to me, was his assumption not only that

---

*Since I am dealing in this book with the *representational* arts of fiction, drama, and film, in which the motivation and behavior of characters are significant, my psychoanalytic treatment of formal elements of art in this book will necessarily always have character as a key form of reference, whether it be showing how the squeeze frame technique in *A Separate Peace* forces the actors into a physical replica of mental symbiosis, or how the two protagonists in *David and Lisa* alternate between harmonious and disharmonious gestures to reflect their emotional states, or how the hiatuses in the Chekhovian narrative dramatically indicate an incomplete gestalt of mourning, or how the decline in patriarchy in successive versions of the Prodigal Son parable inspires the development of new theatrical devices to represent identity diffusion.

imitation is natural but that a sense of harmony and rhythm is equally so:

> Imitation, then being natural to us—as also the sense of harmony and rhythm....(*Poetics*, chap. 4, ll, 20–21)

Thus Aristotle paves the way for dealing with the formal symmetries, tempos, and meters in art as an outgrowth of a *natural impulse* to create patterns.*

We cannot anachronistically accuse Aristotle of not coming nearer to Freud's insights into art as creative wish-fulfilling fantasy because of course he did not know modern psychology. But can we not fault Freud with not coming closer as a psychologist to Aristotle's important clue that the natural impulse to imitate "harmony and rhythm"—an aspect of form both in art and in the "economic" system of the psyche—might unite the structure of the mind with formal patterns of art?

But as far as the humanistic (as opposed to the abstract) arts are concerned, artistic form is not usually conceived of mainly in terms of balance, harmony, and symmetry. It is *not*, as Norman Friedman so succinctly puts it,

> simply a matter of patterns, designs, structures, images, tensions, balances, recurrences, variations, techniques, stylistic devices, and so on—things which are abstractable and discussable apart from any given work in which they appear. It is more a matter of human characters responding to situations in certain ways, and of such actions being calculated to arouse in us certain feelings.[29]

Thus both Freudians and Aristotelians would agree that in the fictional arts action springs from character and that the shape such an action takes will be determined by the laws of psychological probability, in which a generally understood set of feelings and instincts might be conjectured to behave in a particular set of environmental conditions set up by the world of the author's imagination.

*Again Wordsworth emerges as an admirable model for such a way of conceptualizing artistic form. His confession in *The Prelude* that the "beatings of the heart" became for him one of the "grandeurs" of nature that gave "discipline" to pain and pleasure suggests that formal elements (such as rhyme) in art might be adapted from nature or human nature. See *The Prelude, bk. 1, ll. 412*–14.

2

The Fairy Tale as Psychosexual Conflict: Crises in the Phallic Stage in the Grimms' "The Table, the Ass, and the Stick"

> The magic formula "Up stick and at it" suggests phallic associations, as does the fact that only this new acquisition permits Jack to hold his own in relation to his father, who up to now has dominated him.
> Bruno Bettelheim on "Jack and His Bargains"

i

At a meeting of the Vienna Psychoanalytic Society in 1909 Freud casually dropped one of his most provocative pronouncements about aesthetics: that the form of a work of art can be assumed to be "the precipitate of an older content." In literature this would mean that the configuration of a plot, its constellation of interacting characters, and the placing of it dénouement are a transformed, ritualized version of a more hidden, but still dynamic, set of instinctual drives.

Few types of narrative fiction remain as close in form to their primitive contents as the fairy tale, the folktale, and the historical legend. Each of these, as Bruno Bettelheim points out, takes "existential anxieties and dilemmas very seriously and addresses itself directly to them: the need to be loved and the fear that one is thought worthless; the love of life, and the fear of death."[1] But of these three pre-literary genres the fairy tale reveals itself to be the most closely in touch with man's primordial nature, as shown by its continuing appeal to the imagination of the child as he struggles with problems of emotional development and identity.

For these reasons fairy tales have always held a special fascination for the psychoanalyst. For him their color and charm often reside in the ways in which their events and characterizations act as screens for primitive eroticism and aggression. "The Table, the Ass, and the Stick," garnered from German folklore by the Brothers Grimm, is just such a tale—simple in its external trappings but complicated by latent meanings that not only *in*volve infantile sexuality but *e*volve it according to a developmental pattern that shapes its narrative form.

To summarize the plot briefly: a tailor has three sons whom he orders, each in turn, to take the family goat to a choice pasture so that she might continue to provide milk of a very high quality. Even though at the end of the day the goat assures the boys that she is full, she later complains to the tailor that she was put to graze in a barren spot. In great anger the tailor drives each of his sons from the house. But when the goat plays the same trick on him, he realizes her treachery and chases her away with a whip after first shaving her head.

Meanwhile the exiled sons learn various trades: the eldest apprentices himself to a joiner; the second, to a miller; and the youngest, to a turner. At the end of the training period each is given a valuable gift by his master: the oldest receives a table that supplies a feast on command; the second, an ass that spits forth gold coins at the word "bricklebrit"; the youngest, a stick that he can order to jump out of a sack to beat an enemy.

Because the natural process of identification with and idealization of the father has remained for the sons "unfinished business," the sons understandably become anxious to offer these marvelous gifts to him as tokens of reconciliation. However, the first two stop off at different times at an inn where, during the night, the envious landlord substitutes a worthless table and ass for the magic ones. Thus when each lad arrives home and tries to show off his bogus treasure, he is humiliated in front of the tailor and his neighbors. However, the third son is warned about the thieving innkeeper in a letter from his brothers, and when the villain tries to rob, him he summons the stick from its bag to beat him until he restores the magic table and ass.

Thus the father and his sons become truly reconciled, and the wealth provided by the three gifts not only allows the tailor to retire but enriches his neighbors as well.

The end of the story chronicles the goat's fate. Humiliated by the baldness inflicted on her by the tailor, she hides in a dark fox-hole. Her glowing eyes frighten away both the wary fox and his stolid friend the bear, but a brave bee stings her on her shaved head and sends her out into the world screaming.

ii

At first glance, the tailor's rage against his sons for their alleged behavior with the milk-producing goat seems to be a traditional enactment of the male child's Oedipal fantasy that his father threatens him with castration because of his erotic interest in the taboo mother. That the tailor should brandish his yardstick at his sons seems to confirm this. As Ferenczi points out in his brief essay "The Sons of the 'Tailor',", the male offspring of tailors, and to a lesser extent of others who handle sharp instruments (e.g., barbers, soldiers, butchers, and doctors), suffer "a monstrous exaggeration of castration fear."[2]

In "The Table, the Ass, and the Stick" the result of the tailor's aggression against his sons' sexual maturity is to force their regression to earlier stages of sexual development—more primitive levels from which they must strive to progress once again toward genital maturity, but this time with an ego that is strong enough to tolerate their feelings about the real and imagined threats of the father. This is one aspect of sound maturation in real life and often a goal in psychotherapy.

Mythic "decomposition" complicates what would ordinarily be straightforward characterization in the tale. As Freud[3] and Jekels,[4] and later Rank[5] and Jones[6] observed, fairy tales and myths reverse the condensing process of dreams by atomizing or decomposing figures in the family constellation. Traits of a single personage are divided into their components, then represented or personified by separate figures. I illustrated this in chapter 1 when I summarized Jones's view that the Ghost, Claudius, and Polonius can be seen as fragments of Hamlet's father imago.* Decomposition of this kind provides the mind with a means for sorting out the acceptable from the unacceptable, the syntonic ego from the alien ego. As Rank points out, this "splitting" in myth always derives from interrelationships within the nuclear family, between the hero and his parents[7]

---

*Usually we can discover some vestigial link or common denominator pointing to their previous integration into a single being, as, for example, the pomposity and inclination to give advice found in all three of Hamlet's "fathers." In the Grimm tale we are considering, the brothers not only share common destinies—betrayal by the same goat and innkeeper, for instance—but are tied together by their casual relationship to a particular object. At the inn the common-room dining table (a symbol of parental nurture) is the initial focus of activity for each son: the first lures the other guests from it to his own magically furnished one; the second takes the cloth from this table to gather the gold coins that the ass will spit; and the third son displays his stick and sack upon this same table for the benefit of the deceptive innkeeper.

In the tale I am considering, the deceived and angry tailor and the suave and deceiving innkeeper are inverse sides of the same repressive father imago, while the master joiner, miller, and turner are at the other end of the spectrum as the nurturing father to be identified with. The three sons, as they are forced into regression, come to represent the different stages of sexual development in a single individual: the eldest son exhibits orality in his command of the magic table that is a cornucopia of nourishment; and the second son continues the maturation into the next phase—anality—by his control of the ass that spits gold coins, a common displacement type of dream symbol for feces (the appropriate orifice becoming replaced by its opposite for the sake of decorum). Finally, mature sexuality is illustrated by the third son's successful use of the stick and sack.

The wicked landlord is the narcissistic and envious part of the father that would overwhelm and defeat the infant son—his potential rival—at every step of maturation,[8] while the tailor is the superego father, both instilling sexual guilt and seemingly threatening castration.

iii

Yet, is "The Table, the Ass, and the Stick" merely another conventional instance of the son's fear of being castrated by the father because of his own sexual designs upon the mother? Such an interpretation of the story becomes suspect when we realize that here the original threat seems to come from the mother (as represented by the goat) rather than from the father. And a purely Oedipal view of the tale becomes almost untenable when we note that insatiability and deception are *her* chief attributes, whereas in the dynamics of this complex they would normally belong to the son, or, by projection, to the father. Also, the image of the seductive mother is usually generated in instances where the father is weak or nonpresent. This is not the case in this tale.

They mystery begins to clear up when we examine the details of the sons' interactions with the goat. Each boy lets the creature satisfy her hunger *in solitude* until the day's end, then after hearing from her that she is "so full/ [she] cannot pull / Another blade of grass," leads her home and fastens her to her stall. If we take the goat, in one of its most traditional meanings, to mean lechery, and if we recall that it satisfies its appetite in isolation, then we might very well conclude that masturbation is the form of eroticism hinted at. Although physically satiated, the goat, like the solitary masturbator, complains an instant later of emotional unfulfillment.

A moment's further thought, however, will suggest that the auto-eroticism actually applies to the sons rather than to the goat, which is here merely a symbol of the sexual drive.* There is nothing strange about this displacement or transference of erotic feeling in folklore or fairy tales. Just as a mythic character may become decomposed in order to separate what is acceptable in the personality from what is heinous, so also may archetypal actions become fragmented and disassociated into more manageable parts. In this way the ego can separate its "good" activities from its "bad" ones in order that it might accept the former and deny the latter. Thus the sons, who direct the goat to eat in an isolated and unobserved place, are themselves being satiated by their secret "sin" (i.e., "can no more pull"). And the "betrayal" they suffer in the form of the creature's ever-renewed desire (untrammeled even when confined to its "stall") is both the awakening of their guilt about masturbation in the presence of the father-superego and the resurgence of the drive that causes the "crime" to be repeated and punished.

Psychoanalysts frequently equate the phallic stage of development with the Oedipal phase because the boy's recognition of his penis as the primary zone of pleasure soon leads him to fantasize gratification from his first love object, his mother. However, some theorists see phallic ascendancy as a more distinct precursor to the Oedipal phase—a narcissistic period in which the boy merely glories in the pleasure and erectile power of his genital organ. While it is true that some castration anxiety may soon be brought on by his impression that girls may have been deprived of a penis for some "crime," his first fantasy in the phallic stage is probably that everyone (including girls) has this magic appendage. His next reactions are probably first astonishment and then disappointment, upon finding that his father's is much larger. This little backstage drama of self-absorption presumably occurs before the curtain is rung up for the main performance, that is, before he sees his mother as an object of libidinous love and his father as an object of envious hate.

---

*Although the goat, as a symbol of lasciviousness, is usually depicted as male (cf. the half-goat satyr of mythology), here her femaleness provides an Oedipal smokescreen for her true phallic nature, in which her milk-producing ability is really the power to ejaculate sperm.

Since the tailor in our story really seems to drive out his sons for their auto-eroticism rather than for their mother-lust, we may conclude that the tale dramatizes conflicts at the phallic rather than at the Oedipal point of development. In this regard it is interesting to note that the father does not threaten his sons with scissors, the most dreaded instrument for Ferenczi's castration-anxious "sons of the tailor," but lays about them with his yardstick—both a phallic image and, by its nature, a suggestion of superior size. Moreover, the youngest son—who defeats the wicked landlord-father and successfully presents the tokens of all stages of sexual development (table, ass, and stick) to his tailor-father—symbolically asserts that he is now a phallic match for him. His magic stick and sack not only are indicative of male genitalia that are fully mature and functioning but also subsume all other stages of maturation since they have enabled him to regain the table and the gold-producing ass as well.

The youngest son's ability to win his father's praise for his profession of turner is also a sign of his phallic triumph. Whereas the tailor either denigrates or undervalues the trades learned by his other sons—those of joiner and miller—he labels the third son's ability to fashion a piece of wood on a lathe "a very ingenious handicraft." Thus the tailor-father finally acknowledges the value of his son's penis and his son's right to manipulate it, and consequently can begin to enjoy the benefits of the boy's maturity and independence by being able to lay aside once and for all his own yardstick and needle.

The coda to this dramatization of the phallic stage of sexuality is provided by the vignette depicting the final disgrace of the deceitful goat, the emblem of the unquenchable and uncontrollable lust that leads to masturbation. The tailor's retributive acts of shaving the creature's head and then ostracizing her amount to a two-fold defense against erotic desire: first desexualization, then denial. His avoidance of his own temptation to masturbate is shown in his forceful dissociation of his yardstick (penis) from the goat: we are told that he selects a whip to drive the goat away instead of his yardstick. Even though he considers the latter to be a suitable instrument with which to intimidate his sons, he feels it to be "too honorable a weapon" to use on the goat.

Despite the tailor's attempts to ostracize (i.e., exorcize) the goat (libido), she symbolically remains a threat. As two fiery eyes in the foxhole (the id), she continues to wage successful assaults against the imperfect censor-band of the ego (the wily fox) and repression (the stolid bear), but is ultimately subdued.

But what is the nature of this mastery? The bee does not seem to represent the relatively conflict-free process of sublimation carried out by such activities as social adaptation and industry, two characteristics usually associated with this creature. Instead, the bee acts like a very sudden and very brutal nemesis of fate, inflicting a kind of primal wound that sends the goat leaping "like mad into the world."

This certainly violates the tableau of social harmony previously achieved by the tailor and his sons, where those who are overtly strong in their possession of instruments of punishment gladly place them aside. The third son, instead of continuing to have the landlord beaten by the magic stick, had decided to "be generous instead of just," and the tailor in becoming reconciled with his sons had locked up in his cupboard his threatening yardstick and needle. In the coda, on the other hand, the bee, seemingly the most ineffectual force, emerges, like the ironist in a classical comedy, as surprisingly virulent. Like some dormant aspect of the tailor's psyche returning unexpectedly in disguise to exact a heavy toll for a previous libidinous expression, it argues its case before the ineffectual bear:

> I know you despise me. I am a poor feeble creature, but I think I can help you.[9]

It is as if some severe Protestant ethic has to reassert itself so that some previous loosening of sexual expression will not end in complete moral decadence.* This ultimate "sting of conscience" in the tale is the message of both the theme and title of Freud's *Civilization and Its Discontents*: that the social harmony of the civilized occurs only at the expense of the forceful superego repression of emotional life.

iv

Fairy tales, like any other product of the individual or collective mind, may of course be interpreted from a variety of psychological viewpoints. Jungians, for instance, might see the goat in this tale as the anima, the female principle in man, usually shown as the creative life-force of the unconscious but here shown as malevol-

---

*It is possible that this ending is a superimposition made by a later, more super-ego oriented culture.

ent because it remains isolated or unintegrated with the Self.
Adlerians, on the other hand, would stress the "social cooperation" of the sons (all want their neighbors to share in their good
fortune) and might try to differentiate their life-styles on the basis
of sibling birth order, for in fairy tales it is the youngest son who
invariably succeeds, while his older brothers are punished for their
cruelty or lose out because of their stupidity. Such critics would
probably stress Adler's notion that the youngest sibling stands a
greater chance of winning because he has not suffered displacement from the center of the family's attention.

However, "The Table, the Ass, and the Stick" does not seem to
be either replete with archetypal symbols or shot through with
refinements in social behavior. It does not seem (like many Grimm
tales) to be archaic enough to be of much interest to Jungians, nor
civilized enough to intrigue Adlerians. For this tale at least,
Freud's view of the psychosexual stages of development, together
with the neo-Freudian notion of mythic decomposition, seems to
provide the richest psychological insight.

In the works analyzed in succeeding chapters, character motivation can of course still be seen to grow out of adventures encountered along the road of psychosexual development. However,
the greater complexity of character that emerges in these fictions in
the context of an equally complex society and culture make an
exclusive adherence to a psychosexual view inadequate. In
"Rothschild's Fiddle," for instance, Yakob's obsession with
money can certainly be recognized as an anal fixation, but to stop
here is to neglect much else that is moving and meaningful in the
story: his revived feelings for his dead child, to name one incident.
A psychology that includes object relatedness and focuses on
adaptational as well as on defensive skills, on how feelings
synthesize as well as atomize, and on the joys of autonomous
functioning as well as on the pleasures of erogenous zones is
clearly needed.

3

The Myth Play as Psychosocial Drama: An Adlerian Perspective on Sophocles' Oedipus Plays

> What animal is parricidal in the morning, incestuous at noon, and blind at night?
> The drunk in A. Robbe-Grillet's *The Erasers*

i

Ever since Freud hit upon the plight of Oedipus as a metaphor for one of the most decisive psychosexual dramas in human nature, both psychologists and literary critics have been mesmerized by this mythic hero. If, as Freud suggested, Oedipus continues to fascinate because the fate that the gods marked out for him really symbolizes a universal wish for mother-incest and parricide, then it is no wonder that he has become one of the most scrutinized figures of the literary classics. In popularity he vies only with Hamlet, who became his spiritual brother when he repressed these same impulses.

Observers of Oedipus's psyche have generally become polarized into either ontogenetic or phylogenetic interpreters. They either focus, somewhat clinically, on the signs and symptoms of his sexual feelings or view all his actions as a mythic composite of almost forgotten ancient rituals or systems of social adaptation. Typical of the former is Mark Kanzer, who views the entire Sophoclean trilogy as successive stages of the Oedipal complex. For him the whole of *Oedipus Tyrannus* is a kind of fulfillment of the incest-parricide wish, while Creon's overbearing acts in *Antigone* symbolize the castration threats that cause the repression of such a wish.[1] Finally, Kanzer judges Oedipus's harmonious dealings with Theseus in *Oedipus at Colonus* to be a sign of the resolution of the complex: the blinded hero's successful petition to abide in the sacred grove of Theseus's city suggests mature identification with,

rather than infantile hostility toward, a father-surrogate. From the
other end of the spectrum, these same events are seen by writers
like Rank, Reik, and Roheim as vestiges or distortions of primitive
rites of sexual initiation or of rebirth and resurrection.[2]

My own reactions to the Oedipus myth-plays of Sophocles have
presented me with the opportunity to extend the horizons of psychological interpretation of the arts, for to my mind these dramas
invite a psychosocial—and even psycholinguistic—perspective that
goes beyond the rather conventional Freudian one demanded by
the fairy tale dealt with in the previous chapter.

Of course, the Oedipus story shares some important features
with the traditional fairy tale. Like the typical youngest son of the
fairy tale, Oedipus overcomes a monster—the Sphinx—by his
wits, and the mysterious circumstances of his death in the sacred
grove have the earmarks of a magical metamorphosis. Yet as
Bruno Bettelheim points out, the Oedipus myth, like all myths, is
psychologically different from the fairy tale:

> in fairy tales the hero's story shows how these potentially
> destructive infantile relations [i.e., incestuous attachments] can
> be, and are, integrated in developmental processes. In the myth,
> oedipal difficulties are acted out and in consequence all ends in
> total destruction.[3]

The unresolved (and perhaps ultimately unresolvable) nuclear conflicts in myths give them a greater complexity than is found in
simple wish-fulfilling fairy tales. The artist who makes use of myth
finds himself more deeply involved in the psychological nuances of
his characters and their social context.

All the more astounding, then, that the most immediate "here
and now" aspects of the Oedipus myth, namely, the psycho*social*,
have been neglected. Critics seem to have forgotten that along with
the impact of one's ethos and the intrapsychic forces generated by
the father-mother-child triad are the influences of extended
family, society, and state. This may be due to the unintentional
stranglehold that Freud placed on the story by discovering in it his
own central myth of the culmination of psychosexual phases of
development. Yet Oedipus is not merely prototypical in that he is a
son exhibiting a universal design upon his parents; he is an individual distinguished by being the husband of an older woman and by
having four children, two of each sex. He is not only the third
person in a family triad; he is the third party in a political triumvirate shared by Jocasta and Creon. He is not merely the repre-

sentative of a Hellenistic society that has perhaps undergone a transformation from a matriarchy to a patriarchy; he is an elected king of a particular city-state that is undergoing particular kinds of stress, first a drought and plague, then a civil war. His significant experiential "past" is not only that he has dealt successfully with the Sphinx (perhaps a phallic mother, perhaps a bisexual component in himself); his existential plight is also that he is a cripple whose status as an adored only child is shaken by the suspicion that he may in fact be a foundling. It is my contention that these facts and events, constituting Oedipus's immediate present and past, both affect and reflect his life-style and behavior. A closer look at them throws the Sophoclean myth-dramas of which he is the protagonist into a different, more illuminating light.

Given his special neo-Freudian emphasis on the psychological influences of society on the individual, one might suppose that Erich Fromm in his lengthy study of Oedipus[4] would have seized upon this tragic hero's interaction with family, society, and state as an additional chapter in his psychology of interpersonal relations. Surprisingly, Fromm instead throws in his lot with mythopoeic analysts like Rank and diagnoses the Oedipus plays as a "return of the repressed" on a phylogenetic level—as a resurgence of supplanted matriarchal ideals. Equal rights for all of mother earth's children, female as well as male; passive acceptance of, rather than attempts to magically control, all natural phenomena; and intuitive reasoning—all these may have comprised Sophocles' unarticulated, perhaps even unconscious, themes. According to Fromm they are to be considered assaults upon a despised patriarchy with its male hierarchies, its rational thought, and its attempts to modify nature.

Without a doubt Oedipus's role as a psychosocial being, rather than merely a psychosexual or psychocultural one, has continued to elude the probings of psychoanalytic critics, whether Freudian or neo-Freudian. However, if we turn for inspiration to the more heterodox views of Alfred Adler, we can perhaps restore the balance. Adler's insistence that society as well as the entire family constellation (not merely the Oedipal triangle) provides a meaningful setting for individual strivings highlights two aspects of Oedipus's life normally neglected by Freudian depth psychology and mythopoeic approaches. These are the ways in which his lameness leads him to evolve a faulty self-image and social posture, and the manner in which he alters his feelings when he discovers himself to be a rejected foundling rather than a pampered only child. Besides locating Oedipus's emotional crisis in his struggle for self-sufficiency, an Adlerian interpretation of *Oedipus Tyrannus* and *Oedipus at Colonus* at the same time offers an unexpected bonus: it reveals subtle meanings heretofore locked within the linguistic structures of both plays.

In an article entitled "The Social Meaning of the Oedipus Myth," Frances Atkins[5] has made an admirable attempt to reassess both Sophocles' mythical hero and its prototype from an Adlerian perspective. However, in stressing the resemblance of Oedipus's conduct to Adler's model for the power drive as a compensation for inferiority, she fails, it seems to me, to pinpoint the shifting strategies that Oedipus is forced to adopt as his safeguards against a feeling of worthlessness undergo different kinds of attack. Such variations in Oedipus's reaction to "threats" are, as I shall try to show, not only unfolded dramatically during the course of both plays and in some of the details of their mythological sources, but also reflected in the evolving metaphors of Sophocles' poetic diction.

ii

The key to Oedipus's forceful behavior both prior to and during the action of *Oedipus Tyrannus* is not merely a drive for temporal power—as his title *tyrannus* (tyrant) might first suggest—or even *hubris* (overweening pride), generally taken to be the character flaw of all Greek tragic heroes. Rather it comes almost entirely from his overcompensation for the injury resulting from his having been "exposed" in the wilderness during infancy. In the traditional Greek manner of abandoning unwanted children, his parents had caused pins to be driven through the tendons of his feet, accounting later both for his limp and for his name.

Both literature and legend are populated with heroes who try to overcome similar deformities of the lower extremities. Achilles develops prowess as a warrior to counterbalance his vulnerable heel; Hephaestus (Vulcan) succeeds as a master artisan and as a wooer of the highly prized Aphrodite despite his lameness; and philoctetes renounces his masochistic concern with his unhealed foot in order to return to battle. One can even cite contemporary characters, like Philip Carey in Maugham's *Of Human Bondage*, whose clubfoot moves him to greater sensitivity and insight. Adler himself mentions Loki, Gunther, and Wieland as similarly handicapped figures in German mythology who stoically and heroically override their own crippledness.[6]

That Oedipus's lameness is a probable source of an inferiority complex is shown by the way in which he tries to evade, as if it were a painful narcissistic wound, the Messenger's mention of it:

Oedipus. What pain gripped me, that you took me in your arms?
Messenger. The ankles of your feet will tell you that.
O. Alas, why do you mention that old trouble?
M. I freed you when your ankles were pierced together.
O. A terrible shame from my swaddling clothes I got.[7]

This is what Adler would define as Oedipus's "organ inferiority," a real or imagined sense of deficiency in a part of the body that has to be compensated for in one's drive for wholeness and success. Oedipus's attempts to offset his physical weakness and its attendant feelings of inferiority generate the frustration and rage that can be found in every stage of his behavior in the plays about him as well as in parts of the underlying myth.

As soon as Oedipus hears from the Delphic oracle the dreadful prophecy of his patricide and incest, he bolts off in hysterical flight, not even stopping to secure a horse or chariot for his journey. Armed with a spear, which doubles as a staff to support his halting gait, he encounters an older man arrogantly poised in a chariot and accompanied by a small retinue of men. The particular circumstances of the homicide, as they come down in legend,[8] are especially significant. We must imagine Oedipus as not only insulted by the herald's order to make way for this unknown king (in reality his father, Laius), but also feeling an affront to his lameness by having been addressed both from above and from a vehicle. The latter circumstance, by offering such a blatant contrast to his own painfully slow movements on foot, must have exacerbated his sense of outrage, while the former—the attack from *above*, placing Oedipus in the "feminine position"—was a further threat to the "masculine protest" that underlies all compensatory drives.* Moreover, the trauma of the original injury to his ankles must have been reawakened, for, according to some versions of

---

*Adler's early term for the power drive—"masculine protest"—is more applicable to Oedipus's psychological and social condition than the more encompassing term he later substituted—"superiority complex"—to which Frances Atkins[4] subscribes. Adler's probable reason for abandoning the original nomenclature—that it rested too much on the Viennese middle-class notion of a male-dominated society—is the very reason why I wish to retain it in describing Oedipus. Oedipus's later insistence upon his rights as patriarch and his initiation of a system of primogeniture suggest a milieu similar to the mid-European one from which Adler's notion sprang.

the myth, one of Laius's chariot wheels bruised his foot in passing.[9] Thus the rage with which Oedipus kills Laius and his men, although seemingly unreasonable, has been triggered by a deep-seated sense of inadequacy based on the real but exaggerated imperfection of a part of his body.

But even though oversensitivity to his lameness leads Oedipus to perform destructive, neurotic acts, paradoxically it also shapes his principal successes. Neurotic strivings for wholeness and power do not preclude being productive as well.[10] In fact, had Oedipus not been preoccupied with his childhood injury, he might not have been able to answer the Sphix's riddle, concerned as it was with modes of walking. "What creature goes upon four legs in the morning, two at noon, and three in the evening, but is strongest when borne on the fewest?" the Sphinx demanded of each challenger, for whom an unsuccessful reply meant instant death. Yet this riddle, a paradigm for the life of a normal man, is for Oedipus, because he is in essence as in name "Swollenfoot," a mockery. As the infant exposed in the wilderness, he could not even creep on all fours because his ankles were pinned together. As a grown man he found his independence of movement again frustrated, this time by an enforced flight in which he required a traveler's staff (three "feet" when he should be strongest on two). Finally, in blindness and old age he will rely not only upon his staff but also upon the two additional feet of his daughter Antigone. Because the number of his "limbs" has been both decreased and multiplied—but never with real increase in strength—fate not only has mocked his handicap but also has added this further irony: his intellectual triumph over the Sphinx used as its weapons the very mockeries with which fate assailed him.

This strange victory Oedipus celebrates in various ways, but mainly by showing that as king he can both literally and metaphorically "stand on his own two feet." Unlike the traditional *tyrannus*, he does not rely on heralds but communicates with his people by going directly to them. He converses with them "not through messengers," as he puts it, but in person—and he goes to them on foot rather than by chariot. Moreover, the swiftness of his administrative acts—in sending for Teiresias, for instance, even before the chorus has suggested it—and his impatience with others' slowness imply further attemps to offset his lameness.

iii

That Oedipus's life-style is very much determined by his desire to override his physical defect is shown by Sophocles' metaphors alluding to feet and locomotion. One of the most persistent of these is that of the mountain-climber, with its hint that life is a walk upon precarious heights. The chorus depicts Oedipus's boast of self sufficiency, which seems to be one of the causes for his fall (as it is for most Greek heroes), as a nimble athlete who disables his foot by jumping. Pride, says the chorus, "goes up to the highest ramparts, and leaps into sheer necessity, where it finds the use of its foot of no avail";[11] or as another translator has it, pride will "dash her foot against Fate's stone."[12] After Oedipus's public condemnation of Laius's killer, the chorus envisages the unknown murderer as having to "set in flight a foot swifter than wind-swift mares" but nevertheless marked for capture because he is "a wild beast...with miserable foot"—miserable because moving solitary among hard rocks.[13] Thus the imagery of the play prefigures the self-defeating aggressiveness of Oedipus's overcompensation. The irony within the metaphor is that hunting or climbing, running or jumping—all sports requiring extra strength in the lower limbs—may cause injury to the very parts involved.

But Oedipus, having at the beginning of the play no inkling that he will be identified with either the lonely, groping animal that is hunted or the athlete who loses his foothold, sees himself instead as the agile, sure-footed hunter. Moving through the roads and byways of thought, he hopes to uncover faded "tracks" and "flush" the game "from cover."[14] The chorus, however, obliquely hints at his need to make up for an inadequacy of strength and vision by reminding him that mountain-climbers must use their hands as well as their feet—an innuendo that Sophocles later underscores by having them use the word *chersin* (i.e., hands) for *deeds* rather than the customary *erga*.[15]

The paradox of Oedipus's self-defeat born of overcompensation for his "organ inferiority" is carried beyond metaphor even into the linguistic texture of the play. Puns on words and etymologies connect power with helplessness. Although the name *Oedipus* means literally "swollen foot," *oidi* (swell) is, as Bernard Knox points out, almost identical with *oida* (know),[16] so that it is equally as "Knowfoot" and "Swollenfoot" that he solves the riddle about feet.

Freudian and neo-Freudian critics have traditionally interpreted Oedipus's self-blinding as a symbolic self-castration—an atonement for his "oedipal" crime of killing his father and sleeping with his mother. Some have even gone so far as to give a physiological justification to this interpretation. They argue that because both the eyes and genitals develop simultaneously *in utero*, Oedipus is instinctively prone to displace his sexual loathing upon the organs of sight. But these explanations seem rather fanciful not only because of Robert Graves's point that primitive myths do not usually hedge about sexual maiming[17] but because of the failure of these interpretations to take into account the subtle linguistic ties Sophocles has made between the gouging out of eyes and an entirely different set of associations. For instance, the playwright's unusual choice of the word *arthra*, which means *joints* (i.e., ball and socket), to designate the eyeballs through which Oedipus sticks pins, actually hints at the connection this former man of strength makes between his self-inflicted helplessness and his lameness.[18] With his wife-mother's graphic statement that "Laius pinned his feet together at the joints" (again *arthra*) still ringing in his ears, Oedipus uses a similar set of pins—Jocasta's brooches—to bring his life back to its original condition, that of the helpless foot-bound infant.

If this interpretation at first seems far-fetched, we should remember that it is based on very self-conscious and pervasive wordplay. The more traditional Freudian view that the self-blinding is tantamount to self-castration does not have this extensive linguistic support. The task for the psychoanalytic interpreter here, as elsewhere, is to account for all the parts of the "well-wrought urn."

iv

The way in which a person tries to compensate for a real or imaginary physical inadequacy is, Adler points out, partly determined by his star rating in his own family constellation. Depending on other variables, of course, the eldest son will gravitate toward emulating the father, while the second-born, in direct or indirect rivalry, will rebel, establish a different career, and in general strive to differentiate himself from his older brother and father. The youngest may feel outclassed by the competition of his older siblings but at the same time is so highly valued as the family's communal baby that his primary narcissism receives healthy stimulation.

The only child will probably, according to Adler, gain domination over the household by exploiting the deference that adults pay to miniature size without experiencing some of the salutary effects of having actually to compete for it with siblings. If he has a real defect, such as a clubfoot, his parents are likely to be overly solicitous. Yet like everyone else, he has, according to the Adlerian view, an innate drive toward success. Thus he is neurotically caught up in a contradiction: he uses "feminine" passivity to achieve goals that in the real world are accomplished only by "masculine" assertion. Such a person usually functions well in sheltered positions away from the threat of competition, but when forced more into the outside world either by necessity or chance, will likely become alternately abject and hostile. To those who seem weaker he will be either scornful or overprotective, depending on whether at the moment he wants to be free from, or to capitalize on, his own organic weakness. In his role of patron he sees his helpless protégé as an image of himself, and therefore his oversolicitousness becomes a *persona* for the parent that he himself longs to be coddled by.

It is interesting to note that mythic heroes are traditionally only children, if not in fact, at least operating as such. They are sole rescuers (like Hercules) or lonely renegades (like Prometheus) busily engaged not in defeating siblings but in testing their mettle against institutions or fate. Oedipus fits this category, although in a grotesque way he fathers siblings against whom he will have feelings of rivalry and envy. The fairy tale, on the other hand, almost inevitably stars the youngest of three sons as protagonist who is in direct competition with and in ultimate triumph over his older brothers. This was of course the case with "The Table, the Ass, and the Stick," although the rivalrous aspect was deemphasized.

Both the mythic hero and the fairy-tale hero must overcome the impediments of external objects and events, but the former is driven back more upon himself to deal with the defects, vagaries, and vulnerabilities in his own character. Even heroes of action like Hercules must take time to ruminate on what it means to be effeminized by a Queen Omphale.

Oedipus's predominant view of himself has been that of pampered only child, the sole natural son of Polybus and Merope. Even though he has reacted violently to the drunken wayfarer's suggestion that he is a foundling, the Delphic oracle's evasion of this question by substituting a more horrendous image of him as a committer of patricide and incest pushes this suspicion into the background of his consciousness. Thus his sense of inferiority at the crossroads stems solely from what seems to be Laius's mockery of his lameness and helplessness rather than, as Frances Atkins argues,[19] from his sense of being a foundling who must prove his worth. Sophocles reserves this latter feeling for a point much farther on in the play. As an additional assault upon one of his masculine safeguards, it will constitute, as we shall see, one of the play's final climaxes.

Similarly, Oedipus is not acting in arrogant defiance of the gods, as Frances Atkins claims, when he hits an old man "who could be his father," for he has had no real confirmation from the oracle that Polybus is not his actual father. The more horrible prophecy has also pushed the relatively minor question of legitimacy and of true paternity entirely out his mind. As far as he is concerned, Polybus and Merope are still his real parents; to stay near them, not to kill a mere stranger on the crossroads, is to tempt fate.

Since Oedipus had lived as a pampered only child in Corinth before he was forced to flee all alone from the warmth and protection of hearth and home, his excessive benevolence toward his distressed subjects may at first seem strange. Even though many of those in his presence are old, he addresses all of them as "children," posing as father to the city even though the chorus has appealed to "father Zeus" to quell the plague. But to conclude that Oedipus's paternalism here exemplifies Adler's ideal for mental health—a strong sense of social feeling and cooperation[20] —would be premature. Certainly it is true that in a male-dominated society like Oedipus's, the patriarchal system sets the pattern for a boy's more wide-spread social relationships. But this ordinary kind of character development might become disturbed if too much of his energy is used, let us say, to compensate for inferiority feelings, or is drawn off in battles with threatening siblings or merely in coping with the sense of his own inadequacy. He then becomes too self-centered to have genuine human feeling or to participate cooperatively in society.

A closer look reveals that this is the case with Oedipus. He very soon contradicts the mask of social concern that he wears at the beginning of the play; his "I, Oedipus, who bear the famous name" almost immediately cancels his self-advertised empathy with the plague-stricken citizens. In fact, his paternalism merely projects the kind of shelter and care that he as a coddled only child longs for—a temporary pseudostrength yearning to be its opposite: helplessness. Thus his shaky security vanishes when he is the least bit thwarted or opposed, as he is by Teiresias, Creon, the Herdsman, and Jocasta. In his hopeless attempt to stage a masquerade of strength and self-sufficiency, his mercurial temper alters from that of assertive but kindly father, to humble suppliant, then to enraged tyrant.

V

Part of this masculine protest is expressed by the mental gymnastics that Oedipus sees as his triumph over, and therefore as a compensation for, his lameness. His having answered the Sphinx's riddle about the relative strength of legs is, as we have seen, one aspect of this. He choice of metaphors of locomotion to represent logical thought is another, as in the opening speech just referred to, when he expresses his concern by saying, "I have...traveled many wandering roads of thought."[21]

According to Adler, the normal way every child copes with fluid, intangible life is to reduce it to "measurable entities."[22] Of course, these are purely mental constructs, just as cartologists devise longitudinal and latitudinal lines in order to deal with topography. There is nothing wrong with setting up such "guiding fictions," Adler tells us; on the contrary, they are necessary to solve life's existential problems. The difference between the healthy person and the neurotic in this respect is that the former will apply his coordinates and categories only as far as their limits allow, and abandon them or substitute other "fictions" when they cease to be satisfying or productive. The neurotic, on the other hand, concocts an impractical or an overly rigid scheme to which he allows himself to become irrevocably chained. Or he suddenly swerves away from following "his own lights" in order to defend against some imagined threat to an overvalued aspect of his "masculinity."

Because Oedipus has won his greatest success by his mental powers—which he had to develop in part as compensation for his physical infirmity— it is not surprising that the atmosphere he invokes throughout the play is that of the courtroom, where as prosecutor and judge—and later as defendant—he can try to use inexorable logic to win his case. In fact his "guiding fiction" in the play is that his mind can first encompass, then solve, any problem. As Knox points out, Oedipus becomes "equator and measurer" and will reach the truth about Laius's death by calculation of time, by measurement of age and number of persons present, and by comparison of place and description—all prompted by Pythagoras's idea that "man is the measure of all things."[23] He voluntarily puts his abilities as logician and mathematician to the most strenuous tests.

This kind of self-imposed discipline has special significance for the dependent, pampered, or only child. In Adler's view, such persons may fear arithmetic, and presumably other forms of symbolic logic, because they see solutions to all conundrums as related to themselves in some deep, personal way. They tremble at being forced to find answers to problems in their own heads without even a book to rely upon.[24] Oedipus's almost unrelenting logic as "mathematician," investigator, and answerer of riddles becomes an even greater, braver compensation for his lameness than we have heretofore imagined.

vi

But Oedipus cannot hold to strict logic any more than he can maintain a cool, authoritarian pose. Infantile rage overwhelms his trial-judge composure many times—in his encounters with Creon, Teiresias, and the Shepherd, for instance—just as it surfaced during his confrontation with Laius at the crossroads. Furthermore, the past pleasure of having been coddled for his physical weakness and the present necessity for his masculine protest against it keep him vacillating uncertainly between active and passive roles. Again this is borne out in the pairs of contrasting metaphors applied to him. After the self-blinding, he is spoken of by the chorus as the physician who has become the patient ("the disease is more than he can bear"). Near the end of the play Oedipus the active teacher becomes not only the passive learner ("Instruct me, in God's name") but an inert concept, the "thing pointed out" (*paradeigma*), a paradigm, an object lesson.[25] From master mathematician he is transformed to the algebraic formula itself, equated in various unknown ways:

> ...O wedlock, wedlock!
> ...you revealed
> Father, brother, children in blood relation,
> The bride both wife and mother.[26]

In like manner, Oedipus characterizes his wavering between tyrannical oppressiveness and childlike weakness by an intermixture of active and passive verbs. After the dénouement he complains:

> I *am revealed* unnaturally born and married...*revealed* as unholy...as a father who *ploughed* where he himself *was sown*.[27]

He almost thinks of himself as powerless as a foetus in the womb ("Where am I being carried"), or as played upon like a musical instrument ("How does my voice fly about, carried aloft"). Yet his passivity paradoxically turns into swift executive action directed against himself as object. Note the imperative reflexives in his

> Take me away from this place as quickly as possible.
> Hide me away as quickly as possible.
> Throw me out of this land as quickly as may be,[28]

and the way in which he commands even while he supplicates:

> I order you [Creon] and beg you....[29]

vii

If Oedipus's attempt to compensate for his lameness had stemmed merely from an only-child syndrome, his motives and style of living would be fairly transparent, for vacillations between aggression and submission are merely two sides of the same coin of masculine protest for this type of person. When the Messenger announces Polybus's death from old age, Oedipus's dread of patricide seems to be groundless. But now the way is open for his discovery that the claim of the Corinthian wayfarer that he was a foundling is indeed true. It is a dramatic realization for Oedipus, because it exacerbates the fear that all pampered or only children harbor, namely, that they will be totally neglected or cut adrift from parental ties. Now amazed that Polybus, whom the Messenger confirms to have been merely a foster father after all, could "so much love me," he seems anxious to know which one of his real parents mutilated him, even before he is able to determine who they are:

> *Messenger.* I freed you when your ankles were pierced together....Your very name you got from this mistfortune.
> *Oedipus.* By the Gods, did my mother or father do it [the piercing]? Speak.[30]

This question is never answered; we never discover which parent he is more apprehensive about. Since in the Freudian tradition the mother is regarded as the primary attachment, later developing

into the child's first sex object in the Oedipal complex, the classical
interpretation of this line would probably be that Oedipus most
feared rejection from his mother. However, Adlerians see the so-
called Oedipal complex to be merely a result of excessive stimulation by an overindulgent mother. Because a mother need not
necessarily be a coddler of her offspring, however, this phase of
life is not ineluctable in the Adlerian view. On the other hand,
since a father as well as a mother might be overly attentive to the
child, he, rather than the mother, might, according to Adler,[31]
become the object of his offspring's inordinate attachment. From
Oedipus's strong expression of emotion just a few lines earlier concerning the "so much love" of his foster father Polybus, it would
seem that it is paternal rather than maternal love that he cherishes
most. At this point in the play, Adler's broader perspective of the
"Oedipal" attachment seems to be more serviceable than Freud's.

Now that he has heard the Messenger's revelation that the
Corinthian king and queen were only foster parents, Oedipus has
the additional problem of discovering a new center of affection, or
of indifference, in an as yet unidentified set of real parents.
Whether he was voluntarily abandoned by them, or forcibly torn
away because they were in bondage, becomes very important to
him, for his desire for affection is by its neurotic nature necessarily
boundless.

The latter alternative is, of course, less painful. Love from slave
parents, although naturally incapable of expression after the sale
of their child, nevertheless has its existence assured, and it is to this
line of thought that Oedipus probably clings when he tells Jocasta,
"Take courage. Even if I am found a slave for three generations,
your birth will not be base."[32] But he must soon face up to the
other possibility, that he is a foundling and very likely a bastard,
one who was, in other words, unmistakably rejected by his
parents. The only comfort he can derive from this is to imagine
that his illegitimacy is favored by fate, and he begins to fantasize
that he is "the son of Fortune, giver of the good."[33] Picking up
this thread, which is little more than a desperate attempt at narcissistic reparation, the chorus tries to comfort him further by suggesting first that Mt. Cithaeron, sister of Mt. Olympus, the home
of the gods and the place where he was "exposed," had been for
him a respectable mother as well as an affectionate nurse:

> Cithaeron, by tomorrow's full moon
> You shall not fail, by mount Olympus,
> To find that Oedipus, as a native of your land,
> Shall honour you for nurse and mother.[34]

In the antistrophe the chorus feeds his delusion even more by suggesting that he has sprung from the illicit union of Apollo or Hermes with some nymph—thus making him a demigod—or, if indeed a foundling, one probably adopted by none other than the great Dionysus. As Adler points out,[35] children frequently fantasize about having a "princely origin" when some real or imagined rejection makes them feel "banishment from their 'real' home."* Not surprisingly, the actual confirmation of Oedipus's old fear of abandonment calls for this much stronger compensatory fantasy of royal independence. However, as Adler also reminds us, eventually "reality defies the harmlessness of the fairy tale."[36] We soon find the chorus unconsciously undercutting its own optimism that Oedipus may be of divine birth when Sophocles has it inadvertently choose as its terms for abstract realization the word *eurema* (found), implying the *physical* discovery inherent in *foundling*.[37]

At the end of the play, even though Oedipus's knowledge that he is Laius's lawful son is far more painful to him than finding out that he is illegitimate, it nevertheless allows him to resume—this time without pretense or role playing—his initial posture of kind father greeting the citizens as his children. Now, of course, he has valid grounds, which he lacked as *tyrannus*, for speaking the way a hereditary monarch would, it now being established that he is a direct descendant of Cadmus through Laius: "Let not the city of my fathers be condemned to have me...."[38] This leads us to suspect that his paternalistic concern for the Thebans as scions of Cadmus at the beginning of the play probably sprang not only from his secret desire to be coddled by them in a similar way but from his attempt to disassociate himself—a nonindigenous, elected *tyrannus*—from the notion of foundling or bastard. His defense was to adopt the state as his "family" and see himself as its patriarch rather than as its king.

viii

In her paper "The Social Meaning of the Oedipus Myth" Atkins acknowledges that

the marriage of Cadmus and Harmonia symbolized the begin-

---

*Freud expressed the same idea two years earlier (1908) in "Family Romances." A peculiar inversion of the "family romance"—one in which the fantasizer must imagine himself to be an alienated pauper rather than an attention-drawing prince—is cited in chapter 4, in my discussion of Morgan Moreen in Henry James's *The Pupil*.

ning of the patriarchal family, the basic unit of Greek society, while the city of Thebes represented the whole of that society.[39]

However, she emphasizes the "socially uncooperative" disruption of this system by Cadmus's descendants. After all, had its foundations not been shaken by Semele's participation in Zeus's adultery, by Laius's homosexual seduction of Chrysippus, and by Oedipus's patricide and incest? Yet far more important, it seems to me, was the way in which Oedipus derived from that particular society a life-style that was able to embody his compensatory drives. Obviously Oedipus, in insisting upon his true identity as patriarch of the city, is relying upon traditional respect for the father-authority to intensify the masculinity in his protest.

If we delve deeper into the shadowy origins of the Oedipus myth, we discover that Oedipus may not have been merely leaning upon the patriarchal conventions for support. He may in fact have been initiating a masculine claim of his own: the right of primogeniture. According to Robert Graves, Oedipus's real "crime" may have been the attempt to replace the custom of female succession with laws favoring the male line:

> Did Oedipus, like Sisyphus, try to substitute patrilineal for matrilineal laws of succession, but got banished by his subjects? It seems probable....
> Oedipus of Corinth conquered Thebes and became king by marrying Jocasta, a priestess of Hera. Afterwards he announced that the kingdom should henceforth be bequeathed from father to son in the male line, which is a Corinthian custom, instead of remaining the gift to Hera the Throttler.[40]

In Sophocles' play the customs concerning succession are a bit obscure. It seems that Oedipus was invited to share power with Jocasta and Creon as an equal partner in a triumvirate, but that somehow, because of his stronger personality, he had gradually expropriated most of the authority for himself. His threats against Creon, his scornful treatment of Jocasta, and his strong patriarchal stance among the Thebans imply this and indicate that he has already established the right of primogeniture. The succession of his twin sons Polyneices and Eteocles would thus be assured.

What primogeniture comes to mean for Oedipus becomes exceedingly complex in the light of the main ingredients of his life: his masculine protest against organ inferiority and his position as coddled only child fearing to be revealed as a foundling. As Adler tells us, the only child is most likely to be pampered by his mother, and this in turn causes him to treat his father as a competitor.[41] Roughly speaking, this resembles Freud's Oedipus complex. However, should the father be the pamperer, the child identifies with him and sees him as an ally against the mother.[42] A son would therefore receive the stimulation to his feminine side—protection and passive gratification—from the person whose masculine aggressive characteristics he would normally want to emulate.

I have already pointed out how Oedipus was more concerned with Polybus's love than Merope's, suggesting that most of his coddling came from his foster father. After the denouement, he not only nostalgically remembers Polybus as patriarch but, by associating him with "halls," a female symbol for protectiveness and nursing, subtly defines him as maternal as well:

Polybus, Corinth, halls—ancestral, they told me—how beautiful was your ward [from *trophon*, i.e., nurse], a scar that held back festering disease![43]

Note also the special emphasis Oedipus places on *ancestral*, to reveal his interest in the patrimony of name, property, and authority.

Now the gift of primogeniture is peculiar in that while it pays tribute to the biological fact of masculinity, it panders to the instinct of passive gratification or "feminine" receptivity. It is a male privilege unearned by any male aggressiveness. Since Oedipus is the innovator of primogeniture in Thebes and has won rather than inherited the throne, he can safely boast that his success is due entirely to male assertiveness. But the underlying uncertainty of his masculinity, derived from his inferiority feeling about his crippledness and his fear of being a foundling, marks his real goal as that of wanting to remain the fondled only child who receives all things effortlessly. Ironically, his later discovery is that his unwitting murder of his own father has, in accordance with the new laws of succession that he himself has established, made him a *passive* recipient of his father's throne.

The final unraveling of the mystery of Oedipus's origin strips away the various masculine poses that mask his inferiority feelings, especially the pose of the patriarch of many and the progenitor of a male line. As one who stands revealed as the passive and solitary recipient of Laius's heritage (in reality a curse), he discovers without much surprise that he is not really concerned with the further implications of primogeniture. The bestowal of claims to succession upon his sons is of no interest to him. In fact Polyneices and Eteocles, as male competitors, threaten his feminine identification with the pampering Polybus and arouse animosity rather than paternal love. The child who dreams of succeeding to his father's authority will fear his children's dreams of seizing his, especially when the "feminine"-passive aspects of his claims make theirs appear "masculine"-aggressive.

The fear and hostility that Oedipus shows toward Polyneices and Eteocles are merely hinted at near the end of *Oedipus Tyrannus*, when he summarily dismisses them to their own fate:

> As for my sons, Creon, assume no trouble;
> They are men and will have no difficulty
> Of living wherever they may be.[64]

Since his daughters Ismene and Antigone are, as females, socially determined to offer little resistance to his protest of masculinity, he can afford to treat them the way an established elder brother, confident heir to his father's authority and power, would treat the more helpless youngest born. Still remembering his experience as pampered only child, he can even identify with their helplessness and implore Creon to be the affectionate father that he himself had in Polybus and would like to have had in Laius. But the girls, and especially Antigone, are destined to play an even more complicated role than this in the drama of his inferiority feelings and his masculine protest against them. We must go to Sophocles' sequel, *Oedipus at Colonus*, to see the final working out of Oedipus's concept of himself as superior male, who is in reality harboring fears of weakness and passivity.

Unlike *Oedipus Tyrannus*, in which movement and action are almost entirely psychological, *Oedipus at Colonus* is replete with physical activity and references to Oedipus's footsore wanderings. It is full of preoccupations about where he might rest on the terrain, upon which the city elders have marked off spots that are neutral, and therefore accessible to him, from those that are, like his mother's body, sacred and taboo.

The Freudian view of the play is that Oedipus's end symbolically represents a resolution of the Oedipus complex, for he is reconciled with both parents through surrogate figures and actions. Maternal acceptance of his incest feelings is symbolized by his return-to-the-womb kind of death in the sacred grove (mother earth), and paternal approval is expressed by King Theseus's kind permission for him to die there.

From an Adlerian point of view the nature of Oedipus's end, as well as his final paternal attitude, is the logical outcome of the masculine protest that masks his inferiority feelings. It is seldom noted that King Theseus, Oedipus's benefactor, parallels him in also having been an initiator of primogeniture in Athens, "another patriarchal revolutionary from the Isthmus," as Graves calls him.[45] Thus Oedipus, as Theseus's surrogate heir, receives from him another pampering acknowledgment of his "masculinity."

Clearly, Theseus's gift of welcome at the sacred grove affirms Oedipus's feminine weakness while keeping intact his outward masculine protest. Primogeniture is valuable to Oedipus—a pampered only child—only by virtue of what it confers upon him, not by virtue of what he can confer upon his by now fully mature sons. Since their biological masculinity reminds him of his psychological femininity, he confronts them with hidden fear and open hostility. Not only does he thwart Polyneices by refusing to become an ally in his war against Eteocles, but his curse against both for having reciprocated his own indifference virtually dooms them to death at each other's hands. Since his daughters are nonthreatening because female, he can afford to play a more subtle game with them in using aggressiveness to conceal passivity. By reducing Antigone and Ismene to errand runners, he has made them subservient to what has been the root of his inferiority complex—his lame feet. For Antigone this has been a double humiliation. By making her his nurse and mother in exile, Oedipus has degraded the femininity he detests in himself. And by forcing her to be his personal guide and emissary—and thus become for him another pair of legs—he has incorporated her into a grotesque exemplum of the end of the Sphinx's riddle, that man is weakest when he walks on the greatest number of feet.

Oedipus's strange and unenviable triumph is that he has been able to resume his infantile identity as pampered child by what only seems to be an act of masculine will. His final victory is therefore not a rule of strength but a tyranny of weakness.

ix

Both the fairy tale "The Table, the Ass, and the Stick" and the Oedipus myth-dramas deal with narcissistic wounds inflicted by a father. The Grimms' sons of the tailor suffer a denigration of their sexuality by him, while Sophocles'' Oedipus experiences a gradual loss of autonomy and self-sufficiency because of the actions of a father (as well as of a father's father) in the dim past.

In both cases patriarchal power is a maiming force that goes beyond Oedipal castration fantasies and threats, for it is a more pervasive onslaught on the self, on the son's (or sons') ability to function morally and socially, even on the right to exist.* The Grimms' fairy tale, however, allows reconciliation with the father through experientially gained wisdom, normal maturational growth, and ritualistic exorcism of the uncontrollable id-force. The Sophoclean Oedipus myth-dramas, on the other hand, merely allow the "problem" to resonate in every aspect of the personality, family, society, and language. Actual reconciliation with the father is literally impossible but is spiritually feasible by reconnecting with the generative quality of thought and understanding within. The task of psychological interpretation in the first instance is to gather these "decomposed" and atomized elements in order to clarify the indirectly expressed wish, while in the latter case it is to assist us in feeling the reverberations of the paradoxical loss and gain in every facet of the work.

*In the last chapter, devoted to different versions of the Prodigal Son parable, I discuss how the decline of patriarchy is equally problematical, for the absence of the father-authority lessens the opportunities for identification and thus threatens the son's sense of identity. This is one of the great themes of modern literature upon which a psychology of object relations can throw much light.

4

The Short Story as Case Study: Pathological Precociousness in Henry James's "The Pupil"

Children in James's stories do not grow by normal stages—they have heart failures, ghostly shocks, or rude awakenings to the cruel daylight of reality which bend their small forces toward an immolation
B. D. Horwitz, "The Sense of Desolation in Henry James"

i

The foregoing interpretation of *Oedipus Tyrannus* and *Oedipus at Colonus* from an Adlerian perspective should not be taken as an attempt to bludgeon Freud and his disciples with the weapons of the group's most famous renegade. Rather, as I hinted in my concluding remarks about the Grimms' "The Table, the Ass, and the Stick,"[1] shifting the psychological perspective upon a classic or traditional work can suddenly yield startlingly new, and not necessarily contradictory, insights. Even though it is not commonly acknowledged, Adler's change of emphasis away from Freud's preoccupations with instinctual drives to the social matrix of behavior anticipates some of the later, culturally oriented work of Fromm and Erikson. And his intuitions about the importance of disturbances in the body ego (organ inferiority) foreshadow some of the developmental problems with identification, identity, and self-image that have since occupied the object-relations theorists.

The recent work of such luminaries in the field of early childhood development as D. W. Winnicott, Margaret Mahler, and Jean Piaget has pushed psychological investigation into the more shadowy areas of the pro-Oedipal dyadic relationship of mother and child. It has thus made possible not only the more successful treatment of the so-called "narcissistic" disorders but a deeper understanding of the heretofore veiled mysteries of psychic development in preverbal infancy. For the literary critic this has dramatically opened up another field of vision—one in which the "literary psyche" of author, character, and reader can come into sharper focus.

The object-relations theorists and clinicians encourage us to look more closely at literary works that highlight the struggles of the child-hero, for they have shown us that it is in the minds and emotions of children and adolescents that we see *in process* the conflicts that will later form the characterological armor of our "mature" protagonists.

In this chapter, and to some extent in the two following, I shall therefore pause to look at the crises of early and late adolescence in a set of characters in fiction and film as a step toward seeing more clearly the child-within-the-man found in the anti-hero or failed hero of modern art.

ii

One of the ways in which to understand how Henry James decisively brought to a close the Victorian novel of heroic romantic melodrama and helped to initiate the modern story of unheroic psychological realism is to examine his transformation of the *bildungsroman*. In this traditional type of "apprenticeship" novel the protagonist, usually a sensitive young man, attempts to "learn the nature of the world, discover its meaning and pattern, and acquire a philosophy of life and 'the art of living.'"[2] The internal obstacles to his success are described by some such simple phrase as an "undisciplined heart," which eventually becomes chastened by hardships and enlightened by experience.

The Jamesian hero clearly cannot look forward to such an optimistic future. Not that he does not learn to "discipline his heart." On the contrary, he *obsessionally* disciplines it to such a degree that he increasingly closes off freedom of action and breadth of human feeling, frequently substituting some sort of noble sacrifice for love.

For some time it has been recognized that James, with his highly introspective characters, is essentially the creator of modern psychological fiction. Yet it has been only relatively recently that James's work has been subjected to intensive psychological interpretation. Part of the reason, I think, is that his work does not yield readily to traditional Freudian approaches. To cite one instance, the failure of a Jamesian male protagonist to end up in happy intimacy with a woman does not seem to have an Oedipal configuration. For one thing, the hero's rival for the woman is seldom if ever an older man. For another, fear of maternal incest does not seem to underlie his sexual hesitancy; the reader senses instead (as in the case of Marcher in "The Beast in the Jungle", for example) a deeper dread of oral incorporation by the woman or of loss of identity by close association with her.[3] The emotional maimers are not fathers, as in the Grimms' tale and the Oedipus myths, but mothers or mother-surrogates. The precocious behavior of Morgan Moreen in Henry James's short story "The Pupil"—a kind of anti-*bildungsroman*—dramatically exhibits a form of pathology that is centered in such pre-Oedipal problems of development.

iii

We first meet Morgan in his eleventh year, when the youthful Pemberton, an Oxford-educated scholar, is hired as his private tutor and companion. Morgan's precocity reveals itself foremost in his body language, principally in the way he carries his "elderly shoulders." In the presence of his overbearing mother he exhibits a face that seems to Pemberton to be "infantine, yet...also... under the influence of curious intuitions and knowledge,"[4] and the "disrepair" of his clothes makes him look "elderly and gentlemanly" rather than like an "urchin who plays and spoils his things".[5] As Pemberton gets to know Morgan better, other traits coalesce with this "mature" demeanor: the boy's aptitude for witty repartee; his stoicism in the face of physical pain (he has a chronic heart condition); and his highly developed moral awareness, which is especially focused upon the financial exploitation of his tutor by his parents.

Throughout his whole life Morgan has been deprived of normal peer contact. He has never been permitted to attend school because of his ailment, and although he has three siblings—two marriageable sisters and one twenty year-old brother—he is their junior by enough years to see them neither as potential rivals nor as play companions. Thus one of the key deprivations, and probably one of the chief causes of precociousness in Morgan's character, has been the lack of socialized play. One of Pemberton's first impressions of Morgan is that he had "the air in his elderly shoulders of a boy who didn't play," and he wonders if he as the boy's tutor-companion "should be able to teach him to play." Later, however, Pemberton concludes that somewhere behind the façade of "the little cosmopolite, who liked intellectual gymnastics" and who was acutely observant of "the behaviour of mankind" was the child "who nevertheless had his proper playroom of superstitions, where he smashed a dozen toys a day."[6]

Unfortunately James does not treat us to a direct view of these no doubt vivid mental images, which might have offered the best clue to Morgan's pathology. However, Morgan does share with Pemberton two key fantasies, which not only provide a profile of his psyche but give the story its climax as well. The first is his pretense that he and Pemberton are a pair of homeless derelicts going to the Louvre only in order to find refuge from the cold. (They are in fact somewhat shabbily dressed as they wander through the palatial museum on some of their cultural outings.) It is an interesting reversal of the usual "family romance."[7] Here a "prince"—the way Morgan is often regarded at home—is surprisingly intent upon becoming a pauper, but in a borrowed setting more splendid than the long series of very tarnished "aristocratic" dwellings provided by his parents as they shuttle the family back and forth between Florence, Nice, and Paris in their pursuit of high society. Obviously Morgan's dream is one of self-rescue from his burden of sham luxury and "nobility." Not unexpectedly, freedom consists, in his mind, of the reverse of his reality; it would be better to be a *real* wastrel with Pemberton in an authentic palace than to be "living one year like ambassadors and the next like paupers."[8]

The other fantasy is Morgan's "boy's book plan of escape," in which he intends to go off with his tutor and live with him as an equal. Here he in part projects himself into the heroic role of rescuer of another, for he regards his and Pemberton's flight as just as much an escape for Pemberton, who has allowed the Moreens to cheat him of his wages and to hold him in thrall because of his natural growing affection for the boy.

These two escape fantasies highlight Morgan's attempts at solidifying the "strong little male quality"[9] emerging as part of his identity and in achieving separation from his family. But in order to understand the form these developmental problems take and why they evolve into pathological precocity, we must describe the dynamics of the family constellation.

James's most striking aphoristic characterization of the

Moreens is that they are "a houseful of Bohemians who wanted tremendously to be Philistines." To put it another way, they are a group of irresponsible carefree children—almost symbiotically interinvolved (they have even invented their own secret tribal language)—and seek a social identity by "toadying" (Morgan's phrase) to aristocrats of the international set.

The continual striving of the Moreens to have their worth recognized and verified by the famous and powerful seems to be impelled principally by Mrs. Moreen's unconscious phallicism,[10] shown by her compulsion to penetrate forbidden spheres, whether they be social circles or areas of privacy cherished by family members. Within the household all except Morgan bend themselves to her masculine will, but with regard to "high society" Mrs. Moreen joins her brood, again except for Morgan, in abjectly submitting to the great, or as Morgan perceives it, to "lie down and be trampled on." As is typical of the phallic woman, Mrs. Moreen often parades her reverse side (complete submission to castration) vis à vis a more powerful phallic force.[11]

Mr. Moreen is the stock ineffectual and uninvolved father. He claims "to be intimate with his children, to be their best friend," yet always distances himself both physically and emotionally by his frequent trips abroad, presumably to protect the family's rapidly dwindling fortune. He always adds the final touch to his alienation of feeling by assuming the appearance of "a man of the world," a phrase to which James continually and sardonically returns and which forms the ironic last lines of the story to underline the tragedy of Morgan's death.

The older son, Ulick, has identified completely with the father as "man of the world," and his main responsibility seems to be going to his club, where the family hopes he will recruit acceptable suitors for his two sisters. These latter are kept infantile by the phallic intrusiveness of a mother who never allows them to be alone with men. Thus Mrs. Moreen unconsciously undermines for her daughters the marriage prospects she seems to be constantly working on. Anyway, it hardly matters, for the foreign "princes" (Morgan's phrase) that Ulick brings home are entirely uninterested in marriage and completely insincere in their professed sentiments about it, and they constantly bestrew the Moreen household with flowers instead of proposals.

Morgan ironically comments on his own inability to emulate his shallow older brother (and by implication his father, of whom Ulick is a carbon copy) by suggesting that his brother really tries to "imitate" *him*. (This use of reversal as a defense is, as we shall see, one of the key components in his mask of precocity.[12]) In lieu of finding a good model to fashion himself after, he in fact experiences both narcissistic woundings and reparations at the hands of the whole clan because he is simultaneously rejected and adored by them. The quality of this double message is worth pinpointing, for it explains why Morgan is defensively precipitated into pseudo-precocity rather than into a more overtly regressive infantilism:

> They were wonderfully amiable and ecstatic about Morgan. It was a genuine tenderness, an artless admiration, equally strong in each. They even praised his beauty, which was small, and were as afraid of him as if they felt him of finer clay.... Mixed with this too was the oddest wish to make him independent, as if they had felt themselves not good enough for him. They passed him over to the new member of their circle [Pemberton] very much as if wishing to force some charity of adoption on so free an agent and get rid of their own charge. They were delighted when they saw Morgan take so to his kind play-fellow, and could think of no higher praise for the young man. It was strange how they contrived to reconcile the appearance, and indeed the essential fact, of adoring the child with their eagerness to wash their hands of him. Did they want to get rid of him before he should find them out?[13]

In this passage seems to lie the cause of Morgan's pathological precocity. It also reveals a family profile that has general clinical significance. Parents and those who stand *in loco parentis* frequently wish to create the public image of being nurturing and responsible adults, while at the same time preserving an infantile and totally carefree irresponsibility, the unconscious aim of which is to make the child into a nurturing parent for themselves. They hasten the child out of his dependent phase and make him the embodiment of the socially engendered ego-ideal of responsible adulthood. This is an overdetermined act, for it stems from a four-fold motive: (1) the parents may advertise to the world that they are responsible (i.e., appear grown up); (2) they avoid the responsibility of serving a child's dependent phase (i.e., can themselves remain children); (3) they unconsciously groom the child to be a parent to *them*; and (4) they achieve a secondary narcissistic gain by seeming to have produced a show-piece—one to which they need not, however, devote much energy to maintain. The danger in all of this, of course, is that the child who precociously embodies their ego-ideal may take on the force of their judgmental super-ego as well, and, as James says, "find them out." Erikson summarizes this dynamic as

> one of the deepest conflicts in life: ... the hate for a parent who
> served as the model and the executor of the superego, but who
> (in some form) was found trying to get away with the very
> transgressions which the child can no longer tolerate in
> himself.[14]

This is precisely what happens in James's tale.

Morgan's psychosexual development is oedipally distorted and incomplete. Instead of renouncing the erotically invested "castrated" mother and identifying with the "potent" father, Morgan must ward off the overwhelming phallic mother unsupported in his efforts by the passive father who, when he is needed as an ally, always "melts into space...elusively."[15] Although seemingly entirely the master of his own emotional realm within the family, Morgan defensively averts his eyes from the penetrating gaze of his mother when he addresses her and always manages to evade each of her offered caresses. His cynical sallies of wit keep him safely distanced from her.

iv

But where did Morgan get the refined ethical principles that allowed him to more or less accurately take the measure of men and manners in society? Certainly not from the nearly sociopathic Moreens. No doubt his highly developed moral sense came from what James imagined his earlier associations to be with other tutors like Pemberton and particularly with Zénobie, a nurse he had had years ago who had been, like Pemberton, exploited financially by the Moreens. Also, like Pemberton, she had suppressed until her departure any overt criticism of the Moreens' fecklessness but had nevertheless inculcated in Morgan her moral values.

> "Zénobie was very sharp," said Pemberton. "And she made
> you so."
> "Oh that wasn't Zénobie; that was nature. And experience!"
> Morgan laughed.
> "Well, Zénobie was a part of your experience."[16]

James obviously wants us to suppose that it was the efforts of this stable nurturing being that allowed Morgan to develop what a psychoanalyst would call a reasonably intact ego and super-ego rather than a psychotic or borderline psychotic one. Her influence would probably also account for the refinement of manners that made him appear to be a "little cosmopolite"—a role that is in sharp contrast to his father's and brother's pose as "men of the world," with their gaucheries in etiquette and ultimate ontological emptiness.

Morgan's overt attempt to disavow the influence of Zénobie, who, it is inferred, supplanted his mother as his chief oedipal object, is perhaps more interesting as an adolescent phenomenon than his unconscious identification with her in childhood. This denial of interest in a no doubt erotically tinged maternal imago probably constitutes an important attempt toward his individuation and development now that he has reached middle adolescence. It prepares him to begin a new phase, that of peer identification. But despite Morgan's precocious analytical mind and the temporary beneficial influence of Zénobie, his inability to resolve the oedipal issue with the phallic mother causes him to seek peer identification among the weak rather than among the strong. In compliance with this unconscious need, the passive, emotionally castrated Pemberton seems almost made to order.

Idealized peership for Morgan therefore takes the unusual form of shared vulnerability rather than shared strength, for, as he reasons haven't he and Pemberton been fellow sufferers at the hands of the Moreens?

"Haven't I been conscious of what we've been through together?" [Morgan asked].
"What we've been through?" [Pemberton rejoined].
"Our privations—our dark days."
"Oh our days have been bright enough."[17]

Even though Pemberton shams some resistance to Morgan's romantic notion of them both as victims in a melodrama, he very quickly accepts it as truth, just as he had earlier assented to the two escape fantasies in which Morgan made them picaresque heroes in a world adventure. Yet Pemberton is already an emotionally emasculated Robin Hood—one who has abetted his own robbers—for he has decisively surrendered his will, his money, and his hope for an independent future to Mrs. Moreen.

Seemingly, Morgan's alliance with Pemberton as passive victim of Mrs. Moreen, the phallic mother, would constitute for him a homosexual object choice. Because of James's usual retreat from the sexual questions he raises, there is not enough evidence to tell whether Morgan's sexual interest in Pemberton would remain latent or become conscious.* However, the mutual intensity of Morgan and Pemberton's relationship suggests a protracted homosexual alliance on an oral level, in which Morgan, under the guise of becoming Pemberton's peer, would seek to receive the nurture denied by his controlling mother and left incomplete by the too-soon-departed Zénobie. But he would mask his dependency even further by again taking up the banner of the precocious role forced on him by the Moreens: he would himself provide the model for the parent he wishes to have by trying to become the perfect parent to Pemberton.[18]

v

Pemberton's cooperation in letting Morgan perceive him as victim as well as rescuer allows the boy to take another step in the identification process, one that seems even to increase the precocious "sensibility in abundance" that James extols in his preface to the story, but is in reality regressive.[19] Morgan now discovers in Pemberton one of his ego-ideals—that of self-sacrifice for love and friendship:

> Then [Morgan] said: "My dear chap, you're a hero!"
> "Well, you're another!" Pemberton retorted.
> "No I'm not, but I ain't a baby. I won't stand it any longer. You must get some occupation that pays. I'm ashamed, I'm ashamed!" quavered the boy with a ring of passion, like some high silver note from a small cathedral chorister, that deeply touched his friend.[20]

But these altruistic gestures of Pemberton's are only partly based on his affection for Morgan; they are just as much, if not more, based on a paralysis of will in the face of Mrs. Moreen's awe-inspiring control. Only accidentally and indirectly do these

---

*Richard Hall, a writer of homosexual fiction, thinks that the attraction between Morgan and Pemberton is indubitably homosexual. He feels that the only violation of psychological realism is one that the story shares with Thomas Mann's *Death in Venice*, where the homosexual interest is indeed more explicit. That betrayal of realism consists, in both instances, of the authors' super-ego ridden personalities, forcing them to use death by disease as a nemesis-like ally for their homophobia. See Hall's Preface to *Couplings* (San Francisco: Black Sparrow Press, 1979), p. iii.

"virtues" expose the hypocrisy of Morgan's mother's self-advertised "sacrifice" in committing him to Pemberton's care.

The search for a hero to identify with is of course a crucial aspect of adolescent development. In pre-adolescence it normally serves the useful purpose of allowing the traumatic deflations of the parental ego-ideal to be mitigated by another temporary form of idealization, often homosexual in nature. Normally it is a way-station to a romanticized heterosexual object choice.[21] However, the depth of Morgan's narcissistic wounds and the extent of his vulnerability that the passage betrays prefigure his tragedy: that this attempt at hero worship, especially considering the indecisive, self-castrating model he chooses, will not be enough to alleviate his loss of self-esteem.[22] In fact, it ultimately works against it.

By counting on Pemberton, a male, to fulfill maternal duties, Morgan is perhaps magically reconstructing as well as transforming the phallic pre-oedipal mother. At the same time, by dubbing a man who has allowed himself to be put upon by a later edition of this mother a "hero," he betrays as well a condensed wish to (1) submit as castrated male to the phallic mother and (2) win love and protection from the distant father (the negative oedipal complex).[23] These regressive aspects in the formation of Morgan's ego-ideal are another way of seeing his precociousness as merely illusory.

It is interesting that in the conversation quoted above Morgan uses the word *ashamed* rather than *guilty* in relation to his feelings about his parents. This is probably another attempt at super-ego denial[24] in the service of individuation, for shame, unpleasant as it is, subjects his parents to his moral scrutiny as reprehensible "other," rather than linking him with them as culprit. To put it another way, it is Morgan's attempt to replace the toxic parts of the introjected super-ego with a self-chosen ego-ideal, or as James himself phrases it, "a private ideal, which made him as privately disown the stuff his people were made of."[25] Morgan experiences the more concrete feeling of shame—concrete because one imagines that there are pointing and jeering onlookers witnessing his loss of face—an affect that developmentally precedes guilt, where the incorporated voice of the super-ego is muted and abstract. The possibility of shaming a child grows out of the advantage that large and powerful adults have taken in pointing to the child's smaller size and physical vulnerability.[26] Thus Morgan's outcry that he "ain't a baby," directly preceding his confession of shame, and sounding to Pemberton like a "note from a small cathedral chorister," again betrays a more regressive aspect of character representation than is at first apparent in his precocious behavior.

Morgan's fatal heart attack seems to be brought on by the sudden joy of having his parents' "unexpected consecration of his hope," his wish to go off to live with Pemberton. But one wonders if it isn't perhaps due largely to his unconscious feeling that their "sacrifice" was merely the climax of a lifetime of abandoning him, the true underlying message of their adulation of him as a prince apart. Moreover, their decision took away his initiative in achieving his own separation. After all, a young boy planning to run away from home (a common enough experiment in individuation) does not want his parents to control the arrangements. As James so quaintly puts it,

> the turn taken was away from a *good* boy's book—the escape was left on their [the parents'] hands.[27]

Nor does the runaway want his parents to turn his planned departure into banishment by revealing it to be their own secret wish. That this unconscious fear may underlie Morgan's fatal "joy" is not made absolutely clear, but James implies this ambivalence in the brief argument he gives to the parents at the very end of the story:

> "But I thought he *wanted* to go...!" wailed Mrs. Moreen.
> "I *told* you he didn't, my dear," her husband made answer.[28]

These words, suggesting that the "joyful" liberation was perhaps at the same time a fatal blow of rejection, allows us to see Morgan's heart failure to be less of an arbitrary, *deus ex machina* conclusion and more of a climax to the narcissistic wounding that has assailed his whole psychic life. To be emotionally *orphaned* at an early age, as Morgan in fact was from the beginning of his life, rather than *liberated* when the ego is strong enough, may precipitate a child into a pseudo-precocity—a defensive independence in which the processes of identification leading to healthy separation and individuation in adolescence become extremely difficult, if not impossible. We are clearly a long way from the healthy sensibility of the young hero of the Victorian *bildungsroman*.

For James to have such an intuitive understanding of these psychological truths is not so mysterious, least of all to James himself, who realized that the reported events that caused the story to suddenly spring to life in his imagination had merely triggered "an old latent and dormant impression, a buried germ, implanted by experience and then forgotten."[29] His essentially correct instincts

about Morgan in fact derive from the peculiar brand of precociousness into which he himself was forced by a father "who
wanted so much for his sons to surpass him that he denied them
the common limitations of humanity..., who set no real limits
and goals [and thus] left his sons with a frustrating sense of
omnipotence."[30] This is but a short step away from Morgan's fatal
delusion that, merely by suddenly growing taller, "in a little while
he should stand on his own feet...that in short he should be
'finished,' grown up, producible in the world of affairs and ready
to prove himself of sterling ability."[31] James's capacity to transform so brilliantly his own vicissitudes of precociousness into art
without suffering either the mental breakdown experienced by his
older brother William or a fatal psychosomatic trauma like
Morgan's is a further testimony to the sublimatory powers of the
artistic genius.

5

Film Form as a Mirror of the Self: Merging and Symbiosis in Larry Peerce's *A Separate Peace* and Michal Bat-Adam's *Each Other*

> We've seen in the world how monsters can come to the top and just what horrors they can achieve. And those monsters were once adolescents.
>
> John Knowles, *Peace Breaks Out*

i

Devotees of Henry James ("Jacobites," Max Beerbohm called them) might be astounded by my reference to his work in the title of the previous chapter as a "case study." Yet I believe that I have demonstrated quite extensively that James was interested not only in character conflict but in exploring its genesis in early childhood traumas and in family interactions, even going as far as to analyze the decisive influence of "offstage" figures like the governess Zénobie. The psychological interpreter of James therefore becomes more a collaborator—sometimes even a kind of co-therapist—than a mere elucidator. He must complete the gestalt of motives, filling in what James does not express but always seems to have at the tip of his pen.

The principal works to be considered in this chapter—John Knowles's novel *A Separate Peace* and especially Larry Peerce's film version of it[1]—also deal with the volatile, complex emotions of the adolescent. Yet family background seems here to be carefully excluded, even as a casual allusion. It is as if both the author and his film adapter contrived a microscopic investigation of primitive emotions by isolating them in the remote rural setting of Devon in New Hampshire. This centers the dramatic interest not only in the primitive impulses themselves but also in the elaborate defense mechanisms called into play to control them.

Thus Knowles's novel, despite its greater length, has a narrower psychological range than James's story as far as psychogenesis is concerned, for the whole drama of his fiction focuses on the problem of defending against and sublimating aggression (overt sexual interests are equally absent from both fictions). However, the problem the youthful protagonist has in forming a solid core of identity and a healthy feeling of self-esteem is a paramount issue in both works.

A Separate Peace is probably the closest that any novel has come to recreating that particular love-hate relationship between adolescents that is undergirded with envy and fear-filled rivalry. The apparent deviation from ordinary life in this story merely conceals a deeper, more universal psychological truth: that the boy who never loses his innocence, that is, who does not "grow," does not survive—especially in a world on the brink of total social and moral disruption. In the calm before the storm of World War II Gene and Finny are, whether or not Gene admits it, "best friends." But this is merely the eye of another storm, an intrapsychic one. Gene is stopped from calling Finny his best friend "by that level of feeling, deeper than thought, which contains the truth"—the truth being that Gene hates Finny as much as he loves him. What Gene fails to realize is that at times best friends may be enemies, and must therefore not only nurture their love but work out a "separate peace" for their enmity. But it is first necessary to become aware of the underlying battle. Gene's initial ignorance of this feeds his fear of himself, of his inner aggressions. The distant trumpets of war that increasingly penetrate the ivy-league isolation at Devon coalesce with inner pressures to summon these highly ambivalent motives into the open.

Aggression must be assumed to be a "given" in *A Separate Peace* as it is in life, one of the natural instinctive drives. According to developmental psychology, aggression if properly managed, can become creative assertiveness and may assist the child in individuating himself from early symbiosis with the mother. Thus the word *separate* in Knowles's title—already replete with a rich multiplicity of meanings* may carry an additional psychological charge—

*From a political perspective the phrase *separate peace* is of course commonplace, referring to a nation unilaterally signing a peace treaty, usually in violation of a pact with other nations not to do so. In the novel the phrase carries the added personal meaning that Gene works out his own idiosyncratic brand of peace with Finny, and the more macrocosmic meaning that the school itself maintains a temporary isolationism against the inevitable encorachment of World War II.

The title of Knowles's sequel, *Peace Breaks Out*, contains similar multilevel meanings, a subtle reference to a desire to achieve the stability of a totally separate and individuated self.

That Knowles's novel is essentially a drama of defenses erected against untrammeled hostility is made clear in a number of ways, but most palpably through the metaphorical and symbolic use of trees and of various geometrical patterns and architectural designs. A few examples will suffice. The houses in the town "began to look more defensive" as Gene approached the school, and "then more exhausted" as he entered it. The trees surrounding the campus are "Republican, bankerish...New England elms." The paradox of "contentious harmony" (i.e., aggression defended against or sublimated) is represented on the school's quadrangles by "small areas of order—a large yard, a group of trees, three similar dormitories, a circle of old houses"—all of which are pointedly designed to raise questions about the harmony and cohesion within the personality of Gene.*

The magnificent tree from which the boys jump into the river and from which Finny receives his crippling injury becomes the emblematic epitome of this concept. Majestic in its own right and idealized as a test of manly strength, courage, and athletic ability—but imperfect because of its asymmetrical shape and denigrated by wintry bareness when visited fifteen years later by the adult Gene—it somehow stands for the center of the idealizing capacity (and incapacity) of both Gene and Finny's personalities. When further described as an integral part of the Devon woods, a pattern of trees that in Gene's imagination "reached in an unbroken, widening corridor...to the...far unorganized tips of Canada," it also becomes part of the "tame fringe" that stands

---

*Similar images of ego-defense are found in "Phineas" the short story that Knowles expanded into A Separate Peace: the homes in Finny's home town, "from solid white mansions to neat salt boxes, were settled behind their fences and hedges as though invulnerable to change." As he approaches Finny's front door Gene encounters "an ancient impregnable elm." In contrast to such impermeable defenses associated with Finny, Gene characterizes the fragility of his own: "I wasn't going to be opened up like that suitcase, to have him yank out all my thoughts and feelings and scatter them around underfoot." Phineas: Six Stories (New York: Random House, 1953), p. 28.

---

revolving mainly around the paradox that outward signs of quiescence may harbor unsuspected violence. Taken from a speech in Brecht's Mother Courage, the phrase connects with the central incident in the novel—the shattering of the chapel's war memorial window. A special point is made of the fact that the destructive force was from the inside out (like the eruption of violent emotion) and that it reminds Pete, the history instructor, of the bombed-out churches of Italy during the war.

for one of those necessary bastions formed by the ego against the chaotic onslaughts of the id. The undifferentiated aspect of trees as the timeless id actually becomes personified in *Peace Breaks Out*, Knowles's sequel: "If you just kept trotting along these streets and across these fields and through these woods, then probably you gradually metamorphosed into the Great God Pan, hooved and the soul of mischief, and lurked here forever, causing trouble."[4]

Since the adult Gene is the narrator in *A Separate Peace*, we see everything from his point of view. Although in the film he is retained as narrator per se, he intrudes only at the opening and close, thus depriving us of a retrospective viewpoint most of the time. In neither novel nor film do we know anything of what is going on in Finny's head, but at least he is never shown to contemplate anything deeper than apparent good will to all; to him "there was no conflict except between athletes." Thus his choice of Gene as best friend is not complicated by his friend's reservations.

Out of the rivalry on which this typical adolescent relationship is based springs a not-so-typical, profound identity-projection by each boy of his feelings onto the other. This projection originates with Gene; he wants not only to excel academically, utterly outshining Finny, but also to at least keep pace with him in Finny's own forte, athletics. Adopting a code of warfare and a combat officer's mentality—one of the ways in which the war effort build-up subtly infiltrates Devon (or least provides a chance for Gene to externalize his inner battlefield)—Gene imagines that athletic competition automatically means a desire to annihilate the competitor, a notion unfortunately enhanced by Finny's invention of the game "blitzball" in which "there are no teams; we're all enemies." Thus Gene can never refuse to join Finny in his whirligig of physical activities in order to crush him. When Gene finally puts Finny out of the athletic running by shaking him from the tree, he takes Finny's place, an act symbolized by donning Finny's pink shirt.

This assumption of another's persona amounts to much more than purloining the crown of the champion. It is fraught with such a profound sense of emotional identification with the imagined aggressor—now understood as victim—that it begins the movement toward the psychological climax of the novel. Fueled by irrevocable guilt for crippling his "friend" and unable to bear a feeling of separateness from others brought about by his unneutralized hostility, Gene begins to regress to a kind of prenatal and early post-natal symbiotic fusion, where blissful oceanic feelings inebriate one with a sense of omnipotence.* Standing before the mirror in Finny's shirt he becomes "Phineas to the life." He feels "intense relief" and becomes sure that he "would never stumble through the confusions of my own character again."[2] Not long after, Finny unwittingly brings this fusion fantasy to a climax by insisting on making Gene his permanent stand-in in athletics so that in the highest possible state of euphoria Gene can think, "I lost part of myself of him then, and a soaring sense of freedom revealed that this must have been my purpose from the first: to become a part of Phineas."[3]

The process by which identification with important others in one's life either leads to a solid identity and healthy self-image or eventuates in a pathology that is accompanied by serious regression and primitive defenses like projection is as yet only partially understood by the object-relations theorists. As Alan Roland, summarizing the work of H. Loewald, puts it,

> normal identification processes aid in both the development of an identity and individuality on one hand, while enabling the person to see his interpersonal environment more clearly on the other; while abnormal identification processes both hinder identity formation and distort object relations through projection.[5]

The pathological portion of this statement clearly applies more to Gene than to Finny, despite our ignorance of the actual family dynamics of both characters.

Since Finny accepts the respective gifts with which he and Gene are endowed, he has no reason to consider Gene as athletic competition, much less a hated rival, and he simply bows out of the intellectual competition. He is thus able to be more flexible in deciding what parts of others he can emulate and what parts he cannot incorporate, and thus seems to have a much healthier self-image than Gene. Gene's difficulty in formulating an ego-ideal by means of this process of identifying and dis-identifying is shown, for instance, in his view of Leper: "I wondered. . .whether the still hidden parts of myself might contain the Sad Sack, the outcast, or the coward. . . .we all secretly hoped that Leper, that incompetent, was as heroic as we said."[6] However, when Finny is confronted with a lifetime of physical disability, the greatest possible threat to

---

*As we saw, the orderly in D. H. Lawrence's *The Prussian Officer* also sought escape from mental anguish by regression to symbiosis. But since his "mother" was, unlike Finny, sadistic, he was unable to sustain a "soaring" feeling.

his self-image, he, too, must try to preserve his sense of a cohesive and continuous identity by projecting a part of himself onto another: "Listen, pal," he tells Gene, "if I can't play sports, you're going to play them for me."[7]

But Finny's kind of identification does not seem, like Gene's, to be primitive, regressive, or deeply pathological. It does not rest on a fantasy of fusion to assuage guilt and loneliness and, above all, hostility. It is merely a compensatory drive to overcome the thwarted functions of body-ego. It is not much different from the immigrant father's wish to provide for his son material advantages of which he himself had been deprived, so that he might vicariously enjoy them.

In Knowles's sequel, *Peace Breaks Out*, the rivalry between the two boys Wexford and Hochschwender is far less complex psychologically:

> the fundamental similarity which they. . . sensed and found unforgiveable: it was unbearable to be forced to see an unmistakable parody of yourself in this other creep. That was the source of the hatred, and it would never run dry as long as Wexford remained Wexford, and Hochschwender, Hochschwender.[8]

Here the similarities are real and not illusory, that is, not projected out of a psychological need to merge. These less-involved psychodynamics are part of the reason why the sequel is less interesting than its predecessor.

ii

Film has often been thought to be too gross a medium to portray the subtle workings of the human psyche, unless it be by the essentially nonvisual means of voice-over, printed titles, or dramatic dialogue or monologue. Otherwise it may seem limited to revealing only the photographable externals of reality or doomed to stumbling along with awkward and inadequate metaphors for deeper meanings. Panofsky's famous dictum that in film, unlike the theater, everything must be conveyed through the "dynamization of space"[9] suggests that the visual possibilities of the medium might become immediately overtaxed in trying to portray any subtleties of mind or emotion. It would seem to make film—unless it were frankly being used as a recording device for a theatrical performance—suitable only for rendering crude melodrama and farce. However, the most fleeting recollection of any of the films of a director like Ingmar Bergman would soon remind us that this is far from true. A Bergman film is an especially fortuitous reminder that a face in close-up can itself be the most spatially dynamic means of revealing powerful emotional states.

Of course film, like the other arts, has many devices and techniques at its disposal to render nuances of thought and shadings of feeling. But since it is, more than any other art, a child of the machine age, the technology of its form and structure is inextricable from its meanings and effects. Therefore in discussing Peerce's film version of *A Separate Peace*, as well as the films covered elsewhere in this book, it will be necessary to detail to some extent the ways in which choice of camera movement and angle, as well as styles of framing and editing, reveal those depths and surfaces of mind and mood which are more straightforwardly conveyed in some of the other arts.*

Peerce's film, like the novel, does a good job of conveying the surface camaraderie of the boys, but does not disclose Gene's hatred seething underneath. The film shows the manifestations of identity-projection—Gene's illusion that Finny embodies his own feelings of envy—but not the awakening rivalry so explicitly described in the novel:

> I found it. I found a single sustaining thought. The thought was. You and Phineas are even already: you are even in enmity. You are both coldly driving ahead for yourselves alone. You did hate him for breaking that school swimming record, but so what? He hated you for getting an A in every course but one last term. You would have had an A in that one. Except for him.[10]

These omissions from the film do not seem to be intentional since Peerce does attempt to convey hate, as in the added deliberation (though not nearly agitated enough) with which Gene undresses before climbing up the "funereal tree," supposedly to join Finny in a double jump into the river, but actually to push Finny to his crippling fall. Even in the very opening of the film the mature Gene, seeing the tree again, practically bludgeons the audience with the recollection of the "fear, the anger, the senseless rivalry [that] reminded me of Finny"—words Peerce added. But coming in the beginning as they do, from a narrator whom we do not yet

*In Appendix A of this book I discuss the ways in which both film and theater may even seek to go one step further, that is, to create a faithful replica of the mind itself.

recognize and who does not reappear until the closing, such
suggestions of the emotional cauldron within Gene are far too
skimpy to justify or explain his sudden, malicious deed.

In the same way, we see the manifestations of envious
identification in the easily filmed episodes of Gene's first, perfect
dive (another addition to the novel) after he has caused Finny's
accident, and in the scene in which he subsequently dons Finny's
shirt. But the extent of the identity-projection, indicated by the
concluding words, "I could not escape a feeling that this was my
own funeral, and you do not cry in that case" (followed by a fast
wipe for emphasis), is hardly tapped in any visual or aural way.
The words seem to be an appendage to the main point, instead of
being the main point itself.

A look at Peerce's other attempts to recreate the moods and
emotions in the novel will allow us to generalize further on the
ability that film has to present those subtleties of mind and feeling
which challenge us to interpret it psychoanalytically.

Finny's athletic nature lent itself to visual extravaganzas in the
film, and it is at these points that the film is brilliant. The first is a
day-at-the-beach episode, which opens with a comical ground-
level shot of assorted human legs treading the boardwalk. Almost
literally "upon the heels" of such tableaux of depersonalized joy
come shots of billboards on which "War," "Bonds," "Attack,
Attack" are printed, mute indicators of the incongruency of the
times. This dissonant note is immediately reemphasized in the distorted reflections of Gene and Finny in trick fun-house mirrors.
The wonderfully colorful caricatures that ensue continue the
montage effect: a fortune-teller fantasying to lovers and bar-flies,
matronly mothers minding children, fat old women squawking
when splashed, and, best of all, a shoed and hatted man suddenly
taking a nose-dive—scenes (except the last) so familiar as to seem
trite, yet deliciously voyeuristic. The jazzy music of the 1940s
underscores the wholly carefree, moving tempo of this episode.

The second visual extravaganza is the "blitzball" sequence,
which opens with cinema verité, the camera bobbing up and down
with "the gang," as they run toward the audience, who at first
observe them through a telephoto lens. The camera's seeming to
tussle along with the boys succeeds in recreating the rowdiness of
the scene, and in involving us, the audience, in it even to the degree
of making us feel, in a tactile way, the emerging thematic note that
Finny must articulate: "There aren't any teams in blitzball. . . .
We're all enemies."

A good example of how well adapted film can be in portraying the externals of personality, if not the inward psyche, is the incident when the ball is thrown to Leper, the fragile, sensitive one in the group, who with an underplayed mutter that we can hardly hear says, "I don't want it!", his face and figure instantly cringing from the ball, while the camera focuses on and captures his disgust and annoyance at the melee. Better than the actual words that Brinker may previously have uttered about Leper's having a yellow streak "a mile wide," this expression of total revulsion at mob activity sums up Leper's personality in one sure, swift stroke. Good film acting is, as Dudley Nichols has observed, "the art of reacting"—made possible here by a close-up reading of Leper's "body language."*

The third visual extravaganza is the Winter Olympics. The dominant camera angle is high, as if the madness below were being viewed by the gods from on Mt. Olympus. After Gene satisfies tradition by lighting the garbage-can torch, there is an ingenious shot from Gene's eye level through the flames, which almost transfigures the green-wreathed Finny. Tobogganing, chariot races, and a cider-bacchanal follow in a quick succession that is analogous to the frenetic but dispassionate joy of a day-at-the-beach.

The strength of the film lies, predictably, in the brilliance with which purely physical episodes are filmed. Peerce utilizes montage, cinema verité, a telephoto lens, and symbolic camera angles in this endeavor. How, by contrast, does he attempt to communicate Gene's intangible, psychological experience?

iii

Peerce attempts to communicate such experience chiefly through symbols, visual and aural. The two visual kinds of imagery used most often are close-up shots in general and Gene's hypnotized stares in particular. Peerce favours middle and full shots throughout the film, but depends especially heavily on close-up shots of the face, seeming to support the theory that "tragic emotions, being movements of the psyche, are most clearly registered in the face."[11] The close-ups occur whenever Gene and another person have reached a new level of understanding—when Finny feels betrayal and abandonment at news of Gene's possible

*See the next chapter for a discussion of the use of body-language analysis (kinesics) in the psychological study of film.

enlistment; when Gene tries to explain to Finny that "it was just something blind" that impelled him to push Finny off the tree; or when Gene throws Leper to the ground and Leper tells him that he "always was a savage underneath"; or when Brinker, referring to what happened in the tree, says to Gene, "Nobody knows unless you know."

In retrospect, Gene's hypnotized stares may be said generally to commence when his relationship with Finny is most intimate, for example, when Finny calls Gene his best friend during the night at the beach; when Gene dons Finny's pink shirt; when Gene relieves Finny by reporting that he did not take another roommate; when Gene confesses his guilt in causing Finny's accident; and when Gene is "on trial" with Finny as a reluctant witness.

All these scenes of intimacy suggest a relationship that goes beyond mere mutual identification and projection. From the emotional point of view of the protagonists, they represent, as I have said, an unconscious attempt at symbiosis that culminates appropriately in Gene's comment that he was witnessing his own funeral in Finny's death. From the author's more "mythic" position, they seem often to be "decomposed," complementary parts of the same prototype figure—the elemental splitting of a single figure that Freud, Jekels, and Jones found to be true of Macbeth and Lady Macbeth and of Hamlet's different "fathers."

The text of the novel confirms this in various ways:

Finny...sitting opposite me at the table where we read....the study lamp cast a round yellow pool between us.[12]
Trying to forget where I was, even who I was...I decided to put on his clothes.[13]

Finny: "You look like it happened to you or something."
Gene: "It's almost like it did! I was right there, right on the limb beside you."[14]

[Phineas] said, "Listen, pal, if I can't play sports, you're going to play them for me," and I lost part of myself to him then, and a soaring sense of freedom revealed that this must have been my purpose from the first: to become a part of Phineas.[15]

By constantly framing Finny and Gene in close "two-shot," Peerce has found numerous cinematic equivalents for the circle of desk-light in the novel that inextricably binds the two boys together. The daytime scenes at the beach, dominated by broad lateral movements, are followed by a close two-shot on the beach

Parker Stevenson and John Heyl in *A Separate Peace*, **directed by Larry Peerce, 1972, also starring William Roerisk.** (*Courtesy of Paramount Pictures*)

at night, in which the boys are virtually squeezed together in the frame as Phineas declares his exclusive friendship for Gene.

A similar cinematic representation of their symbiotic tendency occurs in one of the final shots in the trial sequence—a highly unusual two-shot in which Finny and Gene sit close together, but at right angles to each other, separated from their inquisitors, who lurk in the encompassing darkness, by the circle of light that bathes them. The scene of the trial has been changed, to great effect, from the gymnasium to the chapel. It removes the locus of Finny and Gene's conflict from the physical plane of athletics to the metaphysical plane of moral absolutes. Of visual interest here is Peerce's elaboration in the chapel of the circle of desk-lamp light in the dormitory room, as described in the novel. The effect of the two boys in such close proximity is that of a cubist painting in which one sees, simultaneously, both the profile and full-faced view of a single figure.

Two chief exceptions to this kind of two-as-one treatment of the protagonists are notable. The first occurs when Gene goes to Finny's house to confess his murderous intent. Here Peerce purposely holds Finny and Gene to separate frames even though they are conversing together in a small room. This is the one scene of naked verbal aggression in which Gene overtly attempts to distinguish himself from Finny as criminal vis à vis victim. Their physical separateness throughout the scene pictorially adds an irony to the word *separate* in the title.

The other instance dramatizes Finny's sudden disassociation from Gene when Gene's homicidal intent finally strikes home. At the end of the trial scene just mentioned—after Leper's testimony makes everything clear—the camera moves from the side view that showed them as a single merged figure to a position behind them. The boys are well defined in silhouette against the circle of light as sitting on their separate chairs but with Finny's arm extending to the back of Gene's. At the moment of revelation of Gene's treachery, Finny's hand drops like a severed umbilical cord.

No discussion of visual symbols in the film would be complete without further mention of the tree, an archetypal symbol of the source of our knowledge of good and evil. As already stated, the novel provides an elaborate build-up to the meaning of this "tremendous...irate, steely black steeple beside the river" by first describing the "defensive" trees lining the street leading to the college and finally inviting us into Gene's fantasy that all trees in Devon Woods formed the most orderly and civilized fringe of "an unbroken, widening corridor so far to the north that no one had ever seen the other end, somewhere up in the far unorganized tips of Canada." In the context of such a description, I have argued, the massive tree is obviously destined to take on the psychological meaning of a setting for an ego-battle on the margin of the vast incomprehensible forces of the id.

In framing a scene in which the position and play of objects in space will be important to either dramatic or symbolic effects, film makers must pay close attention to the "stage-line"—an imaginary proscenium arch creating an invisible wall in front of the action perpendicular to the eye-level line of vision of the camera. Inadvertently moving the camera between shots to the other side of this dividing line (equivalent to a member of a theatrical audience going back into the wings to witness part of a play) would result in a transposition of objects as they are projected onto the screen and cause a general disorientation of spatial relationships. Intentionally crossing the stage-line at certain points might, of course, contribute to a meaningful, and therefore genuinely aesthetic, discord in mood or disharmony in tone.

Photographing a generally symmetrical tree in a rather nondescript forest would seem to make moot the question of whether or not the stage-line is respected. But this particular tree has a particular identity— a significantly differentiated left and right side—in that it contains the crucial jumping branch extending from one side over the river. Movement toward the tree is always left to right and the view of the tree is usually from the right side, with the jumping bough extending from left to right. However, when the jumping sequences are filmed, when the private world of Gene and Finny is entered into, the camera crosses the stage-line; now the bough extends from right to left. Not only the expected trust in friendship, but also the expected orientation in nature become disrupted in the tree. Significantly, the stage-line is crossed only during episodes involving the tree, suggesting the tree's superiority to the rule, its life outside the law.

Other shots free the tree from the stage-line altogether—those shots in which the camera (presumably in a helicopter or on a large overhead crane) hovers almost directly above the tree and revolves about in such a way as to make it seem to be the pivotal point for scanning limitless surroundings. These shots are intended, no doubt, to emphasize the scary perspective from which Gene must dive and the vertigo he must feel, but they help at the same time to locate the tree as the moral and emotional center of the school-boy world at Devon. Under such circumstances none of the boys could become like Leper's skiers, who "see a lot of trees shoot by, but. . . never get to really look at trees, at a tree." Inevitably so to speak, from his position as spectator on the audience side of the stage-line to the center of the action in an arena, where the stage-line concept loses all meaning. This not only has the emotional effect of the dissolution of some heretofore respected law or code of conduct but portends as well the loosening of ego control in Gene that precipitates Finny's tragic fall.

The second kind of symbol through which Peerce attempts to convey Gene's intangible, psychological experience is aural, the most dominant of which are piano plinks. They are repeated whenever there is psychological turmoil, as in the beginning when Finny, the superstar, befriends Leper, the outcast, much to Gene's puzzlement; and when Gene first approaches the jumping tree, which strikes fear, daring, and manhood into his heart, as well as dizziness (reinforced by the swish-panning of the camera). And these same notes intrude at the time of the "accident"; when Finny hands Gene Leper's foreboding note; and when Leper, his mind gone, folds up in the snow.

Peerce also capitalizes on an aural *technique*, as distinguished from a *symbol*, to enlarge a meaning or to convey a psychological experience or mood: the carryover of a bit of dialogue or a tune from one shot to another. This occurs during the garden party in the beginning of the film, when, as the camera pans from one group to another, voices become detached from their owners—effectively conveying the confusion and idleness of party chatter, the speakers of which are often unimportant. When Gene is in Finny's home in Boston confessing his guilt, the trauma of the scene ends on the note of Finny's boyish whistling, which is allowed to extend to the next scene of Gene returning to school, his scrutiny of his room poignantly ending at the sight of Finny's empty bed. This same sound, which represents Finny's simple, innocent pluckiness in the face of cruelty and unfairness, is later heard again when Gene walks back to the tree after Finny's death.

When Peerce is preparing to shoot the humorous classroom episode, he overlaps the lecture while the camera is still shooting the façade of the school, before cutting to the classroom inside. When the recruiting officer is addressing his prospective candidates, his talk is also heard off-screen while the camera is shooting outside, before the cut to the assembly room. Both these episodes suggest the permeation of the school with academia and convention, to the extent that what goes on within the walls cannot be disassociated from the external appearance.

When the doctor is explaining to Gene the reason for Finny's sudden death, his voice continues after Gene leaves and trudges aimlessly over the campus, providing the extended time Gene needs to digest the words. When Gene attends commencement, the traditional address also continues as he walks past the crowds to Finny's gym locker, the door of which, tagged with Finny's name, swings open at the exact moment that the graduates are being exhorted to meet the challenges of World War II, "to kill an enemy you have never met." Gene already has, however indirectly, killed his enemy-in-competition.

Thus, in every instance in which Peerce employs this aural carryover, he is attempting to communicate a distinct, psychological message.

iv

But do these visual and aural symbols and techniques succeed in conveying subtle psychological experiences? My overall evaluation is that they succeed in signaling the onset of intimacy, or new understanding, or mental turmoil, but that they are incapable of identifying each experience for what it is. For example, we cannot tell from a stare why Gene does not return the best-friend compliment to Finny. Neither does the stare tell us why Gene is suddenly wearing Finny's shirt. There has been no suggestion of Gene's competing with Finny athletically. In what way is he taking his place, now that Finny is crippled?

This confusion as to what the symbol is actually communicating is not the weakness of the symbol, but of the overall context in which it appears. The problem emerges more clearly when we examine together certain aspects of both film and novel.

In the film Peerce alters some elements of the plot in an attempt to cope with the strengths and weaknesses of cinema itself or what Peerce conceives them to be. When Finny unexpectedly roars, "...I've suffered!" it happens before "the gang," not only before Gene as in the novel, thereby multiplying the stricken, visual reactions.

Instead of using the novel's aforementioned skiing scene—in which Leper is allowed a discourse on trees—Peerce composes an unusually long shot in which Leper is discovered in the ludicrous situation of painting in the middle of a snowfield, when he is encountered by Gene on his way to the railroad. This change visually dramatizes the grotesqueness with which the "maladjusted" individualist appears to the "normal" majority. Instead, as in the novel, of unseating Leper inside his family's home, a mere jostling within the womb, Gene delivers a blow to his face outdoors, when the blood trickling from Leper's mouth can contrast with the stark whiteness of the snow—a visual improvement, not to mention the closing shot of that episode with Leper curled up in a fetal position, Gene standing helplessly at his side, both enveloped in unutterably cold, white sterility, as the camera obligingly dollies back to assist Gene in abandoning him.

In the film the railroad carload of boisterous soldiers eerily falls silent at the departure gong. This change from the novel was cinematic shorthand for communicating the pall of war and death that hung over the otherwise blithe world of Devon School.

Other deviations from the novel, instead of strengthening the film as did the above examples, worked against its social and psychological integrity—as, for instance, the failure to indicate that the summer of 1942 was unique at Devon, rules having been dispensed with in order to give the boys their last freedoms before their graduation into the War. This omission was probably the result of expediency. There simply was not time to dwell on the urgency of the war. As a result, the railroad scene is depicted as merely a day's outing; the recruiting officer's pep talk serves as merely the background to Brinker's accusations.

But because of this expediency, the very backdrop to Gene's unprovoked malice toward Finny is diminished in significance, while in the novel it functions as an indispensable, reflective macrocosm. Moreover, the weakening of this backdrop—from which were also subtracted the tug-of-war between Brinker and Gene over enlisting, their disagreement with Brinker's father over the war, and the ski troops movie—weakens the emphasis on, and understanding of, Gene's malice, which is strongly stated in the novel.

The fact is that Gene's inner turmoil is clearly expressed in the film only once, when Finny, reacting to Gene's confession, says, "I'll kill you if you don't shut up," and Gene bursts out, "You see! Kill me! Now you know what it is! I did it because I felt like that!"[16] This weakness cannot be attributed so much to the inability of cinema to portray inner turmoil since soliloquies, confrontations, close-ups of "body language," aural and visual metaphors, suggestive angles and cutting rhythms, or even the voice-over retrospections of the mature narrator might have been more frequently and better employed. It is due, rather, to shortsighted directing. Hypnotic stares and piano plinks cannot succeed as signs of inner turmoil unless a context of turmoil is established to which they can relate. Again Peerce practically trounces the audience with the addition of Finny's lines, "You are the genius and I the horse's ass," but they are not enough to convey the degree of rivalry, especially since these lines appear to be mainly comical.

Consequently, when Gene pushes Finny off the limb, the camera swishpanning to simulate dizziness—and to effect deliberate ambiguity—the audience is not at all predisposed to believe what actually happens. This confusion, true to Peerce's intention (since he added the dizziness to the novel's account), leaves the viewer in suspense, which is what Peerce must construe people to go to the movies for. The suspense lasts throughout the film until Leper's "testimony," which pins the guilt on Gene. However, the viewer is then left in the quandary of whether or not to accept Leper's version of the incident as what happened in reality. This shift in emphasis away from that in the novel detracts from the almost clinical examination of Gene's adolescent psyche, which has been already observed, and reduces the plot to "Did he or didn't he?"

Another significant deviation from the novel that weakens the psychological integrity of the film is Finny's line addressed to Leper: "A man like you is always needed." Apparently, reinforced by the piano plinks and Gene's stare of concentration, this addition was intended to convey Finny's inward charity; it didn't, mostly because Finny's innocence, a major theme in the novel, and the ultimate cause of his demise, is thus introduced in the film, only to be immediately abandoned. All the viewer is sure of is that Finny is betrayed by his friend, who is by now his alterego. Compared to the novel, the film never delves into the uncommon extent of Finny's blind trust. Therefore we are deprived not only of Gene's inner disturbance and the backdrop to it, but also of a true understanding of its victim. And therefore we may miss the whole point of the basic story line.

v

The addition of the "kangaroo court" scene deserves its own analysis, for it creates an atmosphere that transports the film into a different key. It also further illustrates my point that the art of film has the visual and auditory means of revealing the complex depths of the psyche. The film reviewer for *Harper's Bazaar* condemns the scene for "totally disrupting the carefully created atmosphere."[17] She can only be referring to the raucous parade to the tune of "the ball" song, since she does not cite the court scene as a weakness inherent in the original plot, but only in the way it is handled in the film. And the only drastic difference between the literary and cinematic handling is the addition of the parade.

But what, after all, is this "atmosphere"? As we know, a psychological ambience in film can be evoked by the choice of such things as lighting, angle, and the length of time an object is shot. The general action in *A Separate Peace* is horizontal, and the general movement of the camera is panning, a tendency that Peerce thrusts into sharp opposition with vertical action and tilt-craning of the camera, notably during the tree-jumping episodes. Whenever this opposition occurs, an out-of-jointedness is communicated, an unnaturalness in being so high and in such danger. Thus we are jolted by the incongruency of experience vicariously felt. An example of this effect, other than the tree episodes, occurs when the predominantly horizontal movement of the camera during the trial suddenly becomes vertical at the climax of Finny's second fall: now the camera cranes down to the broken body and tilts up to look at the horrified boys, the contrast to the previous angle of shots emphasizing the height of the fall, the sickening gravity of the accident, and the horror at Finny's victimization.

Contrary to the reviewer's assertion, the atmosphere of the court parade is consistent with this horror. The panning of the marching boys is alternated with tilt-shooting of the one being carried, which is dizzying to the point of arousing participation in the debauched revelry.

The film in general, and the court scene in particular, capitalize on light and dark values. The glaringly sunny day-at-the-beach ends with Finny's unrequited declaration of friendship in the dark; the figures of Gene and Leper are the only dark values silhouetted in snow. Brinker, at the entrance to the court room, is spread-eagled in black like a vengeance against the hallway light. After Finny's second accident Gene wanders all over in the dark, in what is a metaphor for the night of his soul, until he reaches the tree, which is visible. Later, when Gene visits Finny, Finny is encased in starched hospital white, outstretched in his bed as if crucified, or at least victimized. All of these examples of dark and light being pitted against each other have moral as well as psychological overtones. Each involves a moral sickness. And, in keeping with this trend, the parade is also a medley of light and dark shadows, of righteousness and evil as well as the ritualized sublimation and release of aggression.

While the parade does not dissolve back into the court proceedings, the atmosphere of interrelation between shots carries over to the interrelation of scenes. The parade is a military one; the trial is military, too. The marching song is obscene; the court prodding for every fact of the accident is obscene, too. (Recall Gene's description of similar prodding by the boy in the Butt Room: "His attitude seemed to me almost obscene....") No longer preppies, the paraders, now coarse, vicious, unrelenting, suddenly resemble the soldiers they will soon become. Gene has already fought his war and caused the accident that will eventually kill his enemy. He has broken the ground for the others to follow—right into the war. This undercurrent of war and violence that we have already observed to be deficient in the film to the point of obscuring the cause of Finny's accident, and, in fact, the very reality of it, breaks out now, near the end, relating the paraders, the court investigators, and the future soldiers, to ugliness.

vi

The filming of *A Separate Peace*, then, while it records physical activity brilliantly, is not true to the novel in its more important, psychological aspects. Yet the same techniques (montage, cinema verité, contrasted angles of shooting) that succeed in conveying the action of physical scenes are used to convey the "action" of psychological scenes—and ultimately fail. Peerce certainly attempts to reinforce the psychological message in a number of ways: mechanically, through close-up shots; dramatically, through Gene's hypnotized stares; aurally, through both the foreboding music of the piano and the carry-over of other sounds. But although all of these certainly preface Peerce's message, they do not deliver it. Gene's rage is never expanded on; we cannot even be certain that it has actually been unleashed. The relation between the evil lurking in the child and in the adult is stated only once, quickly. The film might appear adequate to those who are previously acquainted with the novel, but those who are not are given no true or thorough understanding of the basic story line. Even when the film is considered as a work of art unto itself, most of the war that went on in Gene's head esoterically remained there.

T. S. Eliot spoke of the artist's inability to concretize a character's motives as a failure to find an "objective correlative" in the form and medium of his art:

> The only way of expressing emotion in the form of art is by finding an "objective correlative"; in other words, a set of objects, a situation, a chain of events which shall be the formula of that *particular* emotion: such that when the external facts which must terminate in sensory experience, are given, the emotion is immediately evoked.[18]

The problem of externalizing and depicting psychological states seems to be more hazardous for drama and film than for, say, lyric poetry and fiction. In the latter two genres, the speaker or narrator may pass effortlessly back and forth between a description of surrounding exteriors to a direct view of the inner landscape of feeling and ideation. Drama and film, on the other hand, depend heavily upon the externalizing force of representation and "spectacle." This seems to be especially true of film, which, as Siegfried Kracauer puts it, is committed to the "redemption of physical reality."[19]

vii

One further example will make clearer the difficulty that film has in representing aesthetically, and not merely rhetorically, all the subtle, even unconscious, emotions and motivations that make character interesting. *Each Other*,[20] directed by Michal Bat-Adam (who is also responsible for the much acclaimed *Madame Rosa*) is also an admirable, but not wholly successful, attempt to dramatize the complex mutual involvement of two people of the same sex. In this case, however, it is the growing sexual attraction of two young women—Anne, an Englishwoman, and Yola, an Israeli—and neither is an adolescent. Intense feelings begin to develop as the two wander about Tel Aviv as tourists, and reach a climax some years later when Anne visits Yola in Jerusalem after the latter's marriage.

The basic problem with the movie is that the two principals are so inhibited about expressing their feelings that the writer-director (who also portrays Yola) seems hard-pressed to find objective correlatives in setting, action, words, or cinematic technique to convey them to us. Moreover, since it is obvious that we are expected to regard the growing lesbian relationship as more "natural" than "pathological," there is no clear set of symptoms for us to focus on.

But effective dramatic symbols of course need not be tied to symptomatology. One sequence in which the filmmaker is willing to move away from the surface realism of her story achieves a certain poetic power, although its full meaning can be inferred only in retrospect. The scene is an eerie tour by candlelight of one of Tel Aviv's catacombs, conducted for the two women by a speechless young boy. He is a kind of juvenile Ulysses leading them into a subterranean Hades, which here (as in Dante) can be taken as an analogue for the depths of the human psyche. The silent boy shows them how the Christians were laid to rest in the womblike hollows in the cavern walls, and then he and Yola, their candles suddenly extinguished, disappear into the darkness, momentarily leaving Anne alone.

As in a dream, the meanings of the episode seem richly overdetermined. The mysterious mute boy is perhaps Yola's yet-unborn son, who will later become, by his mere existence, another impediment to the women's inclination to act upon their emerging lesbian feelings. Yola's impulsive disappearance, which she engineers by blowing out her candle and remaining quietly in the dark, adumbrates the many denials of a feeling self that she manifests later. Unlike much else in the film, this scene brilliantly succeeds in rendering a psychological complexity by utilizing a basic element in the film medium, a montage of light and dark.

The Englishwoman Anne seems less confused and more direct about her sexual orientation than her Israeli friend. Her brief affair with the hotel's security guard is a casual fling—a mere excursion along a byway—while she awaits a more tangible response from Yola. Yola, on the other hand, is sexually ambivalent from the very beginning, having come to Tel Aviv to "find herself," in fact to write an autobiographical book in which she hopes to sort out the meaning of her adolescence, part of which encompassed a tentative desire for another woman. Her characterization of her fiancé as her own mirror image suggests a not-yet-individuated narcissistic personality. In such shaky circumstances, it is not surprising that her invitation to Anne to join her and her fiancé in an evening's *ménage à trois* backfires. The devastating feelings that rise to the surface of Yola's consciousness seem to be not Oedipal jealousy but rather pre-Oedipal fears of merging with the mother.

Later in the film, when Anne visits Yola and her husband and son in Jerusalem, the understanding husband discreetly absents himself so that the long-delayed sexual consummation can occur. But again Yola's unconscious view of Anne as the sexually taboo "mother" short-circuits the experience, and the husband finds the pair the next morning sitting on the bed, a window illuminated by the first light of dawn separating them. This perhaps is the film's second most eloquent set of cinematic images—after those of the catacomb sequence—to indicate the couple's intra-psychically determined distance from each other. It is reminiscent both in meaning and effect of Gene and Finny sitting in the circle of light at the trial scene.*

The role of the fiancé/husband (played by Moshe Dayan's son Assaf) is a very sympathetic one, full of compassion and sensitivity mixed with understandable perplexity in the face of the growing

---

*Both these images—the circle of light and the illuminated window—resemble Kurosawa's more complex use of a window and a divided door for images of the mind in his *Throne of Blood*. See Appendix A.

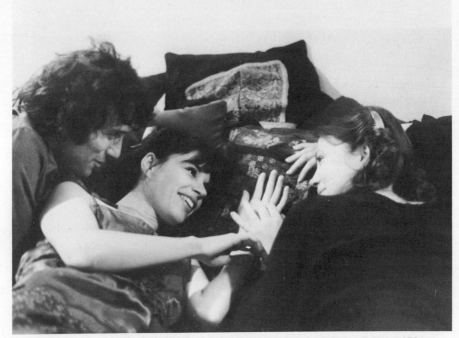

Assaf Dayan, Michal Bat-Adam, and Brigitte Catillon in *Each Other*, 1979, a Moshe Mizrahi production written and directed by Michal Bat-Adam, released by Franklin Media. (*Courtesy of Franklin Media and John Springer Associates*)

relationship that essentially excludes him. Even though he is willing either to sexually satisfy both women or have Anne as an ever-present revered member of the family, he ultimately fears the destruction not only of his marriage but possibly of his wife's sanity as well. It is he who reluctantly requests Anne to leave.

The difficulties in the triadic aspect of the relationships are interestingly underlined by the linguistic problems all three face. The two women communicate with each other in French, a language that is native to neither but is the only one they have in common. The fiancé/husband knows no French but is fluent enough in English to make contact with Anne. Yola of course converses with him in Hebrew, of which Anne has no knowledge. Thus the characters constantly form different linguistic pairs from which the third person must always in some sense be excluded. However, these scenes would have been more effective if these nonconnecting lines of communication had been underscored visually as well, for instance, through the presentation of space as discontinuous or of angles of perception as disharmonious.

As the Israeli woman returns from driving her friend to the airport (a scene that parallels the opening one in which she is driving to pick her up and from which the flashback core of the film takes wing), her voice-over interior monologue informs us that all the remaining moments of her life will be mere waiting periods between her friend's letters. Her encapsulated isolation in the car is not, however, a striking- or unambiguous-enough image to convey the full impact of this message, to show that no emotional catharsis is possible for the two women. It is no more effective than the opening tree-visit scene in Peerce's film in conveying the feeling that certain events will forever permeate one's life and allow of no peaceful sense of closure. In neither case are we left with a visual impression of "open-endedness."

Each Other is a serious attempt to treat a difficult theme of friendship, sex, and intimacy. That it does so without prurience, melodrama, or directorial clichés is much to its credit. That it is unable to do so with a bit more psychological clarity and aesthetic interest—that is, by utilizing more of the devices inherent in the film medium—is rather a pity. The same can be said of Peerce's film version of *A Separate Peace*.

However, my extensive analysis of the shortcomings of Peerce and Bat-Adam should not make us conclude that both directors were doomed by inherent weaknesses in the film medium to give less than full dramatic life to their protagonists' innermost feelings, for as we have seen, the representation of complicated psychological processes was not beyond either. In the next chapter, devoted to kinesics (the study of body language) and proxemics (the study of body distances) as two more modes of psychological interpretation of the arts, I shall be able to explore this question further, for both these taxonomies are especially valuable in describing ways in which mental states can be given a precise form and context in film.

6

Film Images as Symbols of Alienation: Kinesics and Proxemics in Frank Perry's *David and Lisa* and Zenzo Matsuyama's *The Happiness of Us Alone*

> Like the porcupines in Schopenhauer's fable, people like to be close enough to obtain warmth and comrade-ship but far enough away to avoid pricking one another.
> Robert Sommer, *Personal Space*

i

Perhaps two of the most meaningful sounds ever heard in the modern theater are the mysterious snapping of the string and the urgent fall of the ax in Chekhov's *The Cherry Orchard*. But more significant than the passing of the old aristocratic order that these noises herald is the modern void in human communication that they portend. Chekhov dramatically uses these mournful sounds to underline the pathos of a group of people who are not only victimized by change and "progress" and no longer share the same values but are unable to really talk to, or even listen to, each other because each is isolated in his own private world of mourning and melancholia.* Much of our best contemporary art has had at least overtones of this universal predicament of the inability to communicate in a world that is either too fast-paced and fragmented to encourage complete emotional responses or too replete with microcosms of narcissistic self-preoccupation to begin with.**

---

*See chapter 8 for a complete analysis of Chekhov's dramatic use of inhibited mourning in his short stories and plays.

**Christopher Lasch has recently presented the many facets of this new tendency in his *Culture of Narcissism* (New York: W. W. Norton, 1979).

Like the other arts, the art of film has successfully depicted this dilemma—from early German realism (the portrayal of the old ruined councillor in *Joyless Street*) to late Italian neo-realism (in almost all the films of Antonioni, with their strong sense of *tedium vitae*). Moreover, writers and directors of film have embodied it not only in plot, situation, character, and dialogue, but in effective cinematic images as well. In the closing scene of Fellini's *La Dolce Vita*, the inlet of water that separates Marcello from the wind-drowned shouts of the young girl on the beach is just one example of such powerful visual metaphors suggesting the loss of human contact by characters who seem empty or bereft without it.

Indeed, if one agrees with Erwin Panofsky's observation that essential communication in film is via the "dynamization of space," then it follows that film is singularly equipped to deal with themes of loneliness and alienation, for the manipulation of space between actors and objects by means of camera placement and movement and the techniques of editing can provide not only symbols but vivid sensations of separation and loss of contact.

Two film directors—Frank Perry, an American, and Zenzo Matsuyama, a Japanese—have hit upon a subtle apropos image that is not only eminently suited to the motion picture medium but is itself an instrument, as it were, of basic communication. I refer to the human hand and its gesticulative powers. Variously used in *David and Lisa*[1] and *The Happiness of Us Alone*[2] to divulge thought, pose threats, seek knowledge, and reveal affection, hand movements at first compensate the principal characters for the articulate speech denied them by an affliction, but ultimately transport them to a realm of feeling and meaning that is ineffable. In *David and Lisa*, two psychotic adolescents extend their hands first in contortions of fear and menace, and then toward each other in a clasp of affection and appreciation. In *The Happiness of Us Alone*, two deaf-mutes in postwar Japan use their hands not only to eke out a marginal living but also to communicate to each other the intensity of their feelings, thereby maintaining the vitality of their marriage. The emblem for the final achievement of love in the American film is the design of the interlaced hands on the psychiatrist's Italian cigarette box; for the achievement of understanding in the Japanese film it is the silhouette of the disembodied hands flashed on the screen during the credits.

Both of these films reveal, moreover, an artistic synthesis of the performers' overall body language (kinesics) and the spatial relationships in which they are involved (proxemics). These latter include their physical positions relative to other actors, to objects in the setting, to the boundaries of the frame, and to the placements of the camera. The result is a thoroughly cinematic, that is to say nontheatrical, kind of experience. Because such dynamic uses of space transcend the static, nonrevelatory reaction shots characteristic of Larry Peerce's film portrait of Gene in *A Separate Peace, David and Lisa* and *The Happiness of Us Alone* seem to be more successful in mustering the full imagination and resources of cameraman, film editor, and performer for their psychological study of two sets of characters locked into a world of isolated intimacy.

Western psychology has been traditionally insensitive to an individual's body posture and choice of physical distance as vital forms of communication, having followed Freud's lead in analyzing the derivatives of the patient's unconscious in language alone. However, turning aside from the mainstream of depth psychology, Wilhelm Reich took note of body posture and muscle tension as signs of psychic defense that he called "armoring." Recent practitioners of "movement therapy," including psychodrama, primal therapy, and dance therapy, owe something to Reich's respect for the body's connection to the psyche. Like him they recognize body attitudes not only as unconscious communication but as pathways back to the unconscious. That is, they see them as two-way streets: channels of expression but also channels for impression and alteration through exercise and massage.

A parallel awareness of the richness of communication of the body has emerged in the study of infants, whose lack of verbal development has forced investigators to scrutinize their body language. One thinks of the extensive observations of children by the cognitive psychologist Jean Piaget and by the developmental psychologist Margaret Mahler. To the degree that the latter's "subphases of separation" manifest themselves in the child's regulation of his physical distance from the mother, her work has particular relevance to our seeing cinematic space as revealing degrees of alienation and intimacy.*

Finally, there has been the recent impingement of Eastern psychology upon modern life. The practice of Yoga and meditation, with their emphasis upon the harmony between psychic energy and body rhythms, is another attempt to coordinate man's emotional space with his physical space.

*I shall consider the value of Mahler's work in artistic interpretation in the final chapter of this study.

ii

However, before proceeding to a kinesic and proxemic interpretation of *David and Lisa* and *The Happiness of Us Alone*, I should like to remind the reader that a physical gesture consciously contrived to underscore a verbal communication might turn out as well to be an unconscious revelation of motive or character. It may also be a pathological symptom, in which case it is both a defense against a forbidden expression and an unwitting revelation of it. For instance, an hysterical woman waking from a nightmare in which she has been sexually assaulted, but finding her fingers hooked in a clutching gesture even though her arms are extended to ward off her imaginary attacker, may be expressing contradictory feelings of overt fear and hidden desire. Thus in the realm of psychopathology symbolization may take on a very complex function.

Eleanor Perry, who approached her task of writing the screenplay for *David and Lisa* from a solid background in both psychiatry and theater, was able to appreciate the dramatic possibilities in such overdetermined gestures.* It is therefore not hard to understand why she and her director-husband would be attracted to the graphic, and even sometimes poetic, description of the behavior of two disturbed adolescents that was presented as a kind of fictionalized case history by psychiatrist Theodor Rubin in his popular novella *Lisa and David*.[3]

Yet one would be hard pressed to justify Frank and Eleanor Perry's *David and Lisa* as either a clinical case study or a documentary on adolescent psychopathology. Even though the film's principal setting is a mental institution and the two protagonists struggle through the chaos of mental illness in order finally to understand and appreciate each other, neither the background against which they move nor the method of their "cure" is essentially clinical. In a significant deviation from their source material, which contains professional psychiatric profiles and "intake" data on the two youngsters, the Perrys decided to eliminate a scene in which the institution's staff convenes for psychiatric evaluations of all the patients.[4] Seldom are the patients revealed merely as obvious clinical types, and when they are, it is so that the outside world might be shown up as insensitive. The

---

*After receiving a degree in psychiatric social work Eleanor Perry went on to write a series of short plays for the Cleveland Mental Health Association. Her screenplay for *David and Lisa* received a nomination for an Academy Award.

young Don Juan inmate, despite his crudeness, exposes the coldness and snobbishness of David's mother, just as the ones on a field trip find only intolerance in the "normal" couple at the railway station. Therapeutic practices are virtually limited to having the chief psychiatrist leave his door open as a gesture of friendship to David, or to having his assistant rather passively oversee Lisa's play. And of course it would be absurd to argue that the incipient love David and Lisa find for each other in the last scene is in itself a valid cure for severe mental illness. In truth, *David and Lisa* is much less a clinical case study than, say, Henry James's *The Pupil*, where the genesis of character formation is never downplayed or condensed, as here, for the sake of dramatic effect.

Not only does *David and Lisa* carefully avoid a clinical or documentary tone, but happily it also disvows the stage stereotype of a psychiatrist who first overwhelms us with knowledgeable jargon and then omnipotently sets things to rights. Howard Da Silva, as the chief psychiatrist, is commendable for the "expressive restraint" by which he avoids verbosity and domination but reveals instead unsentimental compassion. By having David continually try to taunt him into technical verbalizing and dogmatic diagnoses, Eleanor Perry ironically establishes the credibility of Da Silva's role in a human rather than professional light.[5] In the final scene in front of museum—the one in which David, despite his irrational fears, is able to take Lisa's hand—we have a right to expect the doctor to offer his own helping hand, since it was he who drove David there in his car. Yet he is wisely kept off-camera for the rest of the film. Even the setting for this scene—a wide terrace of marble in front of neoclassical columns—seems propitious for his arrival as the modern equivalent of a Hellenistic *deus ex machina*. But these expectations are purposely aroused, then frustrated, so that our sense of the two adolescents working out their own emotional destiny is what is dramatically underscored.

If *David and Lisa* is neither entirely based upon psychiatric verisimilitude nor descends into melodramatic clichés, what is its essential nature? Thematically, the focus of the film is the resolution of loneliness and the achievement of self-identity through communication with another human being. To be more specific, David, by being able to find in the psychiatrist a father-substitute and ego-ideal, and Lisa, by being able to identify with the mother-and-child in a sculpture group (both feeling motivated by their attraction to each other) are ultimately able to achieve a mature gesture of communication: a firm clasping of hands that implies both trust and love. Because we are shown that this is rarely possible, even in the more "normal world" of David's parents, we value even more highly the accomplishment of such a universally desired human end. What goes on in the film is therefore illuminated more if we pay closer attention to developmental psychology than to nosological descriptions of the psychoses.

Like much contemporary music, the gestures in *David and Lisa* are often nervous, angular, and discordant, although with a definite continuity and pattern. In an early scene, when David's mother brings him to the sanitarium, the camera gives us a close-up of her hand fidgeting with the fingers of the gloves on her lap—a fitting symbol of her cold, snobbish indifference to human contact. Perry gives us a similar synecdoche for narcissistic maternal coldness in *Mommie Dearest* [1981] when he introduces the Joan Crawford character by focusing the camera on an elegantly gloved hand turning off an Art Deco alarm clock.

The scene with David's mother is balanced later on by one in which his weak and rather pathetic father tries to regain his love. We watch the man's hands as they clumsily seek a place to put his burnt match and cigarette ashes. This underscores the point, already made, that there is no real place for the father in David's room (that is to say, in David's *feelings*), nor, for that matter, in the house (that is, in his wife's *affections*). Because David's mental difficulties are, unlike Lisa's, shown against the background of family conflicts, the hand movements of his parents constantly attract the camera's attention in this way. In fact, the need for a lengthy case study of David's home environment is easily, and most poetically, circumvented by the hand imagery.

Throughout the film, the camera often focuses our attention on David's hands as he clenches and unclenches them with fear and frustration or holds them up defensively under the delusion that any physical contact will bring death. But the finale consists of these movements being resolved into their opposite, for David's last gesture is to reach out with assurance to envelop Lisa's hand in his own.

In contrast, Lisa's hands move contrapuntally to David's. Her first dramatic gesture is to assert her power over his when she learns of his fear of being touched. The scene is an excellent piece of cinema. She slowly lowers her extended forefinger like a lance and goes toward him. As she moves closer, the camera catches her from different angles, one of them showing her pointing directly at us. Finally, she pauses and elevates her finger slowly. In counter-

poise to this scene is another in which, after becoming more trust-
ful of David, she slowly lowers her entire hand, palm upward, for
him to read her fortune. From then on to the end, her manual
gestures become less angular, more fluid, and more communicative. The delicate and beautiful scene in which she explores her
breast in the warm and comforting discovery that she is a "pearl of
a girl" becoming a woman, flows naturally to the scene at the
museum in which she caresses the surfaces of the sculpture-group,
probably identifying with both the mother and the child figures.

In these two latter scenes the beauty and gracefulness of Lisa's
movements, together with their musical accompaniment, unobtru-
sively capture all the elegance of a ballet. As she lies on her back in
the semi-darkness, she raises her arm into the center of the frame,
slowly turns her hand, and brings it down to caress her face and
hair, then the contours of her breast. The lighting causes the hand
and arm to appear in chiaroscuro, and the line formed by them is
that of the graceful neck and back of a swan. Many of Lisa's
movements, incidentally, remind one of *Swan Lake*. Whenever she
is frightened, for instance, she bites the back of her wrist, leaving
her hand hanging from it like the drooping wings of a bird. Thus
the ballet aspect of her hand movements contains both
symptomatic and defensive elements as well as move toward
healthy integration.

In the comparable scene at the museum we first see her in close-
up tentatively exploring the surfaces of the woman-with-infant
statue; then from above we watch her cradling herself in the entire
sculpture-group, rearranging the lines of her body and limbs so
that she becomes an artistic part of the whole. Having achieved
this good symbiosis, she can now proceed in her emotional
development on a more even keel, foreshadowed by her
willingness to now let David grasp her hand.

iii

The Happiness of Us Alone also delineates character and theme
by means of moving hands. As in *David and Lisa*, the gestures not
only help to define a character's personality but engage cinematic
space in such a way that they constantly indicate the conflict of
both avoiding and reaching out to other selves. In depending upon
the rhythmic movement of visual forms to convey these
psychological states, the directors of both films have constructed a
kind of cinematic ballet, each in a very different style. Stanley

Kauffmann has attested to the special joy in having the form and spirit of the dance in film:

> It is obvious, once you see it done, that dance is a felicitous method for film storytelling. A form that is motion...belongs in motion pictures.... Those who saw this in *Modern Times*...in which every movement and gesture was molded by Chaplin, who always dances,...will recognize...the effect is of visual music.[6]

One might easily term *David and Lisa* a modern dance movement, whereas *The Happiness of Us Alone* could be considered a form of *traditional* dance. These contrasts in form reflect psychological differences that are both personal and cultural.

In *The Happiness of Us Alone* the more ritualistic kind of dance evolves from the movements of hands of the two deaf-mutes, proceeding from the beginning with more formalized grace and restraint than in *David and Lisa*. The special cinematic quality of their sign-language is that pictorially it is as stylized as the Japanese ideograph itself. Being the means by which the two principals converse throughout, their gestures form such an integral part of characterization and tone that they defy complete analysis. However, the main crisis in the plot offers a fine illustration of the many dimensions of these moving images as a symbol and symptom of the difficulty of communication in the contemporary world.

The scene builds up as follows. After many emotional and financial difficulties, the young wife has managed to buy a sewing machine to enable her to supplement her husband's income, but upon returning home one day she sees her brother loading it into a truck in order to pawn it for gambling debts. Distraught, she runs after the vehicle. The brother ends the pursuit, however, by smashing her hand on the tailgate with his shoe. In despair, and with fingers bandaged, she writes a suicide note and takes a commuters' train away from the city. The husband finds the note, rushes to the station, and barely manages to squeeze into a car before the automatic doors close. He elbows his way through the crowd of commuters searching in vain, until from the end of the aisle he sees his wife standing in the next car. The locked communication doors prevent him from reaching her, but he is able to attract her attention through the windows.

What follows is a long poignant scene during which the couple talk to each other in sign-language through the glass windows of both cars. The facial and manual expressiveness of the man's appeal and of the woman's despair conveys direct and simple pathos. Both touch upon their isolation and loneliness in a world without sound, and the man convinces the woman of their exceptional need for each other. With her permission the husband tears up the suicide note and casts it to the wind.

The dramatic effect of the scene is enhanced by underlying ironies that are brought out by certain visual images. At frist the compartmentalization of the two figures in the two locked coaches seems to emphasize the mutual isolation that they accept as their lot. Like David and Lisa they too suffer "abnormalities" in social adjustment, and their symbolic meanings therefore become suffused with symptomatic overtones. However, it seems to me that their pathology does not extend much beyond the "exceptional need" for each other mentioned above. That is, their mutual dependence does not show regression to merging and symbiosis, as in the case of Gene and Finny in *A Separate Peace*. Here each character remains uniquely "self-actualized." As in *David and Lisa* there is an eventual shift to a kind of Laingian "anti-psychiatry," the surrounding world taking on the coloration of pathological narcissism, alienation, and prejudicial behavior (e.g., David's mother and the railway station couple in *David and Lisa*), while the protagonists gradually exhibit more humane attributes.

In *The Happiness of Us Alone*, a glance at the commuters hanging woodenly from the hand-straps, self-absorbed, indifferent, unable to bridge the distance between the separate coaches even if they wished, shows us that the pair are, with their hands, unknowingly communicating more profoundly than most. (A similar irony occurs earlier when the woman's sign-language at first humiliates and alienates her son but later wins his complete affection by making him a superior interpreter of pantomime at a children's charade.) In the train episode, the injured and bandaged fingers of the wife, which will temporarily impair her ability to sew, cannot mar the grace and effectiveness of her manual "speech."

The word *alone* in the title of the film seems to have the same kind of ambiguity of meaning as does the word *separate* in *A Separate peace*—that is, it could mean *lonely and isolated*, or *distinguished by being set apart*. On the one hand, the title seems to say, "We struggle for happiness while alone"; on the other, it implies, "Only we, among our peers, are really happy." The film really evolves from the first meaning to the second one.

Perhaps   the   essential   difference   between   the   "dance movement" of *David and Lisa* and that of *The Happiness of Us Alone* can be summed up as the difference between the romantic ideal of heightened emotion and the classical one of predictable form. Whereas the excited spasmodic gestures in the American film resolve themselves in evitably in a close-up of physical contact, the tempo of the Japanese one struggles toward calm repose in which neither gesture nor touch is any longer necessary for communication. In the closing scenes of Matsuyama's film, the husband and wife stand peacefully and happily apart, watching their son receive his high school graduation honors. The wife's mother enters the auditorium to tell her that the infant she once saved from an air-raid and had to give up to the orphanage has now returned as a young soldier to thank her. The camera tracks her as she runs excitedly across the yard toward him. We perhaps expect the film to violate its tone (in Hollywood fashion) by ending with an embrace shown in close-up. But the woman and the boy formally bow to each other, and she, at a short distance, merely circles around him in admiration as the camera discreetly moves back into long-shot.

The gradual curbing of gesture when peace and understanding are reached is perfectly natural to the flow of *The Happiness of Us Alone*, just as the sudden release from the paralysis of fear when love and trust are achieved is the only correct rhythm for *David and Lisa*. The two adolescents substantially create a new psychic life out of the nightmare of a developmental disorder; the Japanese couple merely find a way to further adapt essentially healthy personalities to a difficult environment. Both films are superb because their "visual music" not only offers us the beauty of form in motion (the basic element of motion pictures) but has a transforming effect as well, for it causes us to feel that we have transcended the narrow clinical focus on the protagonists that had been the starting points for both films.

iv

The preceding analysis of the ballet of hand gestures and of the poetry and drama of space play, as the performers in these two films move toward, away from, and around each other, also illustrates in a general way how the two recently developed branches of anthropologically oriented psychology I have been using—kinesics (body language) and proxemics (body distance)—can offer fresh insights into works of cinematic art. Because the body language in

David and Lisa and in *The Happiness of Us Alone* emanates from characters who are in some sense "abnormal" in their ability, as well as in their inordinate desire to communicate, physical movement is of course exaggerated. However, for this very reason it complies most readily with the ability of film to do what it does best: to convey meaning and feelings by means of the dynamization of space. In the case of *David and Lisa* the mental disturbances themselves provide some of the cues for creative cinematic form. David's obsessional defenses against death find their correct pace in the even tempo of ticking and the relentless movement of the minute hand in the clock dream, while Lisa's schizophrenic feeling of depersonalization finds its best expression in the aforementioned hand ballet close-ups—the close-up itself being a film technique that by its very nature "dismembers" the part of the body under scrutiny. Paradoxically, the beginning of Lisa's struggle toward emotional integration is also reflected in this same close-up sequence, in the way in which her hand, despite its being disjoined from the body, is given a well-functioning life and compositional completeness of its own.[7]

Finally, because health for Lisa requires an integration of ego functions and a self-identity greater than the harmonious function of her body that is presaged in the hand ballet sequence, it seems cinematically appropriate that in the museum episode the camera should be set at a distance that allows us the best gestalt of her body interweaving itself into a larger whole, into the compositional harmony of the sculptured family group. And because David's fear of touching and of being touched has been dramatized by his wariness about the concentric boundaries of his intimate, personal, and social space, it seems cinematically fitting that his psychological breakthrough should occur in a place where enclosures and territories scarcely exist: on the broad open steps of a public museum.

v

For us, as Westerners, the kinesics and proxemics of *The Happiness of Us Alone* stand out in greater relief than they would for a Japanese audience because they represent in part a transcultural experience. The Japanese feeling for bodily contact and social distance *vis-à-vis* the American one has been amply discussed by Edward Hall:

As an old priest once explained, "To really know the Japanese you have to have spent some cold winter evenings snuggled together around the *hibachi*. Everybody sits together. A common quilt covers not only the *hibachi* but everyone's lap as well. In this way the heat is held in. It's when your hands touch and you feel the warmth of their bodies and everyone feels together— that's when you get to know the Japanese. That is the real Japan!" In psychological terms there is positive reinforcement toward the center of the room and negative reinforcement toward the edges (which is where the cold comes from in the winter). Is it any wonder then that the Japanese have been known to say that our rooms look bare (because the centers are bare)?[8]

This account almost equates the warmth of the touching of hands with the warmth of the hearth that gives social cohesion and centrality to the space of the room. It adds a further validity to the "squeeze frame" aspect of the domestic scenes in *The Happiness of Us Alone*, in which hand gestures are the focus.

If the "personal distance" described by the old priest in Hall's statement above seems to an American less space-free than it should be and more like "intimate distance,"[9] we are sometimes, on the contrary, surprised to find greater physical distances between Japenese people than their personal relationship or emotional interaction seems to require. Yet if we can understand that even though the Japanese have no word for privacy, they see space itself not as emptiness but as a "something" that has a meaningful shape and rhythm, equal to that of objects that actually occupy space, we will not marvel too much at what seems to be an exaggeration of personal space and distance in Japanese life and art. In *The Happiness of Us Alone* the camera photographs the wife approaching her foster son at what Hall calls the "far phase of the social distance" (seven to twelve feet) and underlines this by itself moving back to a more discreet sideline view. The proxemic message of these movements and distances (as the camera identifies with the women's calculated unobtrusiveness) seems to be: "Let me take in as much of you as I can; let me show you that for the moment you are the center of my universe; and let me do this in a manner that is graceful and artful. But let me not come too close lest I presume too quickly and too much about a relationship in which time has caused some shyness and feeling of estrangement."

Feelings that are largely inexpressible in words but are conveyed

in either idiosyncratic or culturally determined gestures, movements, and rituals charging space with a dynamic rhythmic flow
seem to find a natural objective correlative in the art of the
cinema. Psychologies like kinesics and proxemics that are devoted
to deciphering the signals of such behavior are admirably suited to
the art of film interpretation.

These kinds of spatial relationships do not, of course, account
for the essential drama of the theater. As Erwin Panofsky has so
well demonstrated, the actor playing Hamlet can spellbind an
audience with language even though he be rooted to a spot as
bland and inelegant as that of a simple couch in front of a black
backdrop.[10] Although no one would discount the importance of
dialogue in film, it seems obvious that this is not its essential means
of expression. In theater, set decor, lighting, props, the blocking
out of a performer's movements, and the style of acting itself are
of course important ancillary factors in the communication of
psychological nuances, but there dialogue is the essential means of
conveying—and sometimes concealing—that special movement of
the psyche that Aristotle felt to be the heart of drama.

7

Social Drama as Veiled Neurosis: The Unacknowledged Sadomasochism of John Osborne's *Look Back in Anger*

> No one, child or adult, was allowed to challenge Cousin
> Tony's domain or his tantrums, flagrant lying and dwar-
> fish bullying.... His name, incidentally, was Tony
> Porter. Perhaps it was a wry remembrance of his per-
> secution to borrow his surname for a character in a play.
>
> John Osborne, *A Better Class of Person:*
> *An Autobiography*

i

No matter how influential John Osborne's role has been in staking out a path of social protest for a generation of dramatists and novelists known as "the angry young men," in *Look Back in Anger*, his first play, he really fails to give a dramatic context to social or political themes. In fact, the situation in which the play's protagonist, Jimmy Porter, is involved not only fails to motivate or support this character's social iconoclasms but even weakens their validity by revealing his drives to be annoyingly infantile and psychologically aberrant.

Here is a case where dramatic dialogue, which ought to be the chief means of unveiling character and uncovering the deepest springs of motivation, actually undermines, despite its obvious cleverness, the dynamic substructure of the play. Psychological interpretation of this subtextual movement reveals it to be not even a harmonious counterpoint to the play's surface pyrotechnics but something that works against the grain of its intended effects. The submerged psychodynamics of character interaction does not even enhance what is made explicit in the lines of exposition much less what is presented as onstage dramatic conflict. This is, as I shall show, what makes *Look Back in Anger* more a piece of striking rhetoric than good theater.

At first we might naively imagine that the object of Jimmy Porter's anger is, as he himself implies, the snobbish materialism of a middle class whose organization of Society has left no niche for his intelligence, talent, and imagination, and has forced him instead into the humiliating role of shopkeeper. But the play fails to underscore this theme dramatically, in spite of Jimmy's carping allusions to it. If one wishes to argue that Jimmy's justified anger becomes dramatically focused when he makes Alison, his wife, a scapegoat for the middle-class smugness of her parents, he must explain not only what the playwright adds by duplicating Alison's degradation in her friend Helena, a similar product of middle-class morality, but also why he lets Jimmy weaken this effect with verbal abuse of his friend Cliff, who stands far outside these circles.

The enemy is everywhere railed at by the protagonist, and with more than enough wit to make him a worthy challenger; but the battle never really takes place, for Jimmy's "antagonists" never appear—or when they do, they come entirely unarmed. They belong either to the "offstage" group pictured for us in Jimmy's game of dropping names (like T. S. Eliot, the Bishop of Bromley, and "Aunty" Wordsworth), or to the "onstage" group who doggedly arouse our sympathy solely by being misrepresented as the enemy and persecuted for it. We may laugh at Jimmy's comic description of Alison's father as "a plant left over from the Edwardian wilderness" and understand at once the way of life being criticized. Yet when "militant...Daddy" later appears, he merely awakens our sympathy for the honesty of his self-examination, for he is genuinely sensitive to the possibility of his failure as an understanding parent and father-in-law. Alison's only "crimes" are that she happened to be a virgin when she married her husband, and that she cannot bring herself—until the end of the play—to crawl in self-abnegation. Helena's *hauteur* before Jimmy is not smugness but justified indignation at his persecution of Alison. It soon dissolves, anyway, into complete physical, and to a certain extent spiritual, submission to him. And Cliff's only fault is that he wants to spend Sunday afternoons reading Sunday morning papers.

"If a play doesn't deal with recognizable human beings," says Osborne in his foreword, "it is nothing and has no place on the stage. You must," he tells the reader, "work out the social, moral and political implications for yourself."[1] Quite to the contrary, this playwright has been only too willing to let his protagonist articulate for him such larger themes and has given us in lieu of "recognizable human beings"—in the sense of people with universal attributes with which we can identify—a set of abnormal case studies. For whether Osborne is conscious of it or not, the theme of *Look Back in Anger* is not the frustration of a healthy intellectual by a social force. It is a morbid picture of the deteriorating effects of sado-masochism. And whether he intends it or not he makes his every character, and almost all his imagery, reinforce this theme.

A considerable amount of the play's dialogue, as well as the author's stage directions, is devoted to convincing the audience that Jimmy's rebellion is seriously directed against a middle class that has grown so complacent with the *status quo* that it has stagnated, and brought all social and intellectual progress to a halt. Jimmy accuses Helena of selling out Reason and Progress for the "old traditions" and "old beliefs"—in short, of "looking forward to the past." Furthermore, he not only identifies his wife, Alison, with these same middle-class reactionaries, but has used her, she tells Helena, "as a hostage" to carry out "raids on the enemy." Moreover, Osborne informs us parenthetically that Helena's appearance as the "royalty of middle-class womanhood" is enough to "arouse Jimmy's rabble-rousing instinct." Of course, Jimmy supposedly has every right to enact the role of tribune because, as his friend Cliff reminds us, he, like Cliff, not only comes "from working people" but is in fact a shopkeeper.

Upon these premises the protagonist establishes his right to rail at middle-class conservatism and emerge as a comic ironist in full possession of satiric powers. But Osborne wishes also to pass him off as the tragic victim of circumstances. Consequently, Jimmy cannot always retain his humorous superior detachment. The view of him as a potentially effective revolutionary with a legitimate cause must therefore occasionally give way to a regard for him as a hero stranded in an unheroic age devoid of worthwhile aims. "I have discovered what is wrong with Jimmy," Helena profoundly announces. "He was born out of his time. . . . There's no place for people like that any longer—in sex, or politics, or anything. That's why he's so futile."[2] Jimmy readily cooperates in giving this tragic cast to his character in what are perhaps the most absurd lines in the play:

> I suppose people of our generation aren't able to die for good causes any longer. We had all that done for us, in the '30's and '40's, when we were still kids. There aren't any good, brave, causes left.[3]

In this frame of mind he can imaginatively metamorphose himself into a bear and complain that "the heaviest, strongest creatures in this world seem to be the loneliest."[4]

But Jimmy Porter is no more credible as a futile "strong creature"—a curbed Samson—than he is as a member of the working class, regardless of what "causes" he can or cannot champion. In fact, Jimmy's alleged strength of character and his occupation as manager of a sweet stall are two of the most glaring flaws of character delineation in the play. His onstage tantrums, rantings, and impracticality leave no room for visualizing him as either a shopkeeper—successful or unsuccessful—or as a hero of the old school. His every action, his every mental impulse, stems not from a mind that is too ideological but from a personality that is too disturbed—a personality that appears as if it were arrested in an early stage of emotional development and were abnormally intent upon its own and everyone else's destruction.

ii

A large part of Jimmy's aberrant behavior can easily be explained by the unresolved Oedipal situation in which he is enmeshed. So explicitly do some of the statements in the play characterize this syndrome and so broad is the dramatic context given to it that it is remarkable it has escaped the notice of critics. Jimmy wants a "kind of cross between a mother and a Greek courtesan," Alison admits to Helena, and his anger and feeling of "defilement" because Alison was a virgin at the time of their marriage would doubtless have been based on his uneasy feeling that she resembled more the sexually taboo mother-figure than the acceptable courtesan-figure. But the other side of this ambivalence—his overt attraction to the mother-image—is emphasized when Helena, whom Jimmy later takes as mistress, is described in the stage direction as having "matriarchal authority" that "makes most men who meet her anxious not only to pleases but to impress," and again when Jimmy becomes very much emotionally involved in the death of his friend's mother.

More relevant to the formation of Jimmy's character than the Oedipus complex, however, is the evidence for his susceptibility to a classic *pre*-Oedipal neurosis, a characterological syndrome of self-punishment. According to one theory, the disturbance in such cases is rooted in early infancy, at a time when the child decides to turn the inevitable fear and resentment felt toward the mother—

the "giantess of the nursery"[5]—into masochistic enjoyment. Any delay on her part in offering the breast or bottle causes the collapse of his infantile "omnipotence" and "megalomania." Because his rage is of enormous proportions and because he is at the same time powerless to direct it effectively against the offending mother, two defensive neurotic mechanisms come into play. First, the rage aimed at the mother is managed by the primitive device of projection, to be followed later by introjection, a mechanism that we saw operating in only a slightly less primitive way in Knowles's *A Separate Peace**. He first imagines the mother to be angry with *him* to the same frightening degree that he is with *her*, and since he is in the oral stage of development, he fantasizes that her designs against him are cannibalistic. Subsequently, he manages another part of the rage by directing it against himself (the introjection of the original projection) and then transforming it into pleasure: "This pain is unbearable," he thinks; "perhaps I can return to my original omnipotence and nirvana by deciding to *enjoy* it. Clearly the underlying motive is to return to the illusion of a blissful symbiosis with the mother. Later he develops a sadistic bent for making others retaliate with punishment, helping to reactivate the punitive superego (maternal threat) that reinforces his opted-for pleasure in mental self-laceration. In order to continue to indulge in this dubious type of gratification in adult life, he forms immature emotional relationships with women so that he can provoke them into heaping "injustices" upon him.

Insofar as all women unconsciously remind such a man of the devouring mother-"giantess," he must avoid tender hererosexual intimacy. Instead, he must either sadistically provoke women into a retaliatory assault that feeds his masochism, or he must *imagine* that they assail him.[6] Thus all the statements in this play concerning the social iniquities against which Jimmy Porter is rebelling are really a subterfuge masking his underlying predicament with women, and it is to this psychological, not social, problem that Osborne, knowingly or unknowingly, gives a dramatic context.

That Jimmy Porter is prompted by some abnormal urge to be a habitual "collector of injustices"[7]—especially from women—is actually suspected both by the other characters of the play and himself. "Don't try to take his suffering away from him—he'd be lost without it," Alison warns Helena. A short while later, Jimmy's question to Alison, "Doesn't it matter to you what people do to me?" is provoked by nothing more serious than Helena's wish that Alison accompany her to church. And several pages later, Jimmy's wail of despair that "somebody," pre-

*See chapter 5.

sumably his mother-in-law, "has been sticking pins into *my* image
for years" is as groundless and as absurd as his "Why, why, why
do we let these women bleed us to death?"[8] In order to insure a
good supply of suffering he must "look for trouble," as Cliff puts
it, and sadistically "must draw blood somehow," as Osborne
indicates in a stage direction. There is nothing Strindbergian in
such misogyny because, unlike a Strindberg play, *Look Back in
Anger* provides no dramatic development of the reasons for it. The
female temperament does not carefully evolve under the author's
hand into the malicious conniving for power and domination
found in characters like Laura in *The Father*. In fact, Jimmy's fear
and insecurity in regard to women, whom he thinks of as "refined
butchers," are merely a hangover from the infantile dread of the
"giantess of the nursery"—the imagined cannibalism of the
mother. Observe the images of oral aggression in his remark on his
wife's passion, the climactic end of Act 1:

> She has the passion of a python. She just devours me whole
> every time, as if I were some over-large rabbit. That's me. That
> bulge around her navel—if you're wondering what it is—it's me.
> Me, buried alive down there, and going mad, smothered in that
> peaceful looking coil. Not a sound, not a flicker from her—she
> doesn't even rumble a little.... She'll go on sleeping and
> devouring until there's nothing left of me.[9]

Not only are the women in *Look Back in Anger* no real threat to
the protagonist but they are in fact propelled toward him, as a
moth is drawn to a candle flame, by the same brand of sadomasochistic impulses. Thus Helena admits to Alison that she finds
Jimmy's hatred of her "horrifying" but at the same time "oddly
exciting." And this reveling in the mutual giving and receiving of
pain reaches its climax at the end of Act 2 when Jimmy's registered
feeling of "horror," "disbelief," then "despair" upon being
"savagely" slapped by Helena ends in her kissing him passionately
and becoming his mistress. Equally addicted to the persecutor-
victim pattern centering in Jimmy are both Alison and Cliff.
Alison articulates her own propensity to inflict pain near the end
of the play: "It was unfair and cruel of me to come back," she
admits, but shortly afterward reveals that her return was designed
to put a sharper edge on her own suffering:

> I want to be a lost cause. I want to be corrupt and futile!...I
> thought if only—if only he [Jimmy] could see me now, so
> stupid, ugly and ridiculous. This is what he's been longing for

me to feel....I'm in the fire, and I'm burning, and all I want to do is die!...I'm in the mud at last! I'm groveling! I'm crawling! Oh God—![10]

Although the sadistic element seems entirely lacking in Cliff's personality, he is inextricably drawn to the harrowing experiences of the Porter household, in which he finds a wealth of masochistic enjoyment.* His expressions of this range from his playful retort to Jimmy, "That hurt, you rotten sadist!"** to his more serious description of himself for Helena:

This has always been a battlefield, but I'm pretty certain that if I hadn't been here, everything would have been over between these two long ago. I've been a—no-man's land between them. Sometimes, it's been still and peaceful, no incidents, and we've all been reasonably happy. But most of the time, it's simply a very narrow strip of plain hell.... *Perhaps I even enjoy being in the thick of it.* (Italics mine.)[11]

Look Back in Anger is therefore a truly disturbing play. But it obviously does not disconcert because, as critics like Mary

---

*Shirley Panken's remarks on the masochistic character's "enjoyment" of suffering seem to be especially relevant to Cliff, Helena, and Alison:

Where masochistic suffering seems to be "enjoyed" or to give pleasure, one must question the subjective meaning, as well as cultural context of such "pleasure." The subjective feeling of being "happy," when not a quality of the state of well being of the entire person, is illusory. What might be meant is need for drama, crisis, sensation, stimulation, or a high tension level, thereby emphasizing one's identity or acquiring a spurious feeling of aliveness (*The Joy of Suffering* [New York: Jason Aronson, 1973], p. 139).

These comments seem to apply particularly to the "Odd excitement" Cliff and Helena feel in their masochistic enjoyment of Jimmy's assaults. The remainder of Panken's remarks apply more specifically to the abject aspect of Alison's suffering:

Genuine or autonomous feelings are, for the most part, deadened or muted in masochistic persons. Life is generally experienced as occurring outside their orbit, as not to be responded to but to be reacted to in submission, at times to the point of self-extinction (See Panken, *Joy of Suffering*, p. 139.)

**The pain-provoking wrestling matches between Cliff and Jimmy suggest desire for homosexual contact defended against, as is commonly done in pubescence, by macho aggressiveness. Another example of this is the sadistic behavior of the Prussian officer in D. H. Lawrence's story of that name (see introduction, above). Given Jimmy's plight with women, such an undercover urge would seem to be inevitable. Allison's suggestion that Jimmy has a kind of Renaissance ideal of male friendship, that "which surpasseth the love of women" (as shown by his devotion to Hugh, the sentiment for whom is safely transferred to Hugh's dead mother), reinforces this. Edmund Bergler, in *Homosexuality*, suggests homosexuality as a likely outcome of the "basic neurosis" from which Jimmy suffers.

McCarthy have argued, it brings to the theater a fresh and long-
needed challenge to ossified social ideas. What is actually dramatized is a complex interaction of sadomasochistic impulses, nearly
every major character fulfilling the dual role of persecutor and
victim. Every intense thought and action springs from this personality trait and appears again and again with relentless predict-
ability. This is a more immediate source of uneasiness than
Osborne's seemingly unrelenting war on conservatism and
Philistinism.

iii

I do not wish to imply that the presence of pathological sadomasochism in a dramatic in a dramatic work is per se inartistic.
The complexities of sadomascohistic relationships have frequently
attracted dramatists and filmmakers, who have dealt with them
with aesthetic sensitivity. The closed circuitry of power and manipulation involving two people oscillating between the poles of
"victim" and "victimizer" has a built-in drama that audiences
often find irresistible. Plays and films of this type that immediately
spring to mind are Albee's *Who's Afraid of Virginia Woolf?*,
Ingmar Bergman's script for *Torment*, and Victor Fleming's overtly sadistic film version of *Dr. Jekyll and Mr. Hyde*. And these are
works whose themes have a deep social as well as psychological
significance, although they are not rhetorically proclaimed as
such.

Since certain social roles in fact provide the opportunity for a
victimizer/victim relationship—such as that of employer to
employee, teacher to pupil, prison guard to prisoner—playwrights
and scenarists do not have to look far for an exterior set of circumstances that will embody their characters' interior motives of
punishment and pain. The point is that these authors seek to
represent the sadomasochistic underpinnings of their social
themes, not *mask* them. Some years ago Joseph Losey gave us in
his remarkable film *The Servant* the bizarre portrayal of a valet
(Dirk Bogarde) gradually assuming complete control over his
master—a struggle and capitulation that had a strong homosexual
undertone despite the servant's cheery introduction of his
mistress—the seductive Sarah Miles—into his master's household.
More recently France gave us Bruno Gantillon's *Maid and
Mistress*,[12] a film that protrays in a heterosexual and less
melodramatic way the slow emergence of impulses of

sadomasochism. These impulses, previously unacknowledged because of the characters' heretofore fixed social roles, suddenly come into the foreground when the roles themselves suddenly shift.

As the film opens, an attractive but somewhat matronly upstairs maid is playing solitaire and munching an apple in an opulent bedroom in which an old man is dying. She interrupts her game twice: first when she wipes the spittle from the man's lips and then a few minutes later when she notices that his labored breathing has stopped. She casually closes the dead man's eyes, coolly stares at him, and continues to munch her apple.

The next day we see the maid, heavily garbed in mourning clothes, being dropped off in front of the mansion by a hearse. It is obvious that she has been the sole mourner at her master's funeral. As the camera follows her through the lonely house, she fingers and caresses various objects as if she sees them in a new light. We wonder if she is merely enjoying the temporary hiatus in which a servant acts as caretaker until legal heirs take possession, or if she has another claim, emotional or otherwise, to all she surveys. The scene ends with her walking out to the garage, removing the tarpaulin from the master's beautiful old Rolls-Royce, and caressing its elegant hood. We sense that she is more complexly involved with the house than is immediately apparent.

A time lapse is indicated by the sight of the woman again dressed in her maid's uniform busily dusting. At this point there enters with traveling bags, the master's nephew and heir-apparent. It is quickly established that the young man—Jerome—has often spent time at his uncle's house, although he has been away pursuing a diplomatic carreer during the few years preceding his uncle's illness and death. When Jerome orders the maid to draw his bath and then "stay a while," it becomes immediately apparent that there has been some sort of intimacy between them.

A later scene clarifies the true nature of this "intimacy." As the maid is kneeling before Jerome in order to remove a stain from his trouser leg, he guides her hand up his thigh and begins to unzip his fly—to which she angrily reacts by announcing that "there'll be none of that this time." The audience now understands that their liaison has consisted not so much of a mutually agreed upon romantic involvement as a quasi-compulsory servicing of the man by the woman.

The maid continues to play the role of domestic servant to the heir-apparent until he orders her to have the Rolls-Royce put back into working order. This allusion to one of the most obviously phallic symbols of the master's legacy (and the one that climaxed the maid's informal inventory in a previous scene) prompts the maid to tell Jerome that the car has been willed to her. In anger Jerome telephones his uncle's lawyer only to find that the maid has been named sole heir and to be told that the only way for him to have the legacy is to marry her.

Since Jerome is temporarily at loose ends, waiting to be assigned to his next diplomatic post, the maid (now mistress of the house) invites him to stay on awhile. The stage now seems to be set for Jerome to woo the lady in a romantic, courtly way, and this expectation is reinforced in the audience by the sight of the pair, formally dressed, sitting down as social equals to an intimate candle-lit dinner. The anticipated tone of the scene is set no more than slightly askew by the woman's insistence upon all the attentions due a lady, for example, in having the man fill her wine glass before his own. However, when by her rigid posture she indicates that he must not lean across the table to light her cigarette, but must get up and stand at her side to do so, we sense that a less apparent scenario may be surfacing.

Our suspicion is shortly borne out. Jerome soon asks for a loan to buy a tuxedo in order to attend the foreign minister's ball—a social move that would aid his faltering career. When we see the woman secretly go to a drawer for money and leave the house— presumably to surprise her "lover" with an instant gratification of his wish, we are once again seduced into expectations of a stereo-typical romance. Will this film turn out, we wonder, to be merely a double-twist of the classic Pygmalion tale: circumstances convert a low-born servant into a "duchess," who in turn becomes a sculp-tress of personality as she remodels her insensitive lover (who also happens to be a failed diplomat) into a suitable husband and successful careerist?

Such notions are soon undercut. The next day the box that arrives from the clothing store contains not a tuxedo but a chauf-feur's cap and uniform. The hidden scenario is now in the open; the former maid wants neither a romantic suitor nor an affection-ate and successful husband but a servant upon whom she can freely act out her heretofore concealed sadism.

Jerome's decision to comply with this arrangement is made dramatically plausible by a few deft strokes: (1) he regards it to be a diverting "game"; (2) he has time on his hands as he awaits his next diplomatic appointment. However, as the days go by, Jerome falls more and more deeply into servitude while his mistress (by now the word has decisively shifted its meaning from *paramour* to *employer*) becomes increasingly more imperious. We see him being forced to perform the tasks of personal maid, cook, and chambermaid, as well as those of chauffeur. Here the mythic allusion in the title of Raynal's novel, *Aux pieds d'omphale*, upon which the film is based, is most fully realized. In these characteristically female roles Jerome is like a feminized Hercules, who was force to sit dressed up in women's clothes "at the feet of [Queen] Omphale."

Enter a young woman (Christine) newly hired by the mistress to act as maid—a decision that we hope is born of her desire to ease up on her sadistic persecution of Jerome. However, we are again mistaken; she is merely seeking an ally to assist in the torture—much in the way that preadolescent children seek out their cronies on the playground to help harass the hapless scapegoat. (Freud's notion in his *Group Psychology* that censure from the superego is lessened by concerted action seems relevant here.) In a tense scene, mistress and maid dine together as equals, while Jerome serves them both. The mistress demonstrates her absolute power by having him pick up her napkin over and over again, then maliciously entices Christine to order him to do the same. The maid's zest for the game soon exceeds her mistress's—to such a degree that Jerome is driven to the point of violently beating her.

The next day Christine leaves in anger and tears, accusing both her mistress and Jerome of being "sick." Clearly servants, like children, look to their employers/parents to place reasonable limits upon their most primitive impulses, not to provide the frightening conditions for an untrammeled release of them. It is the first prelude in the film to the mistress's own tragedy of aggression gone out of control.

A second prelude is a kind of enter'acte in which the mistress seems interested in contracting an alliance (perhaps marriage) with a middle-aged, aristocratic gentleman of the district. Again we hope—and again with eventual disappointment—that her outlook and behavior have taken a healthier turn. But a pleasant day's idyll spent by the couple in the nearby woods (to and from which Jerome, as chauffeur, has driven them in the Rolls-Royce) ends with the mistress humiliating Jerome by having him kneel before the man to clean and shine his shoes. Realizing her lack of *noblesse oblige*, that self-regulating principle by which absolute authorities humanely temper their own aggressive energies, the would-be suitor leaves in disgust.

As the masochistic complement to his mistress's sadistic behavior, Jerome actually fares much better than she. His enforced, and seemingly humiliating labor, actually provide his life with a needed structure. His existence has been rootless rather than free, and his diplomatic career has been an unadmitted failure. (A brief scene in which he assumes that he can see the Foreign Minister without an appointment but is brushed aside by a subaltern informs us of this.) His temporarily dependent position forces him to closely observe the woman for the first time. Having formerly treated her as an indifferent object of sexual release, he now sees her as a unique personality, although one that worries and horrifies him. He also reaches new levels of understanding of her psychodynamics, to the extent that he can inform her that, even though he formerly forced her into sexual compliance, she really *wanted* it. That is, he recognizes the masochistic pole of her present sadism, and he actually begins to worry about her fate.

She, on the other hand, remains emotionally empty, driven more and more to excesses of aggression in order to alleviate her alienation and loneliness. Except for her grotesque attachment to her role of victimizer, she remains as personally uninvolved and as emotionally unconnected as when she coolly munched an apple at her master's deathbed. The underlying pathos of her emotional condition had been obliquely hinted at earlier when she told Jerome that she received the legacy from his uncle because she "happened to be present," not because she was in any way "special."

For Jerome, the mistress's compulsive sadism has ironically provided a temporarily needed symbiosis—one in which he is forced to mirror other lives until he develops an empathy that allows for a less narcissistic self-absorption. When at the end of the film the mistress's excesses of sadistic exertion lead to her death, he is even able to mourn her (a sign of self-object separation). This is something that was impossible for *her* to do when her employer died. For the mistress, social freedom has ironically meant deeper emotional paralysis. That a more serious entrapment is engendered by her sadomasochistic bent is shown by the fact that despite the freedom of movement offered by newly acquired wealth, she leaves the house only to engineer more intense persecutions within it, whereas Jerome's externally enforced confinement to the same physical space leads to meaningful introspection, a developmental step toward maturity hitherto unavallable to him.

iv

Maid and Mistress is made more cinematically fascinating by having generated a complex picture of two characters with a minimum of dialogue. It eschews monologues and voice-overs, as well as mutual verbal analyses on the part of the characters. Thus the film does not even seek to use words to explain its acknowledged sadomasochism, much less to divert our attention away from it, as Osborne seems to do. It achieves much of its psychodynamic development and impact by means of the performers' body language. So significant, in fact, is the actors' interaction with objects and setting (e.g., the touching of the Rolls Royce; Jerome's lighting of the mistress's cigarette at dinner; the mistress's pseudo-freedom in making excursions away from the house), and so significant is the camera's presentation of this through its manipulation of space and distance, that each becomes another instance of the film medium's ability to make brilliant use of the art and science of kinesics and proxemics. When this occurs, *mise en scène*, a theatrical concept, becomes *mise en "shot"*, a purely cinematic transformation.

In a novel like *A Separate Peace*, where the conscious theme is that of emotional development (even though frequently of a pathological nature), the author seeks to represent these intrapsychic dynamics imagistically, as for example through different ways of characterizing trees and forests, or describing the interplay of light and shadow. Or he sometimes offers dramatic confrontations in which deceptions are concocted or exposed. But Osborne, whose true dynamics of character interaction are camouflaged rather than explored, possibly because they represent an unacknowledged or unresolved part of the author's personality,* must rely on rhetoric rather drama, on essentially static verbiage rather than on psychic change.

Both Sophocles, whom we studied earlier, and Chekhov, whom we shall take up in the next chapter, were able to use the words of their dramatic fictions more resourcefully. In the Oedipus plays Sophocles carried the psychological predicament of his protagonist even into the heart of a word's etymology. In both his plays and short stories Chekhov, as we shall see, is able to make the hiatuses and pauses in thought and speech resonate with his character's dilemmas.

In *Maid and Mistress* the subtext of sadomasochism was allowed to shift its balance and then rise to the surface of the plot in a series of revelations that were made ironic by being placed against the grain of our expectations. In *Look Back in Anger*, however, Osborne has allowed a subtext of a rather stalemated sadomasochism to sap the dynamic life from his play's dialogue. To overlay this kind of stagnant atmosphere with a theme of social protest, as Osborne does, is to distort, not sharpen, the real dramatic focus in the play. How pretentious is his claim that his stage hero "speaks out of the real despairs, frustrations and sufferings of the age we are living in, now, at this moment"!

It is possible to laugh at Jimmy Porter's social and political barbs, but we nevertheless wince at his irrational brutality and self-laceration. Unfortunately, this effect is not artistic but in fact merely harrowing. *Look Back in Anger* fails to arouse an aesthetic response because it depicts a situation in which, as Matthew Arnold puts it, "suffering finds no vent in action; in which a continuous state of mental distress is prolonged, unrelieved by incident, hope, or resistance; in which there is everything to be endured, nothing to be done."[13] The momentary escapes by Jimmy and Alison into their imaginary world of squirrels and bears merely underline rather than relieve the agony born of their unchangeable psychological aberration. *Look Back in Anger* becomes, therefore, little more than a half-way glimpse into the shadowy origins and morbid effects of pathological behavior.

---

*Osborne's recently published autobiography, *A Better Class of Person* (New York: E. P. Dutton, 1981), certainly contains ample evidence of a persecutory and devaluating mother and of his own masochistic relation to her. Without apparent resentment he recalls from childhood her characterization of him as "unwholesome" and her regard for "almost everything about me as unsightly" (p. 22).

8

Humanistic Fiction as Inarticulate Feeling: Mourning and Melancholia in Anton Chekhov's "Misery" and "Rothschild's Fiddle"

> I'm in mourning for my life.
>
> Masha in *The Seagull*

i

It would be hard to find a writer whose style and mode of dramatic presentation are more diametrically opposite to Osborne's than Chekhov's. In fact, a perfect description of *Look Back in Anger* could be gained by merely reversing or negating Avraham Yarmolinsky's characterization of Chekhov's short stories:

> The situations he usually presents are at the *opposite pole from melodrama*, as is his style from the melodramatic. His *language, rather slovenly, with rare strokes of bold imagery*, sometimes very expressive, *always free from the emphatic, the rhetorical, the florid.* (Italics mine.)[1]

These differences do not account for why Chekhov's work succeeds while Osborne's fails. The reason *Look Back in Anger* does not ultimately jell is that its melodrama, bold imagery, and rhetoric, despite careful patterning, push against the current of its deeper psychological movement, whereas Chekhov's apparent nonsequiturs of the mind and particularly of the heart," as Yarmolinsky terms Chekhovian psychodynamics,[2] merely *seem* disjointed. Far from being out of joint, the apparent hiatuses in expression and feeling in Chekhov's characters are found to have an underlying connective tissue of primary process thinking when they are subjected to psychoanalytic scrutiny. This is another way of saying what Francis Fergusson said of Chekhov's *modus*

operandi in *The Cherry Orchard*, which also generally characterizes the artistry of his other work, certainly "Misery" and
"Rothschild's Fiddle": ". . . he selects only those incidents, those
moments in his characters' lives, *between their rationalized
efforts*, when they sense their situation and destiny most
directly."[3] (Italics mine.)

In the plays and short stories Chekhov's treatment of grief and
mourning often borders on comedy. A humorous tone is struck
each time the "bereaved" character incongruously or irrelevantly
displays his sadness. Ostensibly he is attempting to achieve a
catharsis of despair, but often we sense that either he is publicly
nurturing his grief in order to capture the limelight or he is under
the sway of some private impulse to express it, much in the way
that characters in a Jonsonian comedy were forced into inappro-
priately rigid behavior by a surplus flow of one of their biles or
"humours." Expressions of longing for the deceased therefore
become encapsulated pieces of noncommunication, for they are
usually uttered out of their social context in a mood of narcissistic self-preoccupation. Bystanders simply ignore such laments
because they have heard them so often.

In the case of minor characters like Shabyelsky in *Ivanov*, who
harps on his desire to visit his wife's grave in Paris, the reiterated
lamentation becomes a kind of Dickensian tag-line to mark off a
comic eccentricity. However, in major characters whose actions
affect the design of the work, bereavement is usually more
complex and frequently more serious, even tragic, in tone. It can
run the gamut from opportunistic posturing to uncontrollable
obsession—for instance, from Popova's resolve in *The Bear* to
become a professional widow-in-mourning in order to make her
dead husband feel guilty for his past infidelities; to Masha's
display of widow's weeds in *The Seagull* because, as she says, "I'm
in mourning for my life"; to the protagonist's suicidal despond-
ency in *Ivanov* over the loss of his creative energies.

Two short stories by Chekov, "Misery" (sometimes translated
as "Grief" or "Heartache") and "Rothschild's Fiddle," can be
seen as opposite ends of a spectrum upon which we can locate the
dynamics of intense grief and quasi-humorous sadness in much of
Chekhov's work. Both stories contain protagonists whose erratic
behavior becomes fully understood when we realize that their
mind and emotions are caught up in a paralysis of uncompleted
mourning. In "Misery" the psychological needs of Iona the sleigh-
taxi driver are fairly apparent at once, for he has already begun
what Freud calls the "work of mourning"[5]—the process by which,

as another writer[6] puts it, "the lost object"—Iona's dead son—"is gradually decathected by...remembering and reality-testing, separating memory from hope" of his return. And since Iona realistically accepts the death as permanent and irremediable, neither his character nor the motives for his actions present a conundrum. "Rothschild's Fiddle,"[7] on the other hand, is not only more complex but is often mystifying because its protagonist, Yakob the coffin-maker, has a profound grief that is buried under a panoply of defenses, most notably denial and displacement. Cut off from consciousness in this way, his feelings more nearly resemble melancholia than grief, and sometimes produce bizarre behavior.

To take the more transparent tale first, Iona's main problem is merely to find a sympathetic ear into which to discharge an account of his loss. Instinctively he seems to know what psychologists have since made explicit, that "the mourner gradually sets free the bound up energy...bound to the memories and ideas that arose from interaction with the dead person...by focusing his mind on the lost person and bringing to consciousness each relevant memory"[8] Each of Iona's encounters with a patron who hails his taxi offers a fresh hope that he might begin that "obsessional review of events leading up to the loss" that is characteristic of the "grief-work"[9]:

> He wants to talk of it properly, with deliberation....He wants to tell how his son was taken ill, how he suffered, what he said before he died, how he died....He wants to describe the funeral, and how he went to the hospital to get his son's clothes.[10]

But the indifference, intoxication, hostility, or simple self-absorption of each rider frustrates this natural and necessary process of freeing the locked-up feelings of bereavement.

The wintry landscape into which the old sleigh-cabbie and his horse are placed—the two of them covered by a mantle of snow that congeals them into a single sculpture of pain—is the perfect analogue for Iona's soulscape of petrified desolation:

> Iona...sits on the box without stirring, bent as double as the living body can be bent....His little mare is white and motionless too. Her stillness, the angularity of her lines, and the stick-like straightness of her legs makes her look like a half-penny gingerbread horse.[11]

The body language of each is in complementary contrast to that of the other, in reality picturing a single ego-state in the protagonist. Defensively and regressively Iona seeks to reduce himself to the foetal position, the nearest a being can come to a state of suspended animation protected from outside interference. On the other hand, the mare is all awkward protrusions into the external world—we could almost say she is "all thumbs"—revealing the outward-reaching, but brittle and maladaptive parts of Iona's ego. But more dynamically considered, Chekhov's verbal description really is the beginning of a condensed portrait of the three stages of grief outlined by Pollock:[12]

1. Shock and regression

"He bends himself double and gives himself up to his misery."[13]

2. The beginning of the grief phase itself, in which a set of movements, like the wringing of hands, is begun to counteract feelings of impotence.

"He draws himself up, shakes his head as though he feels a sharp pain and tugs at the reins."[14]

3. Painful awareness of the inability of the deceased to receive a discharge of libidinal energy.

"He cannot think about his son when he is alone. . .to think of him and picture him is insufferable anguish"[15]

The force of Chekhov's own empathy for Iona leads him into an intentional "pathetic fallacy" that stamps the mare's emotional state as essentially human in nature:

She is probably lost in thought. Anyone who has been torn away from the plough, from the familiar grey landscapes, and cast into this slough, full of monstrous lights of unceasing uproar and hurrying people, is bound to think.[16]

This attribution to the mare of feelings of grief over the disruption of her familiar way of life prepares us for Iona's later projective identification in which she becomes transformed into a fellow mourner.

ii

Two little ironies join together to complicate and crown this otherwise simple tale. The first of these reflects an emotional ambivalence that psychoanalysts frequently find to be an ingredient of mourning: guilt over having survived the departed, arising perhaps from repressed, unresolved feelings of hate suffused with those of love for the deceased. "It's a strange thing, death has come in at the wrong door," Iona tells a passenger; "instead of coming for me it went for my son"[17] He would have had this guilt mitigated by being accepted into a band of survivors who might share with him similar experiences of loss. The psychodynamics of this would be in accordance with Freud's observation of the psychology of groups: that binding oneself to a body of people engaged in a common cause or course of action considerably reduces the tyranny of the individual superego.[18] But Iona's peers, the other cabbies whom he seeks out back at the sleigh yard, prove to be, in their various states of sleep around the old stove, just as inaccessible as his preoccupied fares had been. However, these brusque passengers had, each in his own way, played an important mediating role between Iona's ego and superego, for their rudeness and hostility externalize the chastisement of his own superego and therefore allow him to purchase the right to survive:

> He hears abuse addressed to him...and the feeling of loneliness begins a little to be less heavy on his heart...And Iona hears rather than feels a slap on the back of his neck.
> "He-He!..." he laughs. "Merry gentlemen...God give you health!" [19]

This is, of course, only a partial solution to his problem and a masochistic one, but one that Iona in his desperation welcomes. Several times he attributes the three riders' obvious cruelty to "merriment," and giggles at their remarks as if this were an appropriate response. He thus pardons these harsh allies to his punitive superego by a reaction-formation of deferential glee—behavior that is the precise opposite of the misery he feels.

Consolation also comes through another devious route, that of a mixed set of positive identifications and object transferences. Verbally frustrated by both his passengers and his fellow cabbies, Iona finally pours out to his little mare as he stables and feeds her, a captive audience, the detailed account of his son's illness and death. He tries to achieve greater bonding and empathy by inviting her to imagine that she, too, is a grieving parent:

> Now suppose you had a little colt, and you were own mother to that little colt....And all at once that same little colt went and died....You'd be sorry, wouldn't you?[20]

Yet his tone in this otherwise piece of projective identification is one that a parent uses to a child rather than of an adult speaking to a peer. Moreover, he is intensely aware that the animal's acceptance of food, its grateful breath upon his hand, and its attitude of respectful attention are more like those of a dutiful offspring. Thus her transformation in his mind from peer to child allows for a partial replacement for the lost son.

The animal's gender complicates Iona's identifications even more. Previously Chekhov had casually, and seemingly irrelevantly, inserted into the story three discrete allusions to the meaning of females in Iona's life:

> (1) "Cabman, are you married?" asks one of the tall passengers. "I? He-He! Me-er-ry gentlemen. The only wife for me now is the damp earth"[21].
> (2) It would be even better to talk to women [of his grief]. Though they are silly creatures, they blubber at the first word.[22]
> (3) He still has his daughter Anisya in the country. And he wants to talk about her too.[23]

In Iona's need for further bonding with others to compensate him for the loss of his son, he had subtly revealed an attempt to reestablish two kinds of security with the female: the unbroken link of child/husband to motherly wife, and the connection of a fond father to a still-alive, doting daughter. In the first allusion cited above, "damp earth" suggests the archetypal earth mother of birth and death, whereas the female "blubberers" in the second statement hint at the regressive projection of the infant's tension-relieving cries onto the mother. Now as he feeds the mare, her pleasant warmth, mute and moist, reinvokes the comforting mother of early symbiosis while the animal's obsequious attitude, seeming to exhibit sadness at being displaced from the rural setting where the daughter still resides, symbolically brings the only other missing offspring into his presence to share the mourning ritual.

iii

The character traits and behavior of Yakob in "Rothschild's Fiddle" are more enigmatic because they derive from warded-off feelings in the unconscious. While Iona instinctively understood the process of mourning, consciously sought to engage in it, and suffered because external circumstances prevented him, Yakob is beset by internal conditions that block his expression of grief. He is one of those "fugitives from grief" so aptly described by Joseph Smith as "frantically immersed in everydayness as a way of covering their sorrow".[24] Whereas Iona wants a communal ritual of mourning and can attempt to diminish his anguish by finding the image of it both mirrored and multiplied in numerous others, Yakob, with his unconscious clinging to the imago of his dead child, can only displace his loss in a repetitious and compulsive way onto "neutral" persons and things. For this reason the reader of "Rothschild's Fiddle" may for a long time remain at sea as to why Yakob obsessively totes up the financial "losses" incurred by his self-imposed "holidays," why he is contemptuous of making coffins for children, why he uses his own body as a yardstick for measuring coffins for male corpses, and finally why he must constantly make a scapegoat of Rothschild, the pitiable little Jew who plays with him in the small part-time orchestra.

The first real clue to Yakob's intrapsychic conflict of unexpressed grief is the paradoxical thought that he *does* express: "Only in death are there no losses; all is gain." These words soon take on a terrible irony when his dying wife Marfa reminds him in her last breath that they once had a "golden-haired child" that died. Such forced and unwanted recollections of death, coupled with his begrudging duty to provide a funeral (he bargains for the lowest rate and makes the coffin himself), make him acutely aware of the true nature of his "losses": he had never fully lived and has done all he could to restrict life's joys in others, most of all in his wife.

At first we suspect Marfa's reference to a dead child to be part of the delirium of a dying woman—especially in the light of Yakob's strenuous denial that such a being ever existed. But later an actual memory of the child is evoked in Yakob by the sight of the willow by the river—now old and "with an immense hollow in it"—that Marfa had recalled as part of the setting for a family outing long ago. Now all the impressions associated with the experience are brought into vivid play in accordance with the psychodynamics of lifting the repression of the key affect connected to the event itself:

He sat underneath it [the willow tree], and began to remember. On the other bank, where was now a flooded meadow, there then stood a great birch forest, and farther away, where the now bare hill glimmered on the horizon, was an old pine wood. Up and down the river went barges. But now everything was flat and smooth; on the opposite bank stood only a single birch, young and shapely, like a girl; and on the river were only ducks and geese where once had floated barges. It seemed that since those days even the geese had become smaller. Yakob closed his eyes, and in imagination saw flying towards him an immense flock of white geese.[25]

Yakob's newly awakened awareness brings the anemic realities of the present into dramatic contrast with the idealized richness of the past. The now old willow "with an immense hollow in it"—once a fresh young tree under which mother, child, and father had been happy—reminds him of the wife who had become old and barren. Such a harsh and direct view, all at once, of the meagerness of his lot is of course unbearable, and fantasy and symbolization must continue in order to soften the blow and make tolerable not only the death of others but the death-in-life in himself. In the image of the "single birch, young and shapely, like a girl", the dead child, or perhaps his once-youthful wife, is resurrected on the other side of the river from where the old willow stands.

Other mechanisms of symbolization and denial had been at work to bind Yakob's libido to an unconsciously maintained imago of the child. These prevented not only his "loss" of it through the normal process of mourning but also accounted for his perpetually melancholic disposition. In reconsidering the beginning of the tale, we can see that his open disdain for making coffins for children—supposedly because they were a "trifle" both in effort and in profit—preserves the value of the internalized image of the child by devaluing its consciously perceived counterparts that are subject to decay and "loss." The many holidays he observes allow his physical energy to be converted to the mental energy that is required for this monumental intrapsychic task. And his compulsive use of his own body to measure coffins for commoners would seem to indicate the unconscious denigration of self so characteristic of the melancholic.

Less obvious perhaps is the relevance of Yakob's treatment of his fiddle and of Rothschild, the Jew to whom he bequeaths it. As we shall see, these are two highly overdetermined bits of symbolic action that directly bear on his inability to accomplish the work of mourning.

In "Mourning and Melancholia" Freud commented on how the fear of poverty was often a concomitant of the individual's loss of self-esteem in depression and how it takes on an obsessive quality that clearly marks it as a regression to anal erotism. Of course Yakob's inordinate desire to tot up his financial losses and his declaration of holidays so that he might perpetuate this task actually bring about his poverty. This is not Freud's point exactly but rather its corollary: by willfully causing his own financial losses, Yakob shapes his own destiny of deprivation. The many connotations of the word *loss* in turn allow him to associate it with another kind of loss, the death of his child. Through the medium of this linguistic link he unconsciously hopes to gain magical and omnipotent control over what is uncontrollable.

Yakob's bequest of his beloved fiddle to the heretofore detested Rothschild, his fellow musician in the part-time orchestra, is clearly an attempt at restitution—a last minute effort to relieve his self-induced poverty of feeling and ego-function. Like many other actions in the story, it is a complex, multileveled gesture. In order to appreciate this, one must understand the paradoxical meaning that Rothschild himself had for Yakob. While on the one hand the vision of great wealth conjured up by his name is a constant reminder to Yakob of his own financial "losses," the Jew's depressed countenance, together with his patched clothes, which rule out even modest comfort, and his sad rendition of tunes, which belies basic happiness, tally only too well with Yakob's underlying depression, for the Jew clearly mirrors the impoverished, devalued self-image that lurks beneath Yakob's pose of contemptuous superiority. For the psychoanalyst, Yakob's sudden rages against Rothschild, supposedly "without any tangible cause," are therefore easily deciphered: the repressed rage at the departed loved one still maintained in the unconscious ego as an introject is activated by his unconscious view of Rothschild as a failed ego ideal of masterfulness and control. Yakob erroneously thinks him to be depleted of both wealth and energy *because of* his seemingly perpetual attitude of mourning.

The fiddle has, to a large degree, symbolically taken on the role of the dead child for Yakob, for in his final illness we become privy to his thought that it "must remain on orphan" after his death until it, too, "would decay" as "had happened with the birchwood" forest where there remained only the soon-to-perish "single birch, young and shapely, like a girl"—the recent reminder of his dead child or the young wife of his youth. We can, incidentally, note how the emotional release in mourning for lost objects allows for a general empathy with humanity, impossible within the narcissistic framework of the more melancholic self.

Yet it is as a shifting image of *self*-identification that the fiddle takes on its most striking character. It merely expresses Yakob's outward persona when it "whines" in the orchestra, but comes closer to revealing his inner grief when he plays it as he lies alone in bed. As it fills the darkness with the "melancholy sound which made Yakob feel better,"[26] it becomes the instrument that completes the mourning work for him, dissolving his view of Rothschild as an unconsciously projected deflated self-image and binding the Jew to him as "brother" in sorrow, that is, as a realistically seen fellow sufferer who shares the acknowledgement of deeper losses. So exquisitely and perfectly does the fiddle convey the grief of both men that it almost takes on a life of its own, injecting an almost supernatural note into the story and giving it the flavor of a folktale. Continuing to emit "sounds so passionately sad and full of grief that the listeners weep," even when Rothschild, its new owner, plays it, the fiddle has finally provided the full expression of mourning that obviates for both Yakob and Rothschild the need for displacement onto other kinds of object losses. Therefore it is appropriate—although seemingly ironic—that Rothschild, Yakob's spiritual heir to his new psychic wholeness, should now profit financially, without "losses", from playing his mournful dirges.

iv

Some form of introjection of and identification with the lost object inevitably constitutes a part of bereavement. By thus incorporating a representation of the deceased in the psyche, the mourner paradoxically prepares to separate from it in reality. Presumably to the degree that the object is tinged with ambivalent feelings, to that extent the introject may remain noxious and undigested, an unconscious precipitant for unrelieved depression.[27] At the end of "Misery" Iona accomplishes the task he has always been intuitively working on, the internalization of the idealized image of his son, significantly achieved as part of the experience of oral incorporation:

"Are you munching?" Iona asks his mare, seeing her shining eyes. "There, munch away, munch away...*Since we have not earned enough for oats, we will eat hay*....Yes....I have grown too old to drive....My son ought to be driving, not I....He was a real cabman.... He ought to have lived" (p. 14; italics mine).[28]

Although Iona thinks he has not earned enough for proper food, he proceeds to nourish himself by the identificatory process of fully incorporating his son's idealized image. Yakob, also thinking he has not earned enough, in reality can not *lose* enough. That is, only until he has begun the process of orphaning his child/fiddle, can he start releasing his pent-up anger about once having been himself "orphaned" by the "golden child."

Both Iona in "Misery" and Yakob in "Rothschild's Fiddle" suffer from the inability to express grief—the one unable to do so merely because he cannot find objective correlatives in customary persons and rituals, the other because of an anally fixated inability to let go of a narcissistically invested object of love. The contrast between the more deeply feeling and libidinously outreaching personality of the grieving Iona, on the one hand, and the narrowed-down, more aggression-tinged self of the quietly melancholic Yakob, on the other, is explained further by Edith Jacobson's estimate of the difference between the merely sad person and the melancholic:

> Inasmuch as the sad person cherishes his past, he will feel deprived but not bad and worthless or empty. In other words, the libidinous cathexis of his self in its current situation is reduced, but not in favor of aggression; the libidinous object cathexes are likewise maintained, though they may also be reduced. An increase in the cathexes of the self and the world, that would lead to either angry or depressed mood, is prevented by the previous memories of a happy past and of a previously rich self.[29]

Both Iona and Yakob seek relief in unusual identifications and in strange displacements of feeling. Psychoanalytic interpretation is of more service to "Rothschild's Fiddle," however, because the more deeply regressed and unconscious aspects of Yakob's melancholia and his uncompleted task of mourning submerge the logic of the tale beneath its surface events.

V

Disruptions, hiatuses, and inhibitions in personal communication can be found in almost every work by Chekhov, be it short story or play. The inability of characters to complete the process of mourning, whether consciously experienced as bereavement or unconsciously felt as emptiness and depression, often explains these peculiar ellipses in thought and speech. The self-preoccupation of both mourner and melancholic frequently provides the main thrust of psychological movement—one can scarcely say "plot development" in this author's case—that can best be described as an endless spiraling around an *idée fixe* or obsession.

Frequently in Chekhov's major dramas the problem of unresolved grief within an individual is linked with a class-shared lament for the passing of an era or nostalgia for a lost life-style. In *The Cherry Orchard* there is a joint wish to save the orchard in order to preserve cultural traditions, but each character is prevented from cooperating with others because of his own preoccupation with a personal loss. Liuboff Andreievna, for instance, is held in a paralysis of inaction by the memory of her dead son, who drowned on the estate as a child, and by hallucinations of her dead mother's face appearing among the cherry blossoms. As Freud put it, the "shadows of these objects fall upon the ego," binding up any energy that could be exerted as will upon the external world.[30]

Almost the same could be said of Chekhov's other major plays: *Ivanov, Uncle Vanya, The Three Sisters,* and *The Seagull.* Many of them contain a mysterious and nearly supernatural sound that, like Yakob's fiddle, gives a transcendent voice to grief, uniting the uncompleted work of mourning of individual characters to that of all humanity or of an entire era: the watchman beating his board in *The Seagull*; the twang of the breaking string "sadly dying away" in *The Cherry Orchard*; the wind that howled in the chimney before the father's death in *The Three Sisters*; the humming samovar in *Uncle Vanya*; and the screeching of the owl in *Ivanov*, Chekhov's monumental case study of melancholia.

On the surface these eruptions in the cosmic order may seem to be similar, at least symbolically, to those personal disruptions suffered by Jimmy Porter, for in the work of both Chekhov and Osborne a theme of social significance seems to be instigated by characters unable to have an emotional catharsis. But in Chekhov every gesture arising from a character's genuine feeling generates its own social or cultural context, one that never has to be explained, whereas Osborne hastily "over-predicates" systems of politics, ethics, and sociology upon a character's misrepresentation of his true sensations. The crucial difference is that Chekhov makes this stasis of feeling, and the attempt to either exploit or overcome it—or the pathetic resignation to it—the focus of his drama and the chief means by which his characters achieve their identity, while Osborne defends against it and diverts our attention toward sociological irrelevancies. Chekhov, in short, is intuitively attuned to the inherent drama in such pre-Oedipal mechanisms of introjection and defense as are involved in mourning and melancholia.

9

Searches for Identity in a Prototypal Tale: The Decline of Patriarchy in Seven Versions of the Prodigal Son Parable

> The parable of the prodigal son as told by Christ is uncanny. The plot is familiar—it is, we sense, the story of our own growing up.
>
> David Wyatt, *Prodigal Sons: A Study of Authorship and Authority*

i

One of the most authoritative commentators on the New Testament, A. J. Grieve, says of the parable of the Prodigal Son that "no passage in the Gospels needs less comment than this matchless illustration of God's forgiving love towards the repentant sinner."[1] Yet the story seems to raise more psychological questions tnan the commentator's moral axioms will admit. For one thing, can we describe the younger son as truly repentant when his return was motivated purely by hunger and by envy of his father's servants for their comfort and plenitude? His rehearsed speech requesting his father to make him "as a hired servant" strikes me as having more the air of a confidence man than a remorseful sinner.

What I am suggesting by raising these questions is that if we are to consider the Prodigal Son parable more as a humanistic work of art than as a moral document, we must realize the truth of Aristotle's observation that "perception precedes predication." That is, we are first moved by a direct view of the movement of the psyche before we begin to conceptualize meanings—whether they be ethical, political, or psychological. Yet it is psychology that allows us to talk about those mental dynamics most directly before they are predicated upon a value system. Since the extraordinary feat of Chekhov was, as Francis Fergusson has observed, "to predicate nothing," that is, to show his action "in many diverse

148

reflectors and without propounding any thesis about it,"[2] it was possible to see psychological laws operating almost in a pure, unalloyed way. A tale like the Prodigal Son parable, on the other hand, suffers obfuscation of its psychological movement because of the genre to which it belongs and the didactic uses to which it has often been put.

Besides questioning the sincerity of the Prodigal's repentance I would like to consider another mental state presented in the tale, especially since it is made the core of a dramatic conflict. I refer to the anger of the older brother. Grieve tells us that the elder sibling is clearly wrong for condemning the father's loving forgiveness because the father's generosity does not injure him (the first-born whose inheritance has already been assured), but this moral logic does not account for the illogic of feeling. To be told that one should be content to have one's loyalty and goodness taken for granted because one's legacy is guaranteed hardly satisfies the basic narcissistic wish for adulation that the derelict brother is expropriating.

Since the Parable of the Prodigal Son is part of a group of New Testament parables whose theme is that of the joy of recovering what is lost,* we could argue that the chief point of view that we are asked to identify it is that of the father, who feels the satisfaction of reestablishing closure of the family circle. Yet a psycho-biographical consideration complicates even this simple possibility, for the situation from which the parable springs makes it clear that Jesus was defending his own apparent "prodigality" in dining with wastrels and "publicans," men who were outcasts but who were also repentant.

ii

That it is not merely fanciful to raise these issues of compliance versus rebellion, of anger versus forgiveness, of defensiveness versus assertiveness, of sincerity versus deception underlying this manifestly simple tale is shown by the persistence with which artists and writers throughout the ages have explored these very same permutations of its meaning and form.

In the Elizabethan period we find a whole generation of minor poets—like Greene, Gascoigne, and Lodge—becoming attracted

---

*The other two are the Parable of the Lost Sheep and that of the Lost Coin. See Luke 15:3-10.

to the story of the Prodigal Son and interpreting it in one of two diametrically opposite ways: either as a cautionary tale in which the erring son ends his life in utter despair after perhaps suffering imprisonment, or as a permissive, even revolutionary tale of dis-obedience in which the son is not so much *pardoned* as *rewarded* for his libertinism. Clearly the Elizabethans were not interested, as one literary historian put it, in the original biblical "vision of paternal forgiveness but rather in the paradigm of prodigal rebellion."[3]

But the Elizabethans handled this theme in a number of ways. When the Prodigal's extravagances became a metaphor for the poet's youthful productions of romantic or erotic verses, as it fre-quently did, the author could later seriously disavow his mis-spent youth. Or with tongue-in-cheek hypocrisy he could run with the hare and hunt with the hounds by pretending that his lurid accounts of the son "devouring his living among harlots" were merely being offered as the picture of a life-style to be eschewed.

More serious Elizabethan writers like Shakespeare also in a sense had it both ways. The Prince Hal of *Henry IV*, a prodigal son if there even was one, could enjoy the company of the disre-putable Falstaff in the Boar's Head Tavern, and later reject this way of life in becoming reconciled with his dying father, but finally lets the memory of his past profligacy prompt him to temper his judgment of human foibles. To put it in Northrop Frye's psychoanthropological terms, it is the permissible dis-sipations of carnival and Mardi Gras that make the renunciations and deprivations of Lent both possible and meaningful.[4] Whether the loosening effect of prodigality becomes a full-blown moral revolution or merely a minor social readjustment or realignment to allow for greater freedom is a question that modern art seems intent upon exploring. The frame of reference is usually that of social and familial patriarchy. Frequently this includes the issue of primogeniture with its built-in conflict of fraternal rivalry. Such a theme may of course be handled seriously or comically.

iii

The Edwardian playwright St. John Hankin chooses to handle the Prodigal Son theme in a comic—one could almost say Shavian—vein. In his *Return of the Prodigal* (1905), Hankin has Eustace, the ne'er-do-well younger brother, stage a melodramatic return from Australia in such a way as to first arouse his mother and sister's sympathy (he allows himself to be "discovered" passed out on the driveway in a rain storm), then to irk and embarrass his older brother and father into bribing him to leave. But Hankin is careful to prepare a moral backdrop of economic exploitation and social hypocrisy against which Eustace's machinations seem forthright, clever, and (to the young women) even charming. The father, a cloth manufacturer, installs electricity in his mill only to extend the working day of his employees, and sends donations to contending political groups in order to insure his election to Parliament. Henry, the elder son, seeks to legitimize his parvenu upper middle-class status by marrying the daughter of an aristocrat, and the aristocrat herself, Lady Faringford—a kind of Lady Bracknell—confesses that her social position bestows the privilege of doing nothing useful for a living. A parasitic clergyman and self-serving physician are added to complete the picture of a covert form of prodigality in contrast with which Eustace's rascality is refreshingly honest.

One way to see the psychocultural implications of the original Prodigal Son tale is in terms of the conservation and perpetuation of tribal integrity. The primogeniture aspect of the patriarchal system is designed to insure the unbroken transmittal of the patriarch's property, ideals, and identity. The wasteful activity of the younger son does not directly threaten this intent because (1) his chance of succeeding to the patriarch's property and power is remote, and (2) he is wasting only his allotted share of his father's goods. Yet his temporary disappearance causes consternation because it is a "loss"—both as an object that is in a sense "owned" by his tribe (compare the other parable in the group in which the housewife searches for her lost coin) and that threatens the tribe's values by an unexpected wayward form of behavior.

Thus a new perception of the story can be gained by seeing the father's delight as arising from his sense of conservation and pre- servation: (1) of his "property" (his son), (2) of his reputation (avoiding the black sheep's besmirchment of the family name), and (3) of the energy that would go into mourning a loss (in accordance with Freud's principle that pleasure arises out of the conservation of energy). Conversely, the elder son's anger can be explained as a contrary interpretation of the same events, for to him the father's welcoming of the prodigal is a further loss: a loss of property (the ring that the father bestows on his brother and the fatted calf he kills in his honor) and a dilution of the paternal affection that was directed solely toward him.

In Hankin's *Return of the Prodigal* the playwright comically reverses these perceptions by showing all the conservative forms of living (he even makes the industrialist as well as the clergyman and the aristocrat party *Conservatives*) to constitute a form of political opportunism that conceals various kinds of riotous waste (campaigning with "bread and circuses"[5])—in short, another form of prodigality. Since Eustace is merely despoiling the spoilers, we rejoice to see his blackmail scheme against his brother and father succeed even though his subversions arise more from his character than from his principles.

iv

We do not similarly rejoice in the activities of the prodigal in Robert Louis Stevenson's *The Master of Ballantrae* (1889),[6] described by neo-Aristotelians as a "punitive tragedy." Here the mutations of the basic story occur within a social class structure and hierarchy that is as traditional and ossified as that from which the original parable springs. In this strange hybrid novel of romantic adventure and psychological realism set in mid-eighteenth century Scotland, the laws of patriarchal authority and primogeniture are inexorable. However in the "ancient and powerful" Durie family it is the elder brother James who is the prodigal: he is a spendthrift, popular with the ladies, and forever involved in brawls, but he always escapes undaunted while remaining his father's favorite.

When Prince Charles, son of James III and pretender to the British throne, lands in Scotland in order to depose George II, the Duries decide to protect their titles and domain by fighting on both sides. James and his more sensitive and responsible younger brother, Henry, toss a coin for the honor of fighting with the more popular prince. James wins and goes off to battle, leaving Henry behind as Master of Ballantrae.

Irony begins to complicate the story when, despite the further accumulation of evidence of James's increasing prodigality (including his indifference to his fiancée, Alison, his mistreatment of a girl by whom he fathers an illegitimate child, and his exposure as a spy for George II, as well as his nefarious adventures with pirates), James is idolized and even practically canonized by Alison, his father, and the peasants, while Henry is unjustly vilified as unpatriotic, miserly, and weak.

The core of the psychological mystery of *The Master of Ballantrae* is the question of why the callous ne'er-do-well James charms while the decent, dutiful Henry repels. A clue lies in the universal wish to entertain contradictory feelings of conformity and rebellion, of adherence to patriarchal authority and contempt for it. This has little to do with the parricidal impulses generated in the Oedipal triangle, for on the story's level of intimate action the maternal figure (Alison) is depicted as already "won" by James and in fact is regarded with indifference by him. Rather, the more basic psychodynamics are entrenched in an earlier developmental phase of James's life (clearly alluded to by Stevenson and paralleled by the somewhat primitive era of Scottish history represented in the novel)—that of early individuation from the symbiotic phase.

The situation is rich in psychological ambivalences. Henry, the second born, in being chosen by the fateful toss of a coin to stay at home in support of George II, seems to be more like the first-born in conforming to the expectations of primogeniture. Yet both the Duries and their Scottish compatriots regard George II to be a foreign intruder, and therefore Henry seems to be ignominiously preserving his own peace of mind by "identification with the aggressor."[7] James, on the other hand, seems, in a manner more typical of the second-born than the first-born,[8] to be identifying with the anti-patriarchal, youthful aggressor Prince Charles, yet in the minds of the Scots he is fulfilling the role of patriarchal rescuer and protector because Charles's Stuart ancestry makes him Scotland's rightful patriarch. However, the final revelation that James is a spy in the pay of England's George decisively shifts the balance of this sympathy to Henry, although tragically too late for Henry to benefit.

Another interesting dynamic underlying James's character and behavior explains the misdirected love and devotion showered upon him by his father, his fiancée, Alison, the Scottish populace, and ultimately by his Indian servant Secundra Dass, despite his prodigality. As a result of the pampering he receives first from his parents as potential heir and later from the people as potential rescuer, James develops a deeply narcissistic character at the expense of object-oriented development. While on the one hand the cornucopia of gifts bestowed upon him teaches him to denigrate their value and become a wastrel, on the other hand his awareness that he is also being asked to be a nurturer-rescuer-protector-patriarch (in short a parent to those who seem to be parenting him) encourages him to cleverly cultivate the persona of a charming, caring being. Like Shakespeare's Richard III, he is clever enough to enthrall women (Alison and others) and children

(Henry's daughter and son). At one point he even almost beguiles Henry's faithful retainer Mackellar by tending him in his seasickness.

Overindulgence, by giving a person a certain sense of worth, can carry him some distance into successful management of his life, but the concomitant lack of discipline, of weaning if you will, also fosters an illusory omnipotence that causes him to come to grief. James's feeling that he has "a king's nature and must rule" leads him into such extravagant gestures as attempting two shipboard mutinies and unsuccessfully engineering his own "resurrection" from a burial in a state of suspended animation. This last act seems a fitting symbolic gesture of illusory omnipotence, one suggestive of re-merging with the powerful mother of prenatal life and early symbiotic infancy and re-emerging with greater power and perhaps even Christ-like divinity.

Understanding the dynamics of James's prodigal nature allows us to see a harmony between what critics like Carlos Baker have called the two ill-matched parts of *The Master of Ballantrae*: its being a novel of romantic adventure, on the one hand, and a work of psychological realism, on the other. The reckless (and incidentally bizarre and colorful) adventures of James are extensions of the exhibitionistic personality that must win emotional allegiances at home and persecute the brother who becomes Master because of his, the exhibitionist's, own extravagances. Stevenson's inversion of the biblical parable in making the older brother the prodigal whose waywardness is overlooked by a doting senile father prepares us for a drama in which the return to order will not be the simple feat of profligate youth resubmitting to the moral control of patriarchal wisdom and authority.

v

Whereas Stevenson in *The Master of Ballantrae* inverts traditional elements in the Prodigal Son parable in order to dramatize the reality underlying appearances, André Gide in his five-part dialogue *The Return of the Prodigal Son* intends actually to subvert the values of the patriarchal system. In so doing, he evokes deeper questions about the evolution of identity based on a child's earlier identifications with parents and siblings.

The first part of the work merely embroiders upon the simple parable: the Prodigal's first joyful sight of the parental home with its garden and fountains and suspicious servants is given a richly pictorial and dramatic life. The first variation in the narrative is the father's visit to the Prodigal the next day and his lecture to him in a dual voice, expressing his own feeling of compassion and forgiveness but at the same time following a secret script of reprimands urged upon him by the elder brother. A face-to-face confrontation between the Prodigal and his elder brother than ensues in which the most disturbing words are not the brother's announcement that he still controls part of the Prodigal's inheritance but his prophecy that the Prodigal's lack of "discipline" in wasting his father's goods threatens the very fabric of his own being:

> You will learn, if you do not know it yet, out of what chaos man has emerged. Nor has he emerged completely; he falls back into it with all his uneducated weight as soon as the spirit no longer bears him up. Do not learn this at your own cost: the well-ordered elements that compose you are only waiting for some acquiescence, some relaxing hold on your part to fall back into anarchy.[9]

The father's walled garden and fountain become the dominant symbols for the nurturing boundaries within which the Prodigal is expected to further define and solidify the boundaries of his ego.

There follows a dialogue between the Prodigal and his mother—another addition to the biblical parable. Her function is not, as one critic avers,[10] to seductively reactivate the Oedipal tie in order to reentrap her son within the family circle. Rather, it is to obliterate those distinctions he sees between himself and his elder brother and to enlist his help in getting the youngest brother to cast himself into the same mold of submission.

The climax of Gide's version of the parable occurs when the Prodigal, now completely brainwashed, visits the youngest son to carry out his new mission of preaching complete conformity to patriarchal ideals, implying complete surrender of the individual ego to the tribal ego. To his surprise he finds that the boy has already internalized his, the Prodigal's, formers more daring self, and has been influenced as well by a nomadic swineherd who has brought him a wild pomegranate from a "little abandoned orchard" where "there's no longer any wall separating it from the desert."[11] An interesting contrast to the key metaphor (mentioned above) of the father's walled garden and fountain as the symbol of enforced paternal identification, this image suggests freedom to develop without the fear of ego-loss or diffusion prophesied by the

elder brother. When we recall that the Prodigal Son had himself
become a swineherd out of dire necessity and in near starvation
had had to feast upon acorn husks with his herd, we realize that
the swineherd who has become the youngest son's model is an
archetypal ego-ideal[12] already unconsciously striven for by the
earlier adventurous self of the Prodigal. The boy's determination
to leave home like his brother, but without money and provisions
because "as the youngest, I have no share in the estate," allows
him to become a separate individual without first having to
become a prodigal. Hence he will not have to risk guilt,
repentance, and resubmission to his father. For him it has become
a short step from prodigal to prodigy.

vi

Thus far the different Prodigal Son stories we have been considering have revealed unexpected and nontraditional variations in
sibling interaction and in deeper underlying problems of self-image
and identity. In spite of the subversive nature of some of these
prodigals, the patriarchal system in which they enact their dramas
has remained in the end virtually intact, the prodigal either submitting to the order (the biblical prototype; Shakespeare's Prince
Hal), being ostracized from it (Stevenson's James Durie), or
leaving it voluntarily, if not in actuality, at least in imagination
(Hankin's Eustace; Gide's hero).

The possibility of the patriarchal system itself collapsing or
being radically revised is comically explored by George Bernard
Shaw in *Major Barbara* in terms of a prodigal's return. But here
the prodigal seems to be the father—the estranged munitions
manufacturer Sir Andrew Undershaft, who has for many years
shown no interest in his family. Not only does he hymn the glory
of gunpowder and sing the praises of alcohol, but he also manages
to strike even a rakish note when he seems to forget how many
children he's sired. According to his wife he has done "every
perverse and wicked thing," albeit "on principle."[13]

In the play's opening scene, in which Sir Andrew returns home
after a great number of years, Shaw both parodies the standard
recognition scene of Greek classical and Shakespearean drama
(Undershaft fails to recognize *any* of his children) and plays with
the notion of a *father's* unexpected prodigality (Undershaft's
breezy manner of defying "every social and moral obligation" is
in marked contrast to his son's prudish avowal that he "knows the

difference between right and wrong''[14]). Of course, as is usual in Shaw, appearances mask an opposite paradoxical truth. Undershaft's apparently immoral manipulation of the great powers by means of his munitions contracts makes possible an ideal socialist factory community, whereas his son Stephen's shallow politics and priggish morality thinly veil a prodigality of chronic malingering with regard to preparing for any real profession. Shaw's *coup de grâce* against the remnants of socially sanctioned patriarchy and primogeniture is to have the law of succession for Undershaft property based on the rule that only an adopted foundling can be designated as heir.

vii

The comic presentation of the *seemingly* prodigal father in *Major Barbara* prepares the way for Harold Pinter's rather sinister exploration of an emotionally regressed version of him in *The Homecoming*. Teddy, the eldest son, returns home to introduce his wife, Ruth, to his father, brothers, and uncle in order to reaffirm his identity as a member of the clan and to measure his own patriarchal independence (he too has by now fathered children) against his father's vestigial authority. The latter, being a widower, now performs for the family all the standard homemaking tasks associated with a housewife.

But as the play progresses, the father's "control" turns out to consist of giving permission to the other two sons, as well as to himself, to act out their sexual fantasies with Teddy's wife. With regard to stages of development, usually these tendencies have a pre-genital cast, ranging from the father's verbal denigrations of Ruth to Lenny's desire to be cuddled like a babe in arms.

Soon Ruth becomes the nucleus for her new "family," deriving her great power from her role as fantasy projection for all the men, imaginatively taking the place of the dead mother Jessie.*[15] While her husband, Teddy—the logical heir to the mantle of patriarchal

---

*Actually Ruth in this way belatedly supplies to her "children" what Jessie had given in a defective or incomplete way—what writers on object relations in early childhood refer to as "mirroring," an essential part of healthy emotional development and ultimate individuation. This consists of the mother selectively reflecting back to the child certain "cues" presented to her. Thus by rejecting some communications and confirming and objectifying others, she helps mold the core of the child's "self." Thus the "absurdist" tone of this play, insofar as it relates to the unorthodox behavior of Ruth and the sons, becomes rational when we see it as standing for part of the process of psychological maturation.

authority—dwindles into a confused bundle of academic and bourgeois clichés about the pleasant life. Ultimately it is he who must be excluded as the misfit.

In the various mutations of the Prodigal Son myth that we have been tracing, this is the first instance of the female-wife-mother figure's becoming dominant—in essence converting apparent patriarchy into matriarchy. In Gide the influence of the mother was to bind the son more strongly to the patriarch's desire for conformity to his ideals; in Pinter she, or her surrogate, exists to release the deepest "polymorphous perverse" fantasies that always threaten to make anarchy of patriarchy.

In the work of some of our contemporary play-wrights—particularly some of the American ones like Albee and Kopit—the power of the female is not simply that of allowing herself to become everyone's fulfilling fantasy. Rather, she often becomes the embodiment of the infant's deepest dread-carried-into-adulthood, that of the devouring "giantess of the nursery," discussed in chapter 7 as the unconscious *bête noire* of Osborne's Jimmy Porter. With these kinds of dramas in which a young man/son fears the voraciousness of a woman/wife/mother, we are a long way from social patriarchy, but rather in a realm of primordial matriarchy that both ontogenetically and phylo-genetically predates it.

viii

Ed Bullins's *A Son, Come Home* is one of the author's series of plays "about black people who have been crushed by the system...because they were denied knowledge of themselves and a place to grow."[16] The mother that greets the son upon his return after nine years is not the overly intrusive woman of Albee and Kopit's "mother-kill" plays. Nor is she, like Ruth in *The Home-coming*, one to offer herself as a projection screen or malleable object for her child's fantasies of sexual possession. Rather she is simply indifferent and emotionally unavailable, concerned with securing her own "home" in the religious sisterhood she has joined and with pleasing the mother superior she has come to idealize.

Thus the prodigal son Michael in returning home finds that he has no home—a place to which he can have a sense of connected-ness—and in fact discovers that he has never really had a home. This is revealed to him not only by his present awareness that his mother has fashioned a life for herself in which he can have no part but also by a series of dramatic reenactments of past events. These latter are expressionistically presented by two characters, a boy and a girl, alternately depicting the interior world of both mother and son as well as significant characters from their past. A flashback triggered by the mother's inquiry into the son's relationship with her sister in Los Angeles allows us to witness his unsuccessful attempt to make a surrogate mother of the aunt when he tries to get her to sign a bail bond. The pleading telephone voice of the son and the denying one of the aunt are played by the ubiquitous boy and girl.

In Bullins's play emotional impoverishment seems to be the general ambience that has been internalized, so that no sense of having a "home" is ever possible. As the son's encounter with the mother proceeds, we realize that she can not offer a home because she too has probably never had one: the father of her child would not live with her; a later paramour would not marry her; and her son was always away. In accepting the surrender of self-determination demanded by her religious order, she becomes more like a hopeful inmate of an orphanage than a house dweller or homemaker.

The Prodigal Son theme is given another interesting dimension in this play by the role of fathers. The boy, unlike the son in the biblical tale, is not looking for the *restoration* of security, cohesion of family, and sense of identity that were temporarily lost, but for the *first experience* of these things. This is shown by his "defamiliarized" perception of the city:

> This town seems so strange....
> Yes, home...an anachronism.[17]

But the son, even though he has been in trouble with the law, has not been the real prodigal; the *father* has, and in the most conventional terms: alcoholic, philandering, impecunious, noncommittal, ultimately indifferent. And the surrogate father, the lover with whom the mother lived, could not serve as a good masculine role-model for the boy because of the mother's open denigration of him:

> He wasn't much...when I thought I had a sense of humor I us'ta call him just plain Will.[18]

So when the mother accuses the returning son (although in a veiled way) of being prodigal, it is really the "fathers" she is thinking of. Here we are made to feel that a strong patriarchal stance might have served to solidify the son's identity rather than to quash its uniqueness. As a socially aware black writer Bullins suggests further that black men are even more likely to be failed fathers because society has not provided a dignified way for them to test and define their manhood.

The experimental form of Bullins's play hints at one of its undeclared themes—the identity diffusion of its characters. The ways in which the boy and girl slide in and out of different personas feel like more than dramatic devices. Rather, they suggest the unstable ego-boundaries that result from the failure to have internalized well-defined imagos of "good enough" nurturing parents. It is possible that such splitting of characters into components of private self and public self, of self present and self past, of the child at various developmental stages within the adult—a device found in experimental plays dating from O'Neill's *Strange Interlude* to the present—may be needed by the modern theater to give dramatic voice to poorly integrated introjects in characters facing serious problems of identity. Hence a dramatic technique may have unconsciously evolved to mirror deeper psychological dilemmas now being unveiled more and more frequently in our psychoanalytic consulting rooms.

ix

With Rilke's retelling of the Prodigal Son tale[19] we are once again back to the home as the ultimate assault upon personal identity. Here the son leaves home not so much to lose himself in pleasure as to get relief from the pain of an oppressive, all-intrusive love. And after his departure, his squandering of money is not, as may be the case of the Bullins character, to acquire objects and sensations to make up for a lack of attention in childhood. On the contrary, he lavishes gifts upon others in order to create obstacles to their expression of love toward him, managing to "hurt them with his gross paying."[20] In this respect he identifies with "the troubadours who feared nothing more than being answered" in their offerings of love sonnets to the lady of the manor.[21] This reversal of our more usual expectation, that the spendthrift may seek to ward off intimacy with his money and gifts rather than purchase it with them, marks the Rilke version of the Prodigal Son story as another unusual variation.

At the very beginning of the Prodigal Son vignette, which concludes *The Notebooks of Malte Laurids Brigge,* Rilke immediately characterizes the Prodigal's dilemma as that of a man "who did not want to be loved." We soon learn that his aversion is based upon his family's unvoiced "expectancy" that he assume a persona they wished to project upon him. As a child he felt that even his pet dogs by their fawning affection "drove one together into the person they believed one to be:"[22]

> And the house did the rest [he goes on to say]. Once one entered into the full smell of it, most things were already decided.[23]

As ego-psychologists have recently discovered, houses in dreams frequently stand for the ego itself, and the soundness of their structure can be taken as a touchstone of the soundness of the personality, the degree of its self-cohesion, and its ability to function in reality. (This is borne out empirically in the house-tree-person projective tests frequently administered together with the Rorschach test to patients in psychotherapy.)

Whereas architectural soundness in the house with which one identifies would seem to be the most favorable sign of mental health, the Prodigal's childhood memory of the solid gable "that always did loom up at last" as he reluctantly returned from playing in the fields was anathema because it signaled a bombardment of intrusions ("the first window up there kept its eye on one"[24]). And as he was dragged into the lamplight by family members who remained amorphous and depersonalized in the shadows of the room, he was revealed, in "all the shame of having a face,"[25] guilty of attempting to have a unique identity of his own.

Therefore it is not surprising that his refuge lay in incorporating images of architectural fragmentation and de-structuring. Earlier in the novel Malte (of whom the Prodigal Son is of course an alterego) acknowledges that his most creative and poetic self stems from his recollection of discrete and fragmented images of his grandfather's house:

> As I recover it in recalling my child-wrought memories, it is no complete building; *it is all broken up inside me* [italics mine]; here a room, there a room, and here a piece of hallway that does not connect these two rooms but is preserved, as a fragment, by itself.... It is though the picture of this house had fallen into me from an infinite height, and had shattered against my very ground.[26]

We soon discover that this atomization of the house is a necessary defense against a much more threatening wholeness:

> There remains whole in my heart, so it seems to me, only that large hall in which we used to gather for dinner every evening at seven o'clock....This lofty and, as I suspect, vaulted chamber was stronger than everything else. With its darkening height, with its never quite clarified corners, it sucked all images out of one without giving one any definite substitute for them. One sat there as if dissolved; entirely without will, without consciousness, without desire, without defence. One was like a vacant spot. I remember that at first this annihilating state almost caused me nausea.[27]

One could hardly find more powerful images of the fear of the loss of ego boundaries and of merging with another entity.

Clearly the strangely unsettling, though certainly hauntingly beautiful, images of parts and fragments of things and experiences that one finds everywhere in Rilke are more than a conscious poetic device. They come across as a desperate attempt to achieve some sort of catharsis: either to dispel demons of despair or more likely to ward off fears of disintegration. In the Prodigal Son episode of *The Notebooks* the full mechanism of this psychological maneuver becomes operative. As part of his childhood play out in the fields away from his father's oppressive house, the son willfully conjures up discontinuous and fragmentary experiences, in his running games trying to "master several directions at once,"[28] and he imagines himself to "be nothing but a bird, *uncertain what kind*." (Italics mine.)[29] He toys with the "dedifferentiation" and loss of identity that he most fears, for by bringing them under his conscious will and control (as a child) and by placing them into the logical structure of language (as an adult) he gains a semblance of mastery over them. This is a very primitive—one could even say psychotic*—attempt to avoid

---

*These plunges into an undifferentiated fragmented self occur several times elsewhere in *The Notebooks of Malte Laurids Brigge* (New York: Norton, 1949), as well as in some of Rilke's best poetry. The character Brigge, who seems to be Rilke's alter ego (note the alternate title of the book: *The Other Self*) almost courts a schizoid state of alienation in order to gain a fresh poetic perspective on conventional reality. It is not always easy to tell whether this distancing of the self, sometimes bordering on depersonalization (as when he almost loses his identity in the mirror or in the clown's costume) is uncontrolled pathology or a matter of artistic discipline, the latter being an intentional "defamiliarization" of the commonplace to endow it with the freshness of a new perception. In his observation that a nearby object sometimes has

uncontrolled merging with, or perhaps even destructive rage toward, the all-intrusive family in the overpowering house.

Closely allied with the Prodigal's fear of being transfixed and stereotyped into a false identity by love is his dread of being "penetrated" by it in a vampiric gesture of total possession and consumption. Patiently he learns instead (and one would again assume as a defense) "to penetrate the beloved object with rays of feeling, instead of consuming it in them,"[30] clearly a projection of how he himself wishes to be treated:

> How he could weep for nights then with yearning to be himself penetrated by such rays. But a woman loved, who yields, is still far from being a woman who loves.[31]

Traditional Freudians might see these wishes as essentially genital, powered by the Oedipus complex with its built-in inhibition against (incestuous) consummation. However, here the speaker's concerns are really more primordial—based on early introjections and identifications. His preferences for the love that "penetrates with feeling without consuming" is an effective voicing of every infant's need for an empathetic parental introject that can be non-threateningly integrated into the self as a model for identification leading to a firm and secure identity.

That the Prodigal's experience has been the contrary—that of an overwhelmingly bad introject is shown not only by his conscious concern to acquire its opposite, but also by his ultimate failure to see any contact as nurturing ("his greatest terror was that anyone should respond to him, [the fear of] embraces in which everything lost itself"[32]). This results in two kinds of distancing from the intimacy of a threatening "other": a poetic idealization of spontaneously experienced fragments of the self and of self-objects (mental representations of a self indistinguishable from an "other" with which it is merged), and a stoical loneliness in which god is seen as "remote" but potentially capable of revealing an undemanding love.

---

tones of distance, has been taken away and is only shown, not proffered; and everything related to expanse—the river, the bridges, the long streets, and the squares that squander themselves—has taken that expanse in behind itself, is painted on it as on silk, (p. 25)

there is the uneasy feeling that what we regard to be the solid boundaries of things are for Rilke/Brigge always in flux, subject at any moment to evaporation or atomization.

This seems to be about as close as a semi-autobiographical character can come to having a psychotic episode without over-taxing the similarly disposed author[33] who is attempting to embody him in an orderly tale. But for Rilke the continuously observing ego that he gives to the Prodigal (even when it is his own near-disintegration that he observes) is an emotional salvation of sorts, and the narrator is able to speculate accordingly that the Prodigal will now, upon his return, be able to remain in his father's house secure in the knowledge that the family's love for him "had nothing to do with him,"[34] and that he might now be able to better authenticate his own identity by more conscientiously reexperiencing those former childhood flashes of sensuousness, those which had formerly "simply been waited through."[35]

All of which seems to be an admirable attempt on the part of the Prodigal to restore and renew the injured self, described by Malte earlier, but one that is likely foredoomed in its grandiosity, as Rilke himself later admitted of his parallel intent in writing the book.[36] Without the empathic mirroring of a maternal figure or the guiding idealization of an accepting (and accepted) father figure, the Prodigal's efforts will probably come to naught. The cold remoteness of God can hardly make up for the loss of these intimate guiding contacts.

Rilke's Prodigal Son vignette is more of a poetic-philosophical discourse than it is a "story." The aesthetic appeal of its poetic aspect often lies in patterns of imagery that concretely reveal a dynamic psychological state, like the harsh lamplight that etches out the feelings registered on the face that he wants to conceal or the malignant and gentle rays of love that both emanate from him and consume him like fire.

But there is a hidden drama in the rhythms of his movement both away from and back to his father's house—one that finds a unity and meaning in Margaret Mahler's phases of separation and individuation in childhood development. In the first of these stages of normal development—known as the autistic phase—the infant feels undifferentiated from his surroundings and other beings. Through anxieties and delayed gratifications of needs, he slowly becomes aware of the existence of a nurturing being—usually the mother—and of a separate self. However, because of the necessity for dependency in need fulfillment, the child fantasizes that though he and the mother are entities, they share a common ego-boundary, and he revels in the harmony of inter-action that this implies. This is termed the "symbiotic phase."

To pursue Mahler's schema for normal development a bit

further, if the mother has allowed a good (that is, relatively anxiety-free) symbiosis to develop, the child is now ready to begin the four sub-phases of mature separation-individuation that lead to the establishment of a firm, unique identity. In the first of these, known as "differentiation," the child sorts out aspects of himself, including feelings and body parts, as being separate from those he formerly conceived of as a fusion of self and other. With the development of the ability to crawl and walk as well as of the extension of visual perception, he can then enter the "practicing" sub-phase, in which he can explore and test the reality of persons and things in his environment. In this still rudimentary state of ego-development the child remains unsure of his soundings and therefore requires the next sub-phase for his progress along the road to mature identity: that of the "rapprochement," returning to the "safe anchorage" of intimacy with the mother for refueling. In this stage (which of course like the others is subject to repetitions in the normal circularity of development) the child is especially vulnerable. Maternal indifference or rebuff can cause depression, or, contrarily, overwhelming response can regress him to engulfment fears of earlier symbiosis, in other words foster a "borderline" organization of personality. Once negotiated safely, however, this stage leads to the final separation-individuation sub-phase of fixed identity. Throughout the entire process the mother's key role has been that of an empathetic mirror, but a selective one that picks up and enhances certain cues of feeling and conduct from the infant and is neutral to others, thus shaping him to some extent in her own image, in other respects allowing him to develop a configuration of personality in accordance with his innate endowment.[37]

Rilke's Prodigal Son character reflects the successive unfolding of these phases and sub-phases of separation-individuation, negotiated in varying degrees of success and failure. The first two stages, autism and symbiosis, are condensed in a sparse number of lines at the beginning:

When he was a child, everybody in the house loved him. He grew up knowing nothing else and came to feel at home in their softness of heart.[38]

The rest of the piece dramatically extends the remaining stages of differentiation, practicing, and rapprochement—and of course their vicissitudes. The son's forays into fields and woods with the exhilaration of "profound indifference" to the "observation and sympathy, expectancy and solicitude" of those at home allow him to practice individuation. Fueled by fantasies of himself in omnipotent roles of adventure, he is nevertheless able to use his play to explore the reality of his environment while at the same time testing the limits of his physical stamina. The close of day, ostensibly necessitating the return home, in essence ushers in the rapprochement that unfortunately culminates in a trauma: his being violently laid hold of and thrust into a harsh light in order to have the mold of a preconceived personality imposed upon him. That is, he is forced into

> imitating with a lie the vague life they ascribe to him, and grow[ing] to resemble them all in his every feature.[39]

It is this distorted phase of rapprochement—where none of his own cues for emotional development are responded to—that first causes the child prodigal's play fantasies to take on the dire depersonalization aspects already described, then the adult prodigal's flight from home (i.e., from the engulfing part of the reactivated symbiosis) in which the fears of having the boundaries of the self penetrated by rays of "love" had become the chief affect.

The final return of the Prodigal to his home is a last (and again a failed) attempt at rapprochement with nurturing objects, the stakes again being nothing less than self-integration and identity. His way of stating his need almost sounds like a textbook on self-psychology:

> He thought above all of his childhood, and, the more calmly he reflected, the more unachieved did it seem to him; all its memories had about them the vagueness of premonitions, and their counting as past made them almost future. To take all this once more, and this time really, upon himself—this was the reason he, the estranged, turned home.[40]

His ultimate fear of the return to dedifferentiation is, however, reactivated by the family's oppressive love, and his defense can only be the near-psychotic one, the grandiose association with a not-yet-manifested god, whose love will somehow promise a non-destructive binding.[41]

It is possible to see many tales of physical departure and return as myths reenacting the vicissitudes in Mahler's paradigm of separation-individuation, with the rapprochement sub-phase (a

return "home") constituting one of the chief climaxes. This might
include stories as varied as Homer's *Odyssey* and Jack Kerouac's
On the Road.* It certainly would seem to be most fundamental in
the Prodigal Son story, which is perhaps another reason (in
addition to those cultural and familial ones I have already
mentioned) accounting for its persistence vertically through all the
arts and horizontally through time.

X

In turning to our final Prodigal Son story, we come full circle
back to its archetypal beginnings and yet paradoxically reach an
apogee of psychocultural change. Franco Zeffirelli's film *Brother
Sun, Sister Moon* (1973), in chronicling the Christ-like life of St.
Francis of Assisi, returns us to the biblical spirit of the original tale
but at the same time attempts to see it through the eyes of the
flower children of the 1960s. Instead of leaving his father's house
to become a wastrel, then returning to it to seek forgiveness (as in
the biblical version), Francis departs in order to fulfill a
patriarchal and patriotic responsibility—to fight in a war—only to
begin his "prodigal" life upon his return. This he does by first
throwing his father's goods into the streets and then renouncing
his paternity by publicly stripping himself naked and returning his
clothes to him.

Thus Francis essentially reverses the traditional chain of events
of the tale that led from renunciation through prodigality to
paternal forgiveness. However, his break with family ties—"There
are no sons or fathers," he declares, "only brothers and
sisters"—and with convention is, in imitation of Christ, now in
the service of another father: God. Francis's second departure
from Assisi, this time in the company of a contingent of ragged
"brethren," is to seek still another father—the Holy Father in
Rome—to secure confirmation and approval of his thwarted
attempts to restore a ruined church, feed lepers, and in general live

---

*In the *Odyssey* the separation-individuation patterns are most *directly* visible in the
actions of Telemachus (in his separation from his nurse, rapprochement with his mother,
etc.) and more *symbolically* enacted by Odysseus, whose adult-hero status somewhat masks
them. I intend to deal with the nuances of Odysseus's symbolic delineation of Mahler's
phases and sub-phases in a later work.

Kerouac's *On the Road* strikes me as a thoroughly modern work in that a classic sense of
emotional closure is never achieved. I see this imcompleteness to consist of Dean Moriarty's
inability to achieve a meaningful rapprochement, resulting in the pseudo-separation
activity of compulsively dashing back and forth, from coast to coast.

as humbly as Christ. This reconciliation with Mother Church and Holy Father is replete with a number of psychological ambiguities that are transmitted to the audience by way of nuances of acting in conjunction with the moving and framing techniques of the camera. Thus in order to completely understand the full impact of this version of the Prodigal Son tale, it is necessary to discuss the psychological rendering of characters and events in terms of their embodiment in Zeffirelli's cinematic form.

The film's early images are preoccupied with conveying Francis's return from the war and his ensuing illness. The close-up shot of the pain-ridden hand that clutches at the masonry of the city gates initiates a whole train of hand images[42] and gestures that synecdochically convey psychic shifts in Francis. During his fever and delirium, close-ups capture the caring hands of his mother administering to his fevered face (all shown through gauze-like curtains that ostensibly ward off insects but aesthetically help to suggest the removed-from-reality state of his mind).

Francis's recovery is signaled in part by the sight of his hands (again shown in close-up) pursuing a coy bird hopping on the tiled roof outside his window. When the camera backs off to reveal to us and to the horrified gaze of his parents that he is perched precariously at a dizzying height above the paved streets below, we question his sanity. Yet as he stands there in his white nightgown flapping his arms, presumably to maintain his balance, Zeffirelli adds an ingredient to suggest a larger harmony subsuming this seemingly disruptive note. He pulls the camera back and releases a flock of white birds above and behind Francis to pictorially suggest that Francis is really learning to "fly"—that is, to leave home and join another "flock" or family.

This scene provides a photographically beautiful ambiguity that is carried forth throughout the film as the focus oscillates constantly between the possibility of Francis's having become brain-damaged and the likelihood of his having achieved transcendent wisdom about Christianity and insight into nature. (It is also an acceptable modern rendition of his legendary ability to speak to, and be understood by, birds.) Such images take on the force of speech when Francis in his newly found spiritual ecstasy and harmony with nature sees that he rarely needs to verbalize, as for example when, instead of telling his mother that his greatest ambition is to rebuild the ruined church in the valley, he merely takes her hands, which he has been caressing, and arranges them in the form of a steeple. Hands are almost as kinesic in this film as they are in *David and Lisa* and *The Happiness of Us Alone*.

Graham Faulkner in *Brother Sun, Sister Moon*, 1972, directed by Franco Zeffirelli, also starring Alec Guinness and Judi Bowker. Produced by Luciano Perugia, original story and screenplay by Suso Cecchi D'Amico, Kenneth Ross, Lina Wertmuller, and Franco Zeffirelli. (*Courtesy of Euro International SPA and Paramount Pictures*)

The psychodynamic movement in *Brother Sun, Sister Moon* can be seen as a quest to replace a series of failed fathers with a more empathetic and idealized one and to bind oneself to a group of adopted siblings as a way of emotional compensation. (This is by implication also Zeffirelli's characterization of the psychosocial status of the "flower children" of the sixties.) Francis's "prodigality" consists in denigrating the accumulated goods (including the principles and philosophies) attached to such debased father-images.

The mother who is at the center of Francis's life is the antithesis of the emotionally nonpresent mother encountered by the Bullins character. She has continued the symbiotic tie to such an extent that the excluded father sees their communications as telepathic. The stage is being set for a narcissistic grandiosity in Francis with a concomitant problem in gender identity because of an unidealizable father. (The parallels to Christ in this respect are obvious and become even more manifest later.) To Francis his father not only seems contemptible for having profiteered from the war (cf. Christ and the money-changers in the temple) but is ultimately revealed to be repulsively satanic. Not only is this latter trait *realistically* shown by the brutal beating he gives to Francis for throwing his wares out of the window but it is *allegorically* suggested when Francis, in visiting his father's surreal, cavelike cloth mill, simulates a descent into Hell. It is interesting to note that the failed fathers of both Zeffirelli's film and St. John Hankin's play, discussed earlier, are owners of cloth mills who exploit their workers. The anti-patriarchal sentiments of both works therefore harbor rudimentary socialistic protests against inhumane capitalism.

The second failed father is the archbishop of Assisi—himself a legitimatized "prodigal," self-indulgent as he is in rich foods and in all the luxuries of the Church—to whom Francis's own father appeals for help in disciplining him. We are given a behind-the-scenes view of this patriarch as petulant, vain, greedy, and vicious—in sum, as almost totally infantile. His politically motivated action against Francis and Francis's band of friars leads eventually to the tragedy of the burning of their church and the murder of one of the group. This is what precipitates Francis's journey to Rome to seek affirmation of his way of life from his third and final sire: the "Holy Father of Rome."

For the Church prelates gathered around the Pope, receiving Francis and his ragged band in public audience at the Vatican is mostly a political event, and the crucial question is whether Francis and his increasingly influential group can be profitably absorbed into the fold or should be declared heretics. Thus the appearance of the humble friars amidst the baroque splendor of the Papal court is like the conclusion of the traditional Prodigal Son tale, except that it is a *group* Prodigal seeking rapprochement with a *group* father.

After Francis's innate candor causes him to abandon the prepared Latin text of contrition urged on him by his Vatican-connected friend and to reveal the true Christian humility of his heart, the physically as well as spiritually aloof Pontiff slowly descends the long flight of steps from his throne (the camera highlighting his elegant slippers) and kneels to kiss Francis's feet. A short while later, Francis and his band return to the fields to do their work, accompanied on the soundtrack by the popular balladeer Donovan's singing the title song "Brother Son, Sister Moon."

From the bald account I have given of these concluding moments of the film, one would think that Francis had achieved an auspicious reconciliation with a good "father." However, Zeffirelli had added certain dramatic flourishes and cinematic touches that cast considerable doubt on such an upbeat ending and has hinted at a more cynical conclusion that is more in keeping with the mistrust of authority shown by the youthful dropouts of the sixties, whose attitudes the film self-consciously reflects. As will be seen, my interpretation of the ending is also more consonant with the existential feeling of skepticism and isolation seen in the Prodigal's return by Hankin, Bullins, Gide, and Rilke—whose treatments of the tale, diverse as they are, nevertheless reveal an underlying pessimism.

After kissing Francis's feet, the Pope makes a significant gesture that triggers in himself a train of reminiscences. The hand he places on Francis's rough sheepskin jerkin—emphasized by the camera shooting in close-up—puts him in mind of his long-forgotten youth, in which he felt connected to the humble and faithful, a type of experience that the hypertrophic growth of Church administration has contravened. But a parenthetical shot inserted into these scenes spoils our joy in witnessing this revitalized bond between "father" and "son": one of the prelates whispers to another that this condescension from the Pope is for the purpose of recapturing the allegiance of the masses. And a moment later we realize that the Pope's reminiscences of a more convivial youth, instead of propelling him forward into further contacts with his most wretched and humble "children," merely regress him into an encapsulated reliving of his distant past. As Francis tries to reach out to him under the illusion that at last he has found his "father," the pontiff's face clouds over into the blank gaze of senility, his attendants quickly surround him, and the camera hastily retreats from the scene and (in reverse angle) from Francis's face and extended hand to emphasize the still impossible distance between "father" and "son." Despite the promising signs of a rapprochement, the Pope is ultimately revealed to be another failed father.

The film closes with shots of Francis and his homeless band again wandering over beautiful and harsh landscapes. As the camera captures dolefully distant shots of fields and sky, interspersed with close-ups of bare feet digging into the soil and clambering over rough rocks, the sound-track resonates with the voice of Donovan wistfully singing of having a "brother son" and a "sister moon" as one's sole companions. The tone is not unlike that struck by Oedipus as he concocts a final desperate "family romance" (Fortune is his mother, the years his siblings) to restore his self-esteem upon discovering himself to be a foundling.[43] Like Oedipus, Francis and his group of "prodigals" find their orphaned state temporarily assuaged by adopting the most majestic forces of nature as their siblings.* It is a gesture that is at one and the same time both grandiosely narcissistic and pathetically defensive.

xi

Because of both its universal appeal and its persistence in literature and art throughout the centuries, the Prodigal Son tale has proved to be an excellent lens through which to observe the demands made upon psychology to interpret art that reflects ever-changing society and culture. One of the key alterations in modern life has been an attack upon and an ultimate decline of patriarchy, often with an added complication of increased sibling rivalry brought on by the slackening of paternal control or interest and an erosion of identity with tribe, clan, or family.

The youthful rebellion of the sixties was therefore not simply "oedipal" in its hostility to paternalistic authority. Rather it was

---

*We can see how such a wistful "solution" would have a special appeal for Zeffirelli when we reflect that, as an illegitimate child himself, he acquired the fabricated name Zeffirelli, meaning "little gentle breezes."

more probably a pre-Oedipal, narcissistic disturbance bordering on identity diffusion and psychopathy and caused in part by a lack of truly empathic paternal guidance.[44] Throughout the ages, whenever patriarchal authority becomes eroded, so does the structure of the nuclear and extended family (as well as of larger tribal coherence*), and the nature and tone of *prodigality* take on a different form and meaning. The sensitive artist reflects these changes, as I have tried to show in this chapter.

It might also have served my purpose to trace the theme and variations of father-son relations in a number of traditional fairy tales, such as the father-and-his-three-sons motif found in the Grimms' tale dealt with earlier in this book, where sons were falsely accused prodigals. However, modern versions of the parable have the added advantage of bringing into play problems of identity diffusion and loss as patriarchal authority not only is resisted in the Oedipal fashion—so characteristic of fairy tales—but also is found wanting as a basis for emulation, the crisis of our contemporary society, and a frequently undetected ingredient of the past. Our newer psychologies of object relations, of cognitive perception, and of the ego and self have evolved from the necessity of looking at personality formation and distortion when integration of the self is more at issue than regression and fixation. But it is generally true that psychoanalytic criticism—rooted as it is primarily in drive theory and defense and in the Oedipal triangle—has not kept pace. I hope that my attempt in this chapter to systematically modify the frame of reference by which these kinds of changes in "prodigal" behavior should be seen will go some distance in providing a model for the psychological critic to follow.

*It is interesting to note that the "flower children" who band together in *Hair*, the rock musical of the late sixties, are known as "the tribe."

Appendix A

Images of the Mind in Theater and Film: Tennessee Williams's *Kirche, Kutchen, und Kinder* and Kurosawa's *Throne of Blood*

i

Before it becomes an artifact, art exists as a state of mind in its creator. Between that state of mind and its expression lies the art medium itself, with its various aids as well as impediments to communication.

Both the lyric poet and the writer of fiction have found their chosen media to be the least resistant to embodying the images, dynamics, and tone of their own mental processes. Few conventions stand in the way of the lyric poet—especially since the iconoclasms of nineteenth-century Romanticism—in expressing the depths of his feeling and thought in verse. In fiction, both the first-person and the omniscient third-person narrative technique allow the reader direct access to the inner sanctum of the minds of characters, and, by inference, the minds of their creators.

Very early in his development the dramatist, by allying himself with the lyric poet,* gave himself a greater latitude for expressing inner turmoil or bliss. The Messenger whose chief task it was to report Oedipus's self-blinding in *Oedipus Tyrannus* could at the same time indulge in images and metaphors that revealed his own reactions. In choosing images like *hail, bedew*, and *fountain* for the bleeding eye-sockets, he not only mitigates the raw violence of the deed by elevating it to an elemental force in nature (*dew* and *hail*) but "manages" his initial helpless awe by seeing the outcome as a work of art (a *fountain*), and therefore orderly and comprehensible.

---

*It was in fact the lyrical dithyramb, used in the worship of Dionysus, that later developed into the choral ode of Greek tragedy.

174

Later, with the introduction of the soliloquy, the lyric poem had its most direct expression onstage and therefore was able to verbalize images of the mind with greater immediacy.

With the appearance of expressionism in the theater in the 1920s, metaphors for mental states were able to make their way directly into the *mise-en-scène* rather than appearing merely in the delivered lines of the play. Elmer Rice's *The Adding Machine*, an American classic in theatrical expressionism, allows the obsessional configuration of the accountant-protagonist's personality to be literally projected onto the walls of his bedroom in the form of the huge numbers on an adding machine.

In the cinema, expressionism as a way of conveying internal states gained a foothold that was more precarious and short-lived. It is generally agreed among film historians that the theater-influenced *Cabinet of Dr. Caligari*, with its obviously painted sets put crazily askew to reveal the title character's insanity, was an interesting experiment in expressionistic cinema, but one that led nowhere. Even when some of the more basic elements of the film medium, like the projection of light and shadow, were given greater self-consciousness by expressionism in the art world, this movement affected the byways rather than the mainstream of film art. The "symphony of shadows" that Murnau announced would permeate *Nosferatu* never really crystallized in that film, except in one or two places, the most memorable being the vampire's enlarged shadow falling upon the wall as he approaches Mina's bedroom. The legacy of such external projections of fear of and obsession with the darker side of life is to be found to some degree in the *film noir* of the forties and perhaps even to a greater extent in the gothic or horror genres.

Film seems to have been more comfortable with surrealism than with expressionism in trying to convey the most secret workings of the mind. From *The Secrets of a Soul* (1926), a film that was approved by Freud and supervised by his disciple Hanns Sachs and that tried to show, among other things, how dreams are formed, to Buñuel's pervasive dream-like states in *Belle de Jour* (1967), film has allowed for distortion of surfaces to reveal the depths of man's inner nature.

ii

The commitment of both theater and cinema to the realistic movement in art has unfortunately brought with it a host of problems for the psychologically inclined artist. How can a play or film that aims to be faithful to the surfaces of life present at the same time the innermost workings of the mind? Dialogue is only part of the means of expression in a performing art like theater and film, in which behavior and gesture, spectacle and setting are equally important to the medium.

For the modern theater of realism the solution has usually been to shift from the naturalistic mode to a frankly surrealistic one when reminiscence or powerful emotion requires expression. Arthur Miller's innovative "area beyond the kitchen" for Willie Loman's recollections of the past in *Death of a Salesman* (similar to flashbacks in film) and his later use of the entire stage as a replica of the mind in *After the Fall*, in which the protagonist-narrator's free associations are presumably addressed to an audience-as-psychiatrist, are particularly memorable. And in the Broadway production of *Da* by Hugh Leonard, a naturalistic kitchen becomes a mind people with the creatures of memory.

Before going on to demonstrate how film in imaging forth the mind faces problems that are uniquely different from those in drama, I would like to focus on a contemporary play that illustrates some of the possibilities that are open to the playwright—an artist who now seems more and more destined to jettison some of the conventions of realism. One of Tennessee Williams's little-known plays entitled *Kirche, Kutchen, und Kinder,** was an interesting experiment in the creation of metaphors and symbols of the mind for the stage.

"Go to church, tend the kitchen, and rear the children"—these three precepts for moral and social conduct that Freud's Vienna assumed to be axiomatic for a woman's well-being even before Hitler's Germany adopted them as national feminine ideals—have in modern times become symptoms of and metaphors for the socially and sexually unliberated woman. Theatergoers might therefore assume from the title of Williams's "play in progress" that they could look forward to an evening of pro-feminist iconoclasms done in the style of social realism. If so, they would be greatly mistaken.

The protagonist of Williams's "outrage for the stage" (the playwright's own subtitle for his play) is neither an entrapped

---

*As performed by the Jean Cocteau Repertory Company at the Bouwerie Lane Theatre in New York City from September 1979 through January 1980. The German word for *kitchen* is *Kueche*, but Williams probably chose *Kutchen* either to indicate German-American dialect or to more clearly distinguish the word in sound from *Kirche*.

Victorian ingenue, like Nora in Ibsen's *A Doll's House*, nor a more recent female disruptor of male complacency, like Ann Whitefield in Shaw's *Man and Superman*. Rather, the spotlight falls upon a "voluntarily" retired male hustler who ultimately feels himself hemmed in by those same above-mentioned female-associated constraints: a *kutchen* (dominated by a scullery-maid kind of wife wedded to her stove and preoccupied with making and eating crullers) and two *kinder* (in the shape of a giggling adolescent son and daughter, twins, still in kindergarten).

The *kirche* is where complex images for the mind enter the picture. Supposedly located in Manhattan's Soho, it is the play's principal *mise en scène*, a refuge for both body and soul. It is where the ex-hustler practices his new profession, minister of some private religion, and where he can feel himself to be enthroned like a "descendant of the old kings of Ireland." Oddly enough, he continues to wear the alluring tight-leather pants of the male prostitute, a sight that casts considerable doubt on his priestly vocation. We also wonder if we can really be looking at a church even though the stage area that is so labeled is dominated by a surrealistic-looking pipe organ. We soon discover the *kirche* to be a compartment of the psyche itself, a "chambered nautilus," a sanctuary for private thoughts and fantasies vaguely dedicated to the god Priapus, and a practical arena for interior monologues about the deleterious effects of time.

In *Kirche, Kutchen, und Kinder* the church as playing area of the mind has been equipped by the minister-hustler protagonist with three walls, each painted in a different primary color (blue, red, and yellow) and each matching one of his varying moods, as for example blue for sentiment and red for violence. Behind the third wall—the yellow one—the ex-hustler has contrived a mechanical device that causes a cheerful artificial giant daisy to open during the day a large night-blooming vine to wend its way in at night.

We soon discover that the church is a psyche that tries to remain dynamically balanced by setting up safeguards against intrusions from without as well as by producing internal fantasies of self-restoration. Externally, the private self is protected by a red light—a kind of anxiety signal—that flashes a warning when someone is about to enter. Internally, the "minister" defends himself further by shamming being a cripple and by taking to a wheelchair whenever the light flashes, in order to maintain his reclusive existence and avoid the burden of further sexual relations with his wife. (In this respect he is a descendant of such former

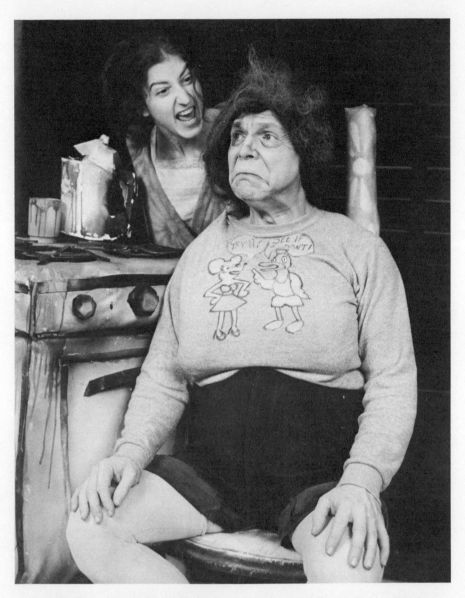

Phyllis Deitschel and Harris Berlinsky in Tennessee Williams's *Kirche, Kutchen,* *und Kinder* **in the Jean Cocteau Repertory 1979–1980 production.** (*Courtesy of* *Eve Adamson; photo by Gerry Goodstein*)

Williams heroes as Brick in *Cat on a Hot Tin Roof* and Kilroy in *Camino Real*.) Meanwhile he enjoys perfecting his physique through secret gymnastics and revels in the clandestine writing of his erotic memoirs.

The "fourth wall" of the *kirche*—that is, the traditional invisible fourth wall of any theatrical performance—is, the hustler tells us, "white, unbesmirched by the vulgarity of this performance." Yet it seems to have its counterpart on stage in the form of the white comic-striplike kitchen that is revealed to exist behind the blue wall of sentimentality. Presided over by an ax-bearing *hausfrau* dressed in white, who constantly cooks white crullers on a white stove, the *kutchen* of the play is the scene for several acts of violence, including its invasion by the wife's ill-tempered father, a Dickensian villain in black suit and top hat with pasty white face—a Lutheran minister from the "Island of Staten" who invades his son-in-law's Irish Catholic household and who is full of primitive rage and sadism. His only acts are to growl ferociously, beat his daughter over the head with his umbrella, snarl over the cooking crullers, and rape (on-stage) a grotesque ninety-nine-year-old woman whom he has already made pregnant. The kitchen is perhaps the walled-off aggressions in the priest-hustler's own psyche displaced into another realm.

But the dramatic climax results from the ex-hustler's ultimate inability to exclude the various threats to his peace of mind, that is, to the defended parts of his ego, represented by the *kirche*. Into this "chambered nautilus" of the mind the wife constantly intrudes, sometimes wielding an ax against him (at one time she is dressed in the yellow of his everyday mood; at another, she appears in the red of his violent mood). And finally into this retreat tumble willy-nilly the rambunctious twins, freshly expelled from their fifteen-year-stint in kindergarten. Their dilemma forces him to initiate an idiosyncratic brand of child-rearing that ushers in the play's dénouement.

The only aid the ex-hustler can give his children is that which is compatible with his past expertise. He orders both to strip and submit their salable wares to his inspection. He teaches the boy how to sell himself to the richest and most generous male clientele on Central Park South, and the girl how to solicit elderly gentlemen of means on a Fifth Avenue bus. But these hasty measures are doomed to failure, and the last remains of his retreat of mind crumble as the *kinder* come to report, amidst giggles and childish shenanigans, that they have given up their virginity for love instead of for money—for the sake of Venus and the celebrating angels instead of in the service of Priapus and Mammon.

The ex-hustler's only solution to this ultimate frustration is to return to his former life of male prostitution, which in a way he had never really given up (witness his seductive leather pants, his secret calisthenics to retain his figure, his offer to the audience at the beginning of the play to unzip his fly). In a perverse parody of Ibsen's Nora's decisively donning her street clothes to leave her "doll house" at the end of the play, the put-upon husband refastens the elegant jewel-studded belt of the high-class call-boy and makes a phone call to an old client at the Plaza.

Ever since Williams's admission of his homosexuality, as encouraged by our new era of sexual candor, critics have been re-examining his treatment of women in a long line of plays in which they have played a key part. The female personae have roughly fallen into one of two categories: tenuously stable and ultimately overpowering mother-types (e.g., Serafina in *The Rose Tattoo*; Amanda in *The Glass Menagerie*) and palpably fragile and ultimately intimidated daughter-types (e.g., Laura in *The Glass Menagerie*; Blanche Dubois in *A Streetcar Named Desire*). Although tending somewhat toward comic-strip burlesque, the women in *Kirche, Kutchen, und Kinder* are still recognizable as Williamsian: the put-upon ax-wielding *hausfrau* belongs to the first type, while the ninety-nine-year-old rape victim is obviously of the latter class.

But Williams sets against these two a strange anomaly: a Miss Rose who periodically appears in crinoline dignity in order to play the organ in the *kirche*. She is like a Blanche Dubois who has been cured of her neurosis and has not only accepted spinsterhood with resignation and equanimity, but has also achieved a sense of self-worth that is rooted in service. Unlike Blanche, her natural habitat is the protagonist's mind rather than a decaying Southern mansion. Early in the play the priest-hustler describes her as "always on cue, nimble and rising like a lark at daybreak," and at the end, as he is about to return to the world of male prostitution, he assures her:

Miss Rose, you have given me all the poetry that exists in my heart.

Those familiar with Williams's life will recall that Rose is the name of his emotionally disturbed sister, from whom the emotionally and physically wounded Laura of *The Glass Menagerie* is both derived and poetically transformed.

Clearly, the Miss Rose of this play is a restored self in both her philosophical and emotional outlook. Her reply to the hustler's despair at having failed to "wall time out of the *kirche*" is that she doesn't "mind eternity." In the light of Williams's direct assertion elsewhere that "it is the continual rush of time, so violent that it appears screaming, that deprives our lives of so much dignity and meaning," it becomes obvious that she is an idealization. Her presence in the play suggests Williams's wish to have not only a sufficiently present and reliably empathic mother-figure at the center of his emotional universe,[1] but to have her bequeath to him the timelessness of primary process thinking that comes with merging. That she makes her final entrance into the *kirche* uncharacteristically by means of a shortcut through the violent and chaotic *kutchen* of the more reality-oriented world betokens the unfulfillment of this wish and strikes the only tragic note (in a very subdued undertone to be sure) in this otherwise farcical play.

Like other plays in the tradition of The Theatre of the Absurd (or in that of its successor, The Theatre of the Ridiculous) *Kirche, Kutchen, und Kinder* does not really involve us on a deep emotional level, but rather appeals to our delight in the unexpected in plot and character and in the outrageous subversion of social and moral convention. In this last respect, it (like other plays in this genre) is more interested in demolition than in construction; or, to put it in terms of Christopher Lasch's recent study of contemporary American society,[2] it seeks to dramatize the discontinuous and shattered selves of our increasingly narcissistic culture. It is not surprising, therefore, that one of its central images for the protagonist's emotional life when the elaborate defenses constructed within the *kirche* break down is "fragments of glass in garbage heaps that catch wondrous glimpses." We may be reminded of Tom's concluding remarks in *The Glass Menagerie* that his memory of his fragile sister is evoked by sights of "colored glass in shop windows, like bits of shattered rainbow," a reminder of the animal figurines that comprised for Williams another image of the psyche.

iii

Given the nature of the film medium, representing the nuances of thought and feeling becomes a special challenge in realistic cinema, unless one settles for essentially uncinematic voice-over exposition or for theatrical dialogue, which for film quickly degenerates into what Alfred Hitchcock derisively called "talking heads." Committed as film is to conveying its effects through the photographing of concrete objects, it faces inherent obstacles in trying to show the internals of thought and feeling. I would now like to examine one of Akira Kurosawa's masterpieces—*Throne of Blood*, a samurai fable based on Shakespeare's *Macbeth*—in order to show how this director has not only been able to meet the challenge with consummate skill but has also provided us with a model for the art of "cinepsychology."

Shakespeare's *Macbeth* has itself had an interesting history in psychoanalytic criticism. Freud became fascinated by its two protagonists as further examples of what he called "characters ruined by success." Addressing himself particularly to the mystery of why the seemingly indomitable Lady Macbeth should suddenly suffer an emotional breakdown, he concluded, along with Ludwig Jekels, that the enigma would be partially solved if we considered Macbeth and Lady Macbeth to be complementary parts of a single prototype. One piece of evidence for this is that even though Macbeth claims that he "has murdered sleep," it is Lady Macbeth who is actually shown having a sleep disorder.[3] This concept of "mythic decomposition" of character in the play is relevant to Kurosawa's treatment of the two principals in this film, and I shall return to it shortly.

In a study of Kurosawa's use of images and metaphors in *Throne of Blood*, Joseph Blumenthal[4] has commented that even though the filmmaker completely jettisoned Shakespeare's magnificent spoken poetry, he created spectacular visual images to replace it. One of these was his transformation of the forest (Birnam Wood in Shakespeare) into a replica of Washizu's (that is, Macbeth's) mind. The labyrinthine paths and byways through which Washizu literally struggles—sometimes in near panic—can be seen, Blumenthal argues, as externalizations of his feelings and his state of mind. What Blumenthal fails to point out, however, is that "objective correlatives" for such internal events extend to specific dramatic encounters as well, thus allowing Kurosawa to integrate the dynamics of theater with the medium of cinema.

Three scenes of dialogue involving Washizu and Lady Washizu beautifully illustrate Kurosawa's ability to create subtle film metaphors to reflect complex psychological conditions. The first is the one in which Lady Washizu implants in her husband's mind the notion of killing "his lordship" (Duncan). It takes place in the large reception hall of their newly occupied North Fortress. Washizu places himself to the left of an open window, which is center-frame and looks out onto a desolate sunlit landscape. Lady Washizu, all signs of emotion enigmatically erased from her face, is seated on the floor to the right of the window. As she speaks and as Washizu begins to take in her words, the illuminated window assumes the role of a *tabula rasa*, a blank tablet of the mind ready to receive impressions from an external source. As her comments begin to register, Washizu walks over to the open doorway, which, unlike the window it replaces, is divided in two by a central wooden strut. As he starts to deliberate whether or not to murder "his lordship," a servant can be seen through the door exercising a white stallion in the courtyard. The movements of the horse, alternating between a circle and a figure eight, project and replicate the fluctuating rhythms of Washizu's disturbed thoughts, their "divided" and oscillating nature made more dramatic by the split construction of the doorway. Following this sequence, Washizu goes back to the *tabula rasa* window to receive further indoctrination from his wife.

The second "cinepsychological" dialogue between the two protagonists opens with Lady Washizu sitting on the floor in the foreground of what has by now been established as her film-space, namely, the right half of the screen. The left-hand side of the frame is filled with the to-and-fro pacing of Washizu, whose figure is seen only from the waist down as he talks, presumably to his wife, but actually to himself.

Opening a scene of dialogue in this manner is of course highly unusual. The conventional method is to begin with a medium "establishing shot" of both speakers, then shift to individual close-ups as needed. In this instance, one feels that the woman, though silent and immobile, nevertheless dominates the frame and is therefore really the power-source that propels the moving legs of the man, whose entire body is encompassed by the frame only when he occasionally stoops down to confer with her and receive a further impetus to deliberation and action. The crucial information that she conveys is that she is now pregnant, a plot element added to Shakespeare by Kurosawa to give more motive to Washizu's killing of Miki (Banquo), whose descendants would rival Washizu's for the throne.

The third interlude of dialogue between Washizu and Lady Washizu that marks another crucial stage in their emergent—and merging—feelings opens with a shot of Washizu again nervously pacing. The set-up differs from that of the previous sequence in that the full form of Washizu is now shown. Lady Washizu is present but *not shown*, although her off-screen voice dominates this part of the scene. Here as before, Kurosawa has violated a film convention by not visually confirming the presence of a key character via a traditional establishing shot. The eerie impression is that Washizu has at this stage completely internalized the voice that is now guiding his every thought and action.

The scene concludes with Washizu moving toward his wife, the panning camera now picking up both figures together at the far right side of the room. (Dare we equate Lady Washizu's continual domination of the right-hand part of the screen with the non-rational right hemisphere of the brain of the composite character of which she is a part?) In a formalized gesture with musical accompaniment, both derived from the traditional Kabuki theater, they turned away from each other and look offscreen, but with their backs touching in a stylized contemplative pose that suggests Siamese twins who might be trying to find their own emotional "space" but who remain inextricably joined in some vital way.

All of these scenes—but especially the final moments of the one I have just described—suggest that Kurosawa intuitively agreed with Freud's and Jekel's view of the Macbeths as "decomposed" parts of a single character or personality. The overall psychological movement extending across these scenes is that of the gradual internalization by Washizu of his wife, but the cinematic representation paradoxically preserves each figure as both a complementary part of the other and a distinct individual in his or her own right.

Throne of Blood is of course replete with other kinds of images of mental functioning. Besides the labyrinthian forest that intrigues Blumenthal, various architectural details of the fortress reflect and interact with Washizu's mind and emotions. From the very moment that a group of common foot-soldiers ruminate on how the foundations of the fort seem rotten and how the rats are beginning to desert it—a low-key prophetic note so characteristic of Shakespeare—we become aware of how skilfully Kurosawa has been able to use architectural structure and space to represent feeling and mood. The low ceiling of the banquet hall, its massiveness exaggerated by the low-angle shot, entraps a flock of frantic birds to give us a graphic image of the feelings of panic and desperation that press in upon Washizu. Other architectural metaphors for feelings of entrapment and isolation come to the fore as the film winds down to its final denouement. As Washizu moves backward in the fighting style of the samurai warrior, he frequently runs into walls and corners. When he runs down a flight of steps to a lower gallery of the fortress in order to address his troops gathered in the courtyard below, the camera becomes choreographed with his movements in such a way that railings and steps seem to impede "our" attempts to reach or observe him. The scene in which the nurse will announce Lady Washizu's mental breakdown opens with the former's hand partially sliding open the double doors to reveal Washizu sitting alone. As the camera dollies back in the middle of this scene, the door panels on either side of him come to dominate more of the frame and seem to press in upon his diminished figure. In the final moments of the film the hundreds of arrows that are shot into the wall to impede Washizu's movement amount to a climactic visual translation of a speech in Shakespeare that is never actually uttered in the film: "...now I am cabined, cribbed, confined, bound in/To saucy doubts and fears."

It is of course impossible to make the visual language of objects, space, and movement speak with the same eloquence and nuance as the written or spoken word. Certain subtleties of connotation and tone may simply be beyond the film medium. However, because Kurosawa chose to tell the Macbeth story as a cautionary tale sung by a chorus of priests, he was able to reduce the moral condition of his protagonists to that of black and white, with only a few shades of gray. But the rather simple and conventional framework of fable or legend provided him as well with a set of vivid and fairly unambiguous metaphors to embody the primitive emotions of two of Shakespeare's most famous characters.

iv

One cannot of course predict what directions will be taken either by dramatists of filmmakers in their attempts to present in their art images of the mind or processes of mental functioning. Probably the theater will continue go along the path of frank divergences from surface naturalism, while the cinema will for the most part try to create images that will be true to the surfaces of life as it tries to mirror the psyche. However, both the theater and film will no doubt continue to use a host of special effects that will markedly depart from naturalism to map out a "chambered nautilus" of the mind. The hallucinatory world characteristic of Bergman's *Hour of the Wolf* or Skolimowsky's *The Shout* will most likely remain as much a staple of film art as a sense of life as "surreal," found in plays like O'Neill's *Strange Interlude* or Albee's *Tiny Alice*, will continue to permeate the theater.

Appendix B
The "Complexes" of Art: Some Contributions Made by Myth and Literature to the Language of Psychoanalysis

i

As Freud so well knew when he suddenly became deeply affected by a theatrical performance of Sophocles' *Oedipus Tyrannvs*, the artist is always ahead of the psychologist in his intuitive understanding of human nature. It is therefore logical that psychologists should look to characters in myth, folklore, and the literary arts to do for them what Oedipus once did for Freud: to delineate and dramatize some of the most pronounced of the complexes they have felt within themselves and clinically observed in others, ranging from the more mildly neurotic to the most morbidly psychotic. After giving a brief history of the development of the concept of the psychological complex itself, I shall present a taxonomy of complexes that come from the writings of psychologists both near and distant in time—those who have discovered in fictional heroes and heroines the perfect embodiment of these bizarre patterns of human behavior. In doing so, I hope to enlarge the repertory of myths and literary vignettes of use to psychologically oriented artists and critics.

ii

So crucial to Freud's thinking was the Oedipus Complex—a condition that he discovered in himself during the exhaustive self-analysis he conducted in the nineties—that many regard him as the originator of the complex concept. Actually it is Carl Jung—the apostle who was soon to become the apostate—who must receive the credit, both for his discovery of the hidden mechanism of the

186

complex and for his development of an extensive theory about its workings. In 1903, shortly before he became involved with Freud, Jung had been conducting a series of word-association tests when he observed that some of the word-stimuli evoked a slower-than-usual response coupled with out-of-the-ordinary physiological changes, as for example labored respiration, a faster heartbeat, and a modification in the skin's level of electrical conductivity. After further experimentation, Jung soon realized that the interference with the word-response was due to a cluster of ideas—that is, emotionally "toned" words and images—that were being automatically and unconsciously linked to a hidden central emotion. Jung went on to investigate and ultimately describe the autonomous split-off nature of such feeling clusters, as well as their relation to the conscious and unconscious self. By 1934 he was able to assert with confidence that the "royal road to the unconscious" was not, as Freud had thought, the dream but, rather, the complex.

Freud's first use of the word *complex* occurs as part of his discussion of the Oedipus Complex in "Contributions to the Psychology of Love"—a paper written in 1910, seven years after Jung's word-association tests. However, Freud had described the dynamics of the Oedipal *situation* long before this—quite extensively, in fact, in 1900 in *The Interpretation of Dreams*—and had hinted at it in letters to his friend Wilhelm Fliess as early as 1897.

In the literature of the early days of psychoanalysis one finds casual but pervasive references to the "mother complex," the "father complex," and the "family complex," along with more systematic analyses of the "vicissitudes" of the Oedipus Complex. However, as Freud's latter-day successors have begun to understand more about the conflicts occurring in stages of psychosexual development earlier than the genital (in which the much-talked-about Oedipus Complex is rooted), and as they have begun to learn more about the child's ordeal of separating from the symbiotic tie with his mother and achieving a sense of his own identity, they have been able to refine their concept of the complexes. As a result they have had to invent more categories to describe these more subtle colorations and nuances of the conflicted personality.

iii

The most famous complex of mythic and literary relevance, Freud's Oedipus Complex, is an emotional phenomenon that is so intricate that it constellates other complexes, which in turn require a whole set of fictional characters to give them dramatic life. Many would limit the Oedipal merely to the sexual attraction of son to mother and of daughter to father, forgetting perhaps the child's hatred and fear of the "rival" parent of the same sex. Others broaden the term to include a parent's reciprocal sexual feelings about the child as well. After all, wasn't Jocasta as interested in Oedipus as he was interested in her? And what about the parent of the same sex, who is regarded by the child as a rival? Is the child's fear of him or of her merely imaginary, or mightn't the parent actually hate the child as a kind of sibling rival, as apparently was the case with Laius, who engineered the exposure to the elements of his son Oedipus? This threefold mixture of feelings at the nuclear center of the family has led some psychologists to invent the term "Jocasta Complex" and "Laius Complex" in order to describe these "reverse-angle" emotions of sensuality and rage that parents direct toward the child—in this case the male child.

As far back as 1920 Raymond de Saussure proposed "Jocasta Complex" as the designation for a mother's "morbid attachment to her son," ranging from "the maternal instinct slightly deformed to a frank sexual attachment in which both physical and psychic satisfaction is found."[1] Presumably the "Phaedra Complex," sometimes cited in psychiatric literature,[2] is identical with the Jocasta Complex, although both in Euripides' *Hippolytus* and in Racine's *Phèdre*, Phaedra is enamored of her *step*-son rather than her son. Nevertheless, her struggle against her passion has all the earmarks of fearing to violate a tribal taboo, and we might therefore conjecture that the *step*-parent relationship is the myth's way of softening or disguising a more deeply forbidden incest wish. To be sure, a myth's usefulness in supplying names to unconscious processes like complexes usually lies in its *manifest* rather than in its *latent* form. Otherwise the myth itself would have to be searched for its own hidden complex. Nevertheless, we must recognize along with Freud that some myths have undergone less repression and distortion than others.[3]

Strangely enough, it is the Adlerians rather than the Freudians who emphasize the inverse side of the Oedipus Complex known as the "Laius Complex,"[4] seeing the hatred of the father for the son as in fact more universal than the Oedipus Complex itself. The attraction of the Laius Complex for Adlerians is that the central feelings are those of power—a concept central to Adler's "individual psychology"—rather than sex. That is, the father is loath to have his son succeed to his patriarchal throne.

Freudians, on the other hand, sometimes refer to the father's death wishes against his children as the "Atreus Complex." However, this is clearly a misnomer since, according to the story, Atreus engineers the slaughter of his *brother's* children rather than his own. Some clinicians therefore prefer the term *Heracles Complex*, referring to one of the less celebrated adventures of Heracles (or Hercules) in which the hero in a fit of madness slays his own children.[5] However, since Heracles is more famous for other deeds, the term obscures more than it illuminates.

Should the mother rather than the father be disturbed by the son's overtures and reject him, she may engender in him an "Orestes Complex,"[6] that is, a feeling of murderous rage against her for "jilting" him. Such feelings, it is believed, may have underlain the acting-out behavior of the Greek hero Orestes when he slew his mother, Clytemnestra, for having murdered his father, Agamemnon.

The more complicated Oedipal situation of the female child also finds its objective correlative in mythological and literary prototypes. Frequently Freudian psychologists refer both to the little girl's initial desire to be the husband of her mother and to her later wish to be the wife of her father as "Oedipal." Jung suggested that this confusion be avoided by referring to the initial phallic wish of the girl to penetrate as "Oedipal" but to her later passive feminine designs upon the father as the "Electra Complex."

According to the myth, as dealt with by Aeschylus in the *Oresteia*, Electra persuaded her brother, Orestes, to help her kill their mother, Clytemnestra, in revenge for Clytemnestra's murder of their idealized hero-father, Agamemnon. The degree of Electra's emotional involvement with her father is underscored by her continued idolization of him and her rejection of all offers of marriage. Eugene O'Neill's suggestion in his updated version of the myth in his *Mourning Becomes Electra* that Electra displaces her passion for her father on to her brother is not a commonly recognized aspect of this complex in clinical discussions.

As we have seen, the Oedipus Complex has its parent-centered as well as its child-centered perspective. That is, as far as the male child is concerned, it encompasses both the mother's libidinal tie to the son (Jocasta Complex) and the father's hostility toward him

(Laius Complex). In like manner, the Electra Complex also has its reverse parental side. J. J. Putnam, an early exponent of Freudian psychology in the United States, invented the term *Griselda Complex* to describe the father's unconscious sexual involvement with his daughter, a feeling that is usually most strongly activated in him by the daughter's decision to marry a younger "rival."[7] This kind of emotional involvement is central to numerous fairy tales in which the father-king places a number of obstacles in the way of the young prince who wishes to win his daughter's hand. In Shakespeare's *The Tempest* Prospero's reluctance to yield his daughter to the care and caresses of Ferdinand may be termed a "Griselda Complex."

Since Griselda was a figure in medieval romance who was widely celebrated for her virtue, chastity, and patience, it is easy to see why Putnam chose the term: by idealizing his daughter as a Griselda, the father puts her on a pedestal beyond the grasp and contamination of earthbound men. However, since the characterization of Griselda describes the fantasied *object* of the father's desires rather than the *embodiment* of those desires, the term *Griselda Complex* is something of a misnomer.

A more accurate designation for the Griselda Complex is the "Lear Complex," coined by Arpad Pauncz and characterized by him as "the other side of the Oedipus Complex."[8] As Pauncz sees it, Lear's angry rejection of Cordelia, as well as of his other two daughters later, is based on his impossible hope that he become their exclusive love-object, which would put him into unconscious sexual rivalry with any of his daughters' husbands or suitors. However, since Lear's reaction formation of hate as a defense against unrequited love complicates the paternal feelings, the "Lear Complex" is also somewhat inadequate to describe the simple unconscious eroticization of the daughter by the father.

Just as the father, at the height of his Laius Complex, might entertain murderous thoughts against his son because of the son's incestuous overtures toward the mother, so too might the mother, in one variation of the Electra Complex, harbor murderous feelings against her daughter as she begins to regard her daughter's emerging sexual interest in the father as serious competition. Fritz Wittels, a member of Freud's original circle in Vienna, seized upon the term *Medea Complex* to represent this state of affairs. But since according to the Greek myth the two children that Medea slew were her *sons* and since her filicide was prompted by revenge for her husband's infidelity, Wittels's mythic borrowing of the term obfuscates more than it illuminates.[9]

iv

In the classical Freudian view the price of Oedipal yearnings is always castration anxiety, a discomfort experienced by girls as well as by boys. For the boy, the fear that the father will castrate him for his sexual interest in the mother normally brings the Oedipus Complex to a close. For the girl, the discovery that she does not have a penis with which to penetrate the mother (i.e., she discovers that she has already been "castrated") terminates the primary Oedipal phase and initiates the Electra phase, in which she accepts her feminine role, with perhaps some vestiges of penis envy.

If anxiety about castration cannot be mastered during the course of the Oedipal phase of development, then the Oedipal Complex gives rise to a "castration complex." In order to clarify this feeling and the defenses against it, psychologist N. D. C. Lewis[10] drew upon the story of the handsome Phoenician god Eshmun who, to escape from the mother-goddess Astronae after she became infatuated with him during a hunting trip, castrated himself. Hence the "Eshmun Complex" describes the male who wishes to ward off the incestuous desires of the Oedipus Complex and rushes forth to accept the castration punishment as the lesser of two evils. Usually the self-punishment is *psychic* rather than *physical* castration, that is, the boy or man thinks and behaves either in a feminine or in a eunuchoid manner.

The female counterpart to the Eshmun Complex would seem to be the "Diana Complex," which is described by *The Psychiatric Dictionary* as simply "the wish of a female to be a male,"[11] that is, to reverse the condition of castration. Presumably Diana (the Roman version of Artemis) is chosen to represent this wish because of her sexual unavailability to men but even more likely because her preoccupation with the hunt is considered to be a masculine pursuit. However, Diana's other key role, that of patroness goddess of childbirth, weakens the appropriateness of her name's being used solely in connection with the central castration complex.

Another way in which the female might try to master her castration anxiety might be to force her penis-bearing mate both to admire and submit to her "mutilated" genital. This perverse form of female exhibitionism is dubbed by Fenichel[12] the "Circe Complex," after the character in Homer's *Odyssey* who turned men into swine by seducing them through her beauty. The lowly nature of the creatures into which the men are metamorphosed in the myth also reveals that humiliation is the Circean's chief mode of vengeance upon the male.

The ultimate revenge that a woman's penis envy can contrive against the male is of course to actually cause his castration. This may be effected physically or psychologically, or it may be revealed as a mere wish to do either. Freud first related this aberration to the character Judith[13] as she appears both in the Old Testament and in Hebbel's tragedy *Judith and Holofernes*, and the emotional configuration of this behavior was later elaborated upon and labeled the "Judith Complex" by Karl Gumpertz.[14] The value of Hebbel's play, both to Freud and Gumpertz, was that it presented the psychological underpinnings of the legend in a less veiled manner than in the Old Testament. Whereas in the biblical account Judith's husband merely dies in a barley field, in Hebbel's play he is paralyzed by fear, that is, sexually dies, on their wedding night and remains impotent. Whereas in the Bible Judith brags that she did not have to sacrifice her chastity to the enemy Holofernes, in Hebbel she is brutally deflowered by him and angrily decapitates (that is, symbolically castrates) him.

For Freud, the different strata of conscious and unconscious disturbance in the Judith Complex would range from the woman's superficial desire to avoid the pain of defloration, to a transferential desire and fear of having intercourse with the taboo father or brother, to the deepest unconscious wish to mutilate the man's genitals out of penis envy.

v

Just beyond the boundaries of the intimate world of the Oedipal triad of father, mother, and child lies the world of siblings and the extended family of aunts, uncles, cousins, and grandparents. And since these figures may also involve an individual in intense personal interactions, it is not surprising to discover that complexes of both eroticization and aggression may spring up in relation to them. Aside from his famous discourse on the "brothers of the primal horde" lusting after the mother and killing the father as well as each other in order to have her,[15] Freud does not deal very much with the complexes of the larger family unit. It remained for the defector Alfred Adler, with his concept of sibling rivalry and his notion of the way in which sibling birth order affected psychological development, and for later analysts and theorists, to deal with conflicts lying just beyond the Oedipal center.

One of these aberrations, known as the "Clytemnestra Complex," concerns the wife 'who kills her husband so that she may possess one of his male relatives.''[16] Concomitant fear of and desire for incest would seem to be the unconscious conflict in this complex, so that in a sense we are brought right back to an Oedipal experience. The wife "hates" her husband because he reminds her of her father or brother, but she can allow herself to "love" her husband's relative because even though on the one hand he mildly reawakens former incest feelings (he appears as a kinsman), on the other hand he is rendered safe by being merely an in-law, a non-blood relative. Unfortunately, the unconscious wish for incest would probably eventually emerge and be transferred to the relative. Thus the defensive feelings of hatred and contempt previously shown for the husband would recur and spoil the new relationship. In the play *Agamemnon* Aeschylus presents only the first part of this scenario—Clytemnestra's slaying of her husband, Agamemnon, and her cohabitation with his cousin Aegisthus—although he hints at the impending denigration of Aesgisthus by having him described as passive and effeminate.[17]

More widespread than the erotic motive among members of the extended family is perhaps the aggressive and rivalrous one. Numerous fairy tales about fiercely competing brothers (e.g., *The Three Feathers*) or sisters (e.g., *Cinderella, Cupid and Psyche*, and *Beauty and the Beast*) would seem to bear this out. That all of these are about rivalry for the sexual possession of the parent of the opposite sex seems unlikely; that most of them concern a more anally oriented struggle for mastery and control of self and environment is more plausible. Whatever the cause, however, the simple manifestation of aggression of brother toward brother is sometimes referred to by analysts as the "Cain Complex,"[18] named of course after the elder son of Adam and Eve who slew his younger brother Abel.

A more complicated version of the Cain Complex is the "Judas Complex," coined by Wilhelm Stekel and described later by F. L. Lucas as occurring in "a man who loves his master and feels himself less loved than [the other disciples and] can be provoked to passionate resentment and betrayal by that jealous love."[19] Thus in considering this complex—and by implication the character of Judas—clinicians emphasize not so much the act of betrayal and ensuing guilt as the underlying dynamics of an all-jealous, all-possessive love turning into hate. It is a form of sibling rivalry in which the master is probably unconsciously viewed as the father and calls to mind the feelings of the elder son in the biblical parable of the Prodigal Son. As a number of Freud's original circle in Vienna, Stekel, the originator of the term *Judas Complex*, was in a position to see this pattern of behavior operating in relation to his own master, as certain members of the group—notably Adler, Jung, and Rank—successively rebelled against the "Professor" with open hostility.

vi

Thus far we have been considering complexes that are primarily neurotic in form and incestuous in content. But many complexes originate in phases of psychosexual development earlier than the phallic-genital, and when they stem from severe stresses during the oral phase may be psychotic in their coloring. Literature and myth have adequately provided fictional characterizations for these clinical entities as well.

Various kinds of struggles for success and self-esteem distinguish a large group of complexes. Since battles with authority figures and attempts to overcome shame for one's excretory functions are earmarks of the anal stage of psychosexual development, one expects to discover anal fixations with obsessional symptoms and defenses of reaction formation and intellectualization as the chief dramatic highlights of these complexes. However, frequently this type of behavior stems from traumas of earlier origin, in problems of disturbed symbiosis with the mother, inadequate weaning and separation, and introjections of destructive parental imagos, resulting perhaps in deep narcissistic woundings.

In a recent article in *Psychology Today*[20] Angus Campbell tries to account for the reason many college graduates, after attaining a certain level of income, become unhappier rather than happier, in contrast to blue collar workers whose happiness seems to increase proportionately to their income. Campbell terms the problem of the college graduates the "Cory Complex," named after the subject of Edward Arlington Robinson's poem "Richard Cory," who after attaining all that money could buy, in addition to being endowed with good looks, went home one day and shot himself. Campbell concludes from his survey that Cory-like disappointments result from nonmaterial ideals having been unconsciously associated with monetary success.

A more intricate kind of conflict equating money with success emerges in the "Midas Complex," named after the legendary king of Phrygia whose god-granted wish to be able to turn everything he touched into gold ultimately caused his ruin. The complex therefore refers to the mechanism by which a person gets what he wants but unconsciously contrives, out of a sense of guilt for satisfying a "forbidden desire," to plant the seeds for self-punishment or destruction. Fenichel[21] identifies the Midas personality as primarily that of an obsessional compulsive neurotic (not surprising, since money and gold are frequent dream images for the anal functions upon which obsessionals are fixated). Midas's "gift" creates a torture chamber of successes that have gone haywire—a parody of a lack of impulse control most feared by the obsessive character and over which he hopes guilt and punishment will provide some disciplinary control.

Another form of overachievement-come-to-grief stems not so much from anxiety about sphincter control as from infantile fantasies of omnipotence—a tendency that Leo Katz calls the "Rumpelstiltskin Complex."[22] In the Grimms' fairy tale involving the dwarf bearing this strange name, a miller foolishly brags to the king that his daughter can spin gold from straw—a task that, to her and her father's despair, she is soon required to perform. In exchange for receiving the necessary magic from Rumpelstiltskin she has to promise her firstborn to him. Later she wriggles out of her bargain by "guessing" the little dwarf's bizarre and almost unpronounceable name when she overhears him utter it in the woods.

According to Katz, the miller in the tale unrealistically overvalues his daughter out of an unconscious disappointment in himself. The girl in turn introjects these illusions of grandeur and joylessly and compulsively tries to conform to this inflated image.

A better name for the Rumpelstiltskin Complex would of course be that of a character who himself harbors hopes for achieving the impossible rather than the character who provides the mechanism for the attempt to act out the fantasy. A more suitable choice would have been a character like Ibsen's clergyman Brand (in the play of the same name), whose overblown and unbending idealism in having to practice his religion in a sunless fjord causes the death of his wife and child, and his exile from his own village.

vii

Other aspirants to a greatly improved condition in life come a cropper not so much because they have tried to surpass their own limitations but because they seem to have tried to surpass those of the gods—a form of irreligious behavior that the Greeks called *hubris*. (In Freudian psychology we would of course read "castrating father incorporated as superego" in lieu of the "gods.") Three characters—one from history and two from mythology—were guilty of the crime of such pride and presumption in different ways and from different motives, and have lent their names to complexes: Polycrates, Promethous, and Icarus.

The first of these, Polycrates, a tyrant of Samos in the sixth century before Christ, feared that the gods would envy and punish him for his long record of successes. To placate them he pretended inadvertently to drop his favorite ring overboard and then feigned grief. But the gods detected the ruse, had a fisherman return his ring, and crucified him. Both Sandor Ferenczi and Maryse Choisy agree[23] that the underlying dynamics of the Polycrates Complex is a guilt over morally unacceptable fantasies of either eroticism or aggression that can only be controlled through external punishment or self-inflicted pain and humiliation (compare the Midas Complex discussed above). Either type of chastisement would be evidence of a harsh primitive superego, the former being disguised as a projection into external reality.

The "Prometheus Complex" and the "Icarus Complex" invite comparison with each other because both the heroes lending their names to them are in defiance of the heavenly force of fire. Moreover, both figures transgress against the wishes of a "father"— Icarus against his real father, Daedalus, Prometheus against the father of the gods, Zeus. On the surface both actions—Prometheus's theft of the immortal fire in a hollow stick, and Icarus's disastrous flight with waxen wings too near the sun—might seem Oedipal: defiance of a "father" motivated by a passion for "fiery excitement" (lust). However, the traditional object of desire, the mother, is missing from both these tales. Moreover, the pervasive feeling seems to be a narcissistic reveling in one's own power and an exhibitionistic display of it rather than an object-directed sexual urge.

In applying the concept of the Prometheus Complex to revolutionary leaders like Karl Marx, Lewis Feuer[24] is able to more fully define it as a strong desire to shape history by creative ideas, followed by impatience in not seeing one's wishes and prophecies come to quick fruition, and a reliance on war to accomplish them. Finally, the cycle ends with a projection of personal anger and frustration as if these were inevitable cosmic or historical forces.

Since Icarus's boldness with fire is punished by another element—that of water (the Icarian Sea in which he drowns)—rather than directly by the father-figure (as in the case of Prometheus, by Zeus), it suggests to H. A. Murray[25] the mechanism of regression to an earlier psychosexual stage of development specifically connected with "water": the urethral phase. In fact, Murray's Icarus Complex is a restatement of his earlier conceived "urethral complex," which involves the pleasurable sensations created by both emitting and retaining urine. As we would expect from the myth, the Icarian character, according to Murray, is marked by an inordinate desire for success (often accompanied by dreams of flying or overcoming gravity) and a strong narcissism and craving for immortality, all of which quickly dissolve into a sense of "falling" at the least sign of an obstacle. Such personalities Murray argues, have a strong attachment to fire as a source of power as well as having a history of bedwetting, which is both a retreat from adult genital activity and a parody of it. Freud, in his essay on "The Acquisition of Power over Fire," somewhat anticipates Murray when he points out that the urinary ("water") function of the penis both predates and continues to dominate, in terms of frequency of performance, its sexual ("fire") function,[26] neither of which is compatible with the other at any single point in time.

Some complexes may be the result of a failure of normal ego functions rather than of a regression from a hard-to-negotiate higher level of development or of the attempt to ward off an unacceptable id-wish. Therefore they can be seen as variations of Adler's "inferiority complex" or sense of "organ inferiority," in essence a failure in the power drive toward mastery of self or environment. One of these, the "Demosthenes Complex"—named after the pre-Christian Athenian who progressed from stutterer to master orator by training himself to speak with pebbles in his mouth—refers to the neurotic's need to overcome inferiority feelings by garrulousness.[27] When a person's feelings of low self-esteem can thus be directly related to an actual physical defect, psychiatrists may instead describe him as the possessor of a "Quasimodo Complex,"[28] in honor of the protagonist of Victor Hugo's *Hunchback of Notre Dame*, whose deformities of face and body made him a recluse, a figure of derision, and an unrequited lover. Freud's essay "The Exceptions,"[29] in which he analyzes the psychology of the crookback King Richard III, is relevant to this complex. Freud felt that individuals so affected saw themselves placed outside the pale of natural, and by extension *moral*, law, and were therefore left free to engage in amoral Machiavellianism.

viii

When we thus begin to view behavior from the point of view of ego integration and function, and trace it to early object relations, we begin to see complexes more as a part of evolving character structure than as a central conflict produced by a trauma. They may range in seriousness and intensity from a mild disturbance, arising from the normal vicissitudes of emotional development, to outright psychotic behavior, revealing an ego structure that is highly fragmented and an identity that is diffuse. For instance, at the relatively benign end of the spectrum is the "Horatio Complex,"[30] a type of self-imposed moratorium or holding pattern in adolescent development in which the acceptance of the role of a "supporting player" or in-the-wings observer to a more exhibitionistic peer betokens an unwillingness to leave the childhood phase of passivity and dependency. In a manifest way this roughly describes Horatio's role in Shakespeare's Hamlet.

A reluctance to reach what Erik Erikson calls "phase readiness" in one's natural course of development is characteristic of three other complexes as well: the "Marschallin Complex," the "Lolita Complex," and the "Cinderella Complex." The first of these, named after the middle-aged female protagonist of *Der Rosenkavalier*, describes a woman who has love affairs with teen-aged boys in order to hold on to an earlier narcissistic stage of life.[31] The counterpart of this problem in middle-aged men has been described by the second named, the Lolita Complex,[32] bringing to mind Humbert Humbert's lust for "nymphets" in Nabokov's famous novel. (Here once again the term is a misnomer, since it primarily defines the *object* of desire rather than the *experiencer* of that desire.) In the Cinderella Complex, a term coined for a recent controversial best-seller of the same name,[33] the author describes women who regress to previously conditioned roles of dependency when they become involved with a professionally successful man. Presumably it is Cinderella's patient and passive waiting to be found and rescued by her assertive prince charming that gives the complex its main coloration. Nothing is said about her submission to the vixens of her foster family (step-mother and step-sisters), that is, to the dominating females in her culture, about which another best seller could be written.

ix

Finally, we come to that group of complexes that arise out of earlier problems of separation, individuation, and identity, that are engendered primarily in the oral-narcissistic stage of development, and that are associated chiefly with the borderline psychotic and the totally psychotic individual.

Following Freud's precept that "the superego is heir to the Oedipus Complex and is the introjection of the parent of the same sex,"[34] Maryse Choisy, a French psychoanalyst, speculated on the nature of the dilemma of the male foundling who because of his illegitimacy lacked the father-figure to introject. Her conclusion was that such a child was likely to develop the "Phaeton Complex,"[36] in which he grandiosely focused upon the sun as the all-seeing, all-powerful, all-punishing father (i.e., the archaic superego). In Ovid's version of the tale, Phaeton insists on driving Helios's (the sun's) dangerous, fiery chariot across the heavens in order to prove himself a true scion of the sun-god, and consequently loses his life. The implication is that in the Phaeton Complex the introjected father superego is so primitive and harsh that it leads to intense masochism or suicide.

The "Dorian Gray Complex," which Otto Fenichel cites in his classic work on psychopathology,[37] has a similar dynamic. Although our knowledge of Oscar Wilde's protagonist may lead us to believe that a narcissistic devotion to hedonistic pleasure and a psychopathic disregard for moral values are the key features of this complex, Fenichel uncovers the underlying configuration as follows. The hideous painting of Gray by his artist friend is a projection of that unconscious aspect of the superego that has been introjected as an evil persecutor, most likely a negative parental imago. Gray's death at the moment he slashes the painting beautifully illustrates the point that the suicidal person unconsciously aims not so much at killing himself as at murdering the bad introject.

The narcissistic reluctance to surrender the infantile illusion of omnipotence lies at the root of the remaining complexes we are to consider. Recently a clinician-theorist gave the term *Monte Cristo Complex* to a form of thievery unconsciously used as vengeance upon a world that deprives one of an "entitled" cornucopia of narcissistic supplies. Even though the Count in Dumas's tale does not literally behave in this way, the writer interprets his acquisition of wealth from a fellow prisoner as a veiled form of a deeper

hostile and immoral intent.[37] Jung's archetypal figure the
"trickster" may be a near kinsman to this character-type.

Closely allied to the maneuver of restoring infantile narcissism
by cherishing and acquiring *other* people's property is that of
falling in love with *one's own* possessions—especially if the objects
are products of one's very own creation—thus giving birth to a
"Pygmalion Complex." Named after the Cypriot sculptor who
fell in love with the beautiful female statue he made, the
Pygmalion Complex may reach psychotic proportions, as in the
reported case of a paranoiac homosexual who devised a
"perpetual motion machine," called it "Albert," and fell in love
with it.[38] The term *pygmalionism* is sometimes loosely applied by
psychotherapists to those among their colleagues who see their
patients as helpless children or as ill-defined beings wanting and
waiting to be molded according to the therapists' ideals.

Although the "Don Juan Complex" is spoken about almost as
frequently as the Oedipus Complex, it is perhaps one of the least
understood. This is because the manifest genital acting-out of the
Don Juan masks a pre-Oedipal narcissistic aim. The Don Juan is
really in love with himself, but most precariously so. He takes on a
succession of women in order to reclaim the ideal maternal figure
and assure himself of continued oral nurturance. His excessive
heterosexual conquests, as recorded in fictional accounts by
Tellez, Molière, Mozart's librettist, and others, may also in part be
a counterphobic defense against homosexual desires.

These, then, are some of the more colorful examples from
among the myriad of complexes to which psychoanalysts in their
role of auxiliary artists have given names from legend, literature,
myth, and art. Many of these disturbances are readily observable
by the layman as an exaggerated aspect of character and behavior.
Other complexes reveal themselves most dramatically in the consulting room at the height of the "transference neurosis." Some
condense the developmental and identity crises of a patient's
whole life—as, for example, the just-cited Don Juan Complex.
Others idiosyncratically mirror the accoutrements of the analytic
process itself, as for example the last complex I shall mention—the
"Harlequin Complex"—a mixed feeling of fear and excitement
that may be reached by women during the height of the transference neurosis when they begin to view death as a dark
mysterious lover. Since the graceful and witty Harlequin of the
Italian Commedia dell' arte stems from the more primitive and
sinister demon-on-horseback Harlequin of medieval France, his
evolutionary nature is important for understanding the full

meaning of the complex. His more modern equivalents, to which excitable women have succumbed in an ecstasy of fear and love, are Svengali, Charles Manson, the Reverend Jimmy Jones, and of course "the dark mysterious foreign psychoanalyst."[39] One speculation is that Freud himself did the most to bring this complex to the surface when he insisted that his female patients lie on the couch, for this physical position fostered in them a desire for sexual intercourse with the male therapist while the confines of the reclining area itself made them simultaneously feel that they lay dead on a bier.

Thus the tools of the psychoanalytic profession sometimes seem to take on a life of their own when they touch upon the seemingly autonomous complexes.

Notes

Introduction

1. S. A. Weiss, "Osborne's Angry Young Play," *Educational Theatre Journal* 12 (1960): 285.
2. Letter from Joyce Carol Oates to Roy Huss, June 22, 1973.
3. See Gilbert Rose, *The Power of Form* (New York: International Universities Press, 1980), p. 206 and passim.
4. Norman N. Holland's pioneering *The Dynamics of Literary Response* (New York: Oxford University Press) appeared in 1968, and his "revisionist" *Poems in Persons: An Introduction to the Psychoanalysis of Literature* (New York: W. W. Norton), in 1973. For his discussion of the "identity theme" see chap. 2 of the latter work.
5. See R. D. Laing, *The Divided Self* (Harmondsworth: Penguin Books, 1965).
6. D. H. Lawrence, "The Prussian Officer," in *The Modern Tradition*, ed. Daniel F. Howard, 2d ed. (Boston: Little, Brown, 1972), p. 209.
7. Rose, *Power of Form*, p. 212.
8. Norman Friedman, "Psychology and Literary Form: Toward a Unified Approach," *Psychocultural Review* 2 (Spring 1978): 79.
9. Roy Schafer, *A New Language for Psychoanalysis* (New Haven, Conn.: Yale University Press, 1977).

Chapter 1: Awakening to the Dream

1. Sigmund Freud, "The Relation of the Poet to Daydreaming" (1908), *Character and Culture*, ed. Philip Rieff (New York: Collier Books, 1963), pp. 34-43.
2. In his study of sexual sado-masochistic fantasies in "A Child is Being Beaten" (1919), Standard Edition, 24 vols. trans. and ed. James Strachey (London: The Hogarth Press, 1962), 17: 175–204. Freud showed that while the immediate precursor of a present fantasy was a consciously remembered one, this latter was in turn a derivative of a "forgotten" pre-Oedipal one. His analysis of the unconscious wishes behind Leonardo da Vinci's "early memory" of the vulture and of Goethe's "childhood recollection" of the crockery-breaking incident also bears this out.
3. Sigmund Freud, *The Interpretation of Dreams*, ed. James Strachey (New York: Basic Books, 1953) p. 265.
4. See Freud's "Psychopathic Characters on the stage" (1905-6), Standard Edition, 7: 308–9. See also Letter 71 to Fliess (written much earlier) in which Freud points out that Hamlet is a projection of *unconscious* material (Standard Edition, 1: 263).
5. Durwood Markle, Jr., "Freud, Leonardo and the Lamb," *The Psychoanalytic Review* 57 (1970): 285–89.
6. Edmund Bergler, *1000 Homosexuals* (Paterson, N. J.: Pageant Books, 1959), p. 235.
7. Ibid., p. 223.
8. Ibid., pp. 227, 234.

9. Sigmund Freud, "A Childhood Memory from *Dichtung und Wahrheit*" (1917), *Character and Culture*, p. 201.
10. Sigmund Freud, "The Relation of the Poet to Daydreaming, *Character and Culture*, p. 42.
11. Sigmund Freud, "The Theme of the Three Caskets," *Character and Culture*, pp. 67–79.
12. However, is it not also true that a dream may represent the dreamer's ego as "decomposed" into several figures in the manner that Freud reports some writers of "psychological novels" split their own egos into several characters? (See "The Relation of the Poet to Daydreaming," p. 41.) We may also note that in gestalt therapy the patient is required to act out all the elements of his dreams, even inanimate objects, because all are presumably parts of his ego.
13. Sigmund Freud, "Some Character Types met with in Psychoanalytic Work, Those Wrecked by Success" (1916), *Character and Culture*, p. 171.
14. Freud later says ("Psychopathic Characters on the Stage," *Standard Edition,* 7: 305) that if the "secret" communicated is repressed (unconscious) rather than merely suppressed (conscious), the audience that enjoys the work must, like the author, be neurotic. By this reasoning all who enjoy *Hamlet* are neurotic.
15. Sigmund Freud, "Psychopathic Characters on the Stage," p. 305.
16. Ibid., p. 306.
17. Sigmund Freud, "The 'Moses' of Michelangelo," *Character and Culture*, p. 80.
18. Sigmund Freud, "The Interest of Psycho-Analysis from the Point of View of the Science of Aesthetics" (1913), Standard Edition, 13: 187–88.
19. *The Interpretation of Dreams*, p. 340.
20. A latter-day neo-Freudian tries to supply this lack by insisting that the psychic shape which defines works as diverse as *Beowulf* and Jane Austen's *Emma* is the interplay of ego, superego, and id (P. Withim, "The Psychodynamics of Literature," *The Psychoanalytic Review* 56 [1969–70]: 556–85). But this tells us nothing about the relevance of the refinements of form and style, of genres and subgenres of literature and art, of the relation of form to content.
21. Pinchas Noy, "Form Creation in Art: An Ego-Psychological Approach to Creativity," *The Psychoanalytic Quarterly* 48 (1979): 229–56.
22. Rose, *Power of Form*.
23. Noy, "Form Creation," pp. 244–45.
24. Rose, "Power of Form," p. 167.
25. William Wordsworth, *Wordsworth's Literary Criticism*, ed. Nowell C. Smith (London: Humphrey Milford, 1925), p. 32.
26. Ibid.
27. Ibid., p. 33.
28. Ibid.
29. Friedman, "Psychology and Literary Form, p. 79.

Chapter 2: The Fairy Tale as Psychosexual Conflict

1. Bruno Bettelheim, *The Uses of Enchantment* (New York: Knopf, 1976), p. 10.
2. Sandor Ferenczi, "The Sons of the 'Tailor'" (1923), *Further Contributions to the Theory and Technique of Psycho-Analysis* (New York: Basic Books, 1952), p. 419.
3. Sigmund Freud, "Some Character Types," *Character and Culture* pp. 170–71.
4. Ludwig Jekels, "The Riddle of Shakespeare's Macbeth," *The Psychoanalytic Review* 30 (1943): 51.

5. Otto Rank, *The Myth of the Birth of the Hero* (1909) (New York: Vintage Books, 1959), pp. 86–90 and *passim*.
6. Ernest Jones, *Hamlet and Oedipus* (Garden City, N.Y.: Doubleday Anchor Books, 1949), pp. 160–62.
7. Rank, "The Myth," pp. 85.
8. Rank has traced the father's fear of, and opposition to, his son's succession to his power and authority in *The Myth of the Birth of the Hero*, pp. 306 ff.
9. Jacob and Ludwig Grimm, "The Table, the Ass, and the Stick," *Grimms' Fairy Tales*, (New York: Pantheon Books, 1944), p. 178.

Chapter 3: The Myth Play as Psychosocial Drama

1. Kanzer's interpretation is summarized by Lester H. Golden in his article "Freud's Oedipus: Its Mytho-Dramatic Basis," *American Imago* 24 (1967): 275–6.
2. See Golden, in ibid., pp. 271–82 for a very enlightening summary of most of these other approaches to the Oedipus myth.
3. Bettelheim, *Uses of Enchantment*, p. 198.
4. Erich Fromm, "The Oedipal Myth," *The Forgotten Language* (New York: Grove Press, 1951).
5. Frances Atkins, "The Social Meaning of the Oedipus Myth," *Journal of Individual Psychology* 23 (1966): 173–84.
6. Alfred Adler, *The Individual Psychology of Alfred Adler*, ed. H. L. and R. R. Ansbacher (New York: Harper and Row, 1964), p. 29.
7. Sophocles, "Oedipus Rex," trans. Albert Cook, in *Oedipus Rex: A Mirror for Greek Drama*. ed. Albert Cook (Belmont, Calif.: Wadsworth, 1963), ll. 1031–35.
8. Robert Graves, "Oedipus." *Greek Myths*, 2 vols. (Baltimore, Md.: Penguin Books, 1955), 2: 9–15.
9. Ibid., p. 10.
10. See Patrick Mullahy's comments on Adler in his *Oedipus: Myth and Complex* (New York: Grove Press, 1955), p. 117.
11. Bernard Knox, *Oedipus at Thebes* (New Haven, Conn.: Yale University Press, 1957), p. 103.
12. Sophocles, *The Oedipus Plays of Sophocles*, trans. Paul Roche (New York: New American Library, 1958), p. 57.
13. Knox, *Oedipus at Thebes*, pp. 110–12.
14. Ibid., p. 111.
15. J. Crossett, "The Oedipus Rex," in Albert Cook, ed., p. 46.
16. Knox, *Oedipus at Thebes*, p. 264.
17. Graves, "Oedipus," p. 14.
18. Richmond Lattimore, "The Poetry of Greek Tragedy," in Albert Cook, ed., p. 109.
19. Atkins, "Social Meaning," pp. 179–80.
20. Adler, *Individual Psychology*, pp. 133–42.
21. Sophocles, "Oedipus Rex," trans. A. Cook, ll. 67–68.
22. Mullahy, *Oedipus: Myth and Complex*, p. 119.
23. Knox, *Oedipus at Thebes*, p. 132.
24. Lewis Way, *Adler's Place in Psychology* (New York: Collier Books, 1962), p. 252.
25. Knox, *Oedipus at Thebes*, p. 132.
26. Sophocles, "Oedipus Rex," trans. A. Cook, ll. 1403–7.
27. Knox, *Oedipus at Thebes*, pp. 150–52.
28. Ibid., p. 188.

29. Sophocles, "Oedipus Rex," trans. A. Cook, 1. 1446.
30. Ibid., ll. 1034–37.
31. Mullahy, *Oedipus: Myth and Complex*, pp. 126–27.
32. Sophocles, "Oedipus Rex," trans. A. Cook, ll. 1062–63.
33. Ibid., l. 1980.
34. Ibid., ll. 1090–93.
35. Adler, Individual Psychology, p. 53.
36. Ibid.
37. Knox, *Oedipus at Thebes*, pp. 131 and 243.
38. Ibid., p. 190.
39. Atkins, "Social Meaning," p. 183.
40. Graves, "Oedipus," p. 15.
41. Adler, *Individual Psychology*, p. 54.
42. Ibid., p. 374.
43. Sophocles, *Oedipus the King*, trans. T. Gould (Englewood Cliffs, N. J.: Prentice-Hall, 1970), ll. 1394–96.
44. Sophocles, "Oedipus Rex," trans. A Cook, ll. 1459–61.
45. Graves, "Oedipus," p. 15.

Chapter 4: The Short Story as Case Study

1. In chap. 2.
2. William F. Thrall, Addison Hibbard, and C. Hugh Holman, *A Handbook to Literature* (New York: Odyssey, 1960), p. 31.
3. The title of a recent psychological study of James's work—Elaine Zablotny's "Henry James and the Demonic Vampire and Madonna," *"Psychocultural Review* 3 (Summer/Fall 1979): 203–24—succinctly conveys my point.
4. Henry James, "The Pupil," *Selected Short Stories of Henry James* (New York: Viking, 1957), p. 169.
5. Ibid., p. 179.
6. Ibid., p. 176.
7. Sigmund Freud, "Family Romances." p. 295.
8. James, "The Pupil," p. 194.
9. Henry James, *The Art of the Novel* (New York: Grosset and Dunlap, 1934), p. 150.
10. B. D. Horwitz, "The Sense of Desolation in Henry James," Psychocultural Review 1 (Fall 1977): 472.
11. As Horwitz (ibid., p. 470) points out, she is unconsciously cast by Pemberton (and of course by James) into the role of the "mutilated phallic mother" when she is perceived as one whose "parts didn't always match."
12. It can also incidentally, be seen as James's revenge upon his older brother William, the philosopher-psychologist, whose fame often seemed to throw him into shadow and whose open contempt he frequently had to suffer.
13. James, "The Pupil," pp. 174–75.
14. Erik H. Erikson, *Childhood and Society* (New York: W. W. Norton, 1950), p. 257.
15. James, "The Pupil," p. 181.
16. Ibid., p. 190.
17. Ibid., p. 191.
18. Anna Freud, *Normality and Pathology in Childhood: Assessments of Development* (New York: Internatational Universities Press, 1966), pp. 190–91.
19. James, *Art of the Novel*, p. 150.

20. James, "The Pupil," p. 191.
21. Peter Blos, *On Adolescence* (New York: The Free Press, 1962), p. 185.
22. Ibid., p. 182.
23. Peter Blos, "The Genealogy of the Ego-Ideal," *The Psychoanalytic Study of the Child* 29 (1974): 56–57.
24. M. Laufer, "Assessment of Adolescent Disturbances," *The Psychoanalytic Study of the Child* 20 (1965): 122.
25. James, "The Pupil," p. 192.
26. Erikson, *Childhood and Society*, p. 253.
27. James, "The Pupil," p. 213.
28. Ibid., p. 214.
29. James, *Art of the Novel*, p. 151.
30. Horwitz, "Sense of Desolation," pp. 484 and 488.
31. James, "The Pupil," p. 199.

Chapter 5: Film Form as a Mirror of the Self

1. John Knowles, *A Separate Peace* (New York: Bantam, 1972). The film version (U.S., 1972), directed by Larry Peerce, starred Parker Stevenson, John Heyl, and William Roerick.
2. Ibid., p. 54.
3. Ibid., p. 77.
4. John Knowles, *Peace Breaks Out* (New York: Holt, Rinehart, and Winston, 1981), p. 138.
5. Roy Huss, Alan Roland, et al., eds., *Identity, Identification, and Self-Image* (New York: National Psychological Association for Psychoanalysis, 1972), p. 36.
6. Knowles, *A Separate Peace*, p. 119.
7. Ibid., p. 77.
8. Knowles, *Peace Breaks Out*, p. 65.
9. Erwin Panofsky, "On Movies," in *Film and the Liberal Arts*, ed. T. J. Ross (New York: Holt, Rinehart, and Winston, 1970), p. 379.
10. Knowles, *A Separate Peace*, p. 45.
11. Roy Huss and Norman Silverstein, *The Film Experience* (New York: Harper and Row, 1968), p. 117.
12. Knowles, *A Separate Peace*, p. 43.
13. Ibid., p. 54.
14. Ibid., p. 57.
15. Ibid., p. 77.
16. Ibid., p. 62.
17. *Harper's Bazaar* 105 (October 1972): 141.
18. T. S. Eliot, "Hamlet and His Problems," *Selected Essays of T. S. Eliot* (New York: Harcourt, Brace and Company, 1950), pp. 124–25.
19. This is the subtitle of his book *Theory of Film* (New York: Oxford University Press, 1965).
20. *Each other* (Israel, 1979), directed by Michal Bat-adam.

Chapter 6: Film Images as Symbols of Alienation

1. *David and Lisa* (U.S. 1962), produced by Paul M. Heller and directed by Frank Perry.
2. *The Happiness of Us Alone* (Japan, 1961), written and directed by Zenzo Matsuyama.
3. Theodor Isaac Rubin, *Jordi/Lisa and David* (New York: Ballantine Books, 1962).
4. Personal communication from Lee Beltzer, based on a conversation with Howard Da Silva.
5. In this aspect of character delineation, Perry took her cues from the novella upon whch her screenplay is based.
6. Stanley Kauffmann, *The New Republic*, Jan. 4, 1960, p. 7.
7. In this respect the film sequence is a perfect expression of the novelist's intention. Theodor Rubin writes: "Then her hand seemed to be separated from the rest of her. It was as if it had a life of its own. She regarded it in a detached way—but at the same time concentrated on it so that it absorbed her completely.

   "It lightly touched her hair and mussed it up in an almost affectionate way. Then it traced the outlines of her nose and mouth almost as a blind person would." *Jordi/Lisa and David*, p. 103.
8. Edward T. Hall, *The Hidden Dimension* (New York: Anchor Books, 1969), p. 150.
9. As Hall points out, the Japanese sense of intimate distance is also more intense than we expect, as is borne out in the film *Woman in the Dunes*, in which the surfaces of the body are almost microscopically examined by the camera (p. 151).
10. Erwin Panofsky, "On Movies," in T. J. Ross, ed., *Film and the Liberal Arts*, p. 379.

Chapter 7: Social Drama as Veiled Neurosis

1. John Osborne, *Look Back in Anger* (London: Faber and Faber, 1957), p. 2.
2. Ibid., p. 72.
3. Ibid., p. 68.
4. Ibid., p. 76.
5. This phrase was coined by Edmund Bergler. For a detailed explanation of the origin and development of this rather common neurosis see his book *The Basic Neurosis* (New York: Grune and Stratton, 1949). The subsequent discussion is a summary of Bergler's concepts.
6. Bergler speculated that a third choice is even more inevitable: that the phobicly regarded breast of the woman will be "safely" displaced to the penis of another man and that the preferred object choice will therefore most likely be an orally tinged homosexual one. See his *Homosexuality: Disease or Way of Life?* (New York: Hill and Wang, 1956). Although there is some indication in the play that Jimmy's relationship with Cliff may be latently homosexual, the evidence seems too scanty to provide a valid contextual interpretation.
7. This is also Bergler's phrase. Its appropriateness here is easily seen in the following exchange in the play: Cliff: "You look for trouble, don't you?" Jimmy: "Only because I'm pretty certain of finding it" (p. 36); or: Jimmy: "There are cruel steel traps lying about everywhere, just waiting for other mad, slightly satanic, and very timid little animals. Right?"(*Look Back in Anger*, p. 77.)
8. Osborne directs these same baseless charges against the female in other plays. In *The World of Paul Slickey* (London: Faber and Faber, 1959) he has his protagonist, Jack, complain without provocation, "We're all being slowly deflowered—deflowered by the female!... crawling and cringing before the almighty tyranny of the bosom (p. 75).
9. Osborne, *Look Back in Anger*, p. 30.

10. Ibid., p. 76.
11. Ibid., p. 48.
12. *Servante et maîtress* (France, 1977), directed by Bruno Gantillon, starring Victor Lanoux and Andrea Ferreol, based on Henri Raynal's 1957 novel *Aux pieds d'Omphale.*
13. "Preface to *Poems*, 1853," *The Portable Matthew Arnold* (New York: Viking 1949), p. 187. See also my discussion of the meaning of catharsis in Freudian aesthetics in chapter 1.

Chapter 8: Humanistic Fiction as Inarticulate Feeling

1. Avraham Yarmolinsky, ed., *The Portable Chekhov* (New York: Viking Press, 1968) p. 24.
2. Ibid., p. 23.
3. Francis Fergusson, *The Idea of a Theater* (New York: Anchor Books, 1953), p. 175.
4. Anton Chekhov, "Misery" (1895), in *The Modern Tradition*, 2d ed., edited by D. F. Howard (Boston: Little, Brown, 1972).
5. Sigmund Freud, "Mourning and Melancholia" (1917), *Standard Edition*, 14: 243.
6. Martha Wolfenstein, "How Is Mourning Possible?" *The Psychoanalytic Study of the Child* 21 (1966): 93.
7. Anton Chekhov, "Rothschild's Fiddle" (1893), in D. F. Howard, ed.
8. I. Glick, *The First Year of Bereavement* (New York: Wiley, 1974), p. 6. See also Freud's "Mourning and Melancholia," p. 166.
9. Glick, "First year," p. 7.
10. Chekhov, "Misery," p. 140.
11. Ibid., p. 137.
12. George Pollack, "Mourning and Adaptation," *International Journal of Psycho-Analysis* 42 (1961): 341-61.
13. Chekhov, "Misery," p. 140.
14. Ibid.
15. Ibid., p. 141.
16. Ibid., p. 137.
17. Ibid., p. 139.
18. Sigmund Freud, "Group Psychology and the Analysis of the Ego" (1921), *Standard Edition*, 18: 117.
19. Chekhov, "Misery," p. 139.
20. Ibid., p. 141.
21. Ibid., p. 139.
22. Ibid., p. 140.
23. Ibid.
24. Joseph Smith, "On the Work of Mourning," in *Bereavement, Its Psychosocial Aspects*, ed. B. Schoenberg (New York: Columbia University Press, 1975), p. 19.
25. Chekhov, "Rothschild's Fiddle," p. 147.
26. Ibid., p. 143.
27. See Otto Fenichel, *The Psychoanalytic Theory of Neurosis* (New York: Norton, 1945), p. 394. Joseph Smith, "Work of Mourning," p. 21, describes this process in a similar way.
28. Chekhov, "Misery," p. 141.
29. Edith Jacobson, "On Normal and Pathological Moods," *The Psychoanalytic Study of the Child* 12 (1957): 89.
30. Pollack, "Mourning and Melancholia," p. 252.

Chapter 9: Searches for Identity in a Prototypal Tale

1. Arthur S. Peake, ed., *A Commentary on the Bible* (London: Thomas Nelson and Sons, 1937), p. 735.
2. Fergusson, *Idea of a Theater*, p. 175.
3. See Richard Helgerson's *The Elizabethan Prodigals* (Berkeley: University of California Press, 1976), p. 3.
4. Northrop Frye, *A Natural Perspective: The Development of Shakespearean Comedy and Romance* (London: Methuen, 1965), chap. 3.
5. St. John Hankin, "The Return of the Prodigal," in *Edwardian Plays*, ed. Gerald Weales (New York: Hill and Wang, 1962), p. 112.
6. Robert Louis stevenson, *The Master of Ballantrae*.
7. This is a classic defense outlined by Anna Freud (see her *The Ego and the Mechanisms of Defense* [New York: International Universities Press, 1966], pp. 109–21) in which the ego can, by identifying with a strong, commanding figure, steel itself against both assaults from without and impulses from within.
8. Alfred Adler was the first to elaborate upon the "dethroning" urges of the second-born in his theories of birth order. A good summary of his theories is presented in Lewis Way's *Adler's Place in Psychology* (New York: Collier, 1962), pp. 30 ff.
9. André Gide, "The Return of the Prodigal Son," in *The André Gide Reader*, ed. David Littlejohn (New York: Knopf, 1971), p. 384.
10. Thomas Cordle in his *André Gide* (New York: Twayne, 1969), p. 84.
11. *André Gide Reader*, p. 392.
12. C. G. Jung associates the rescuer-redeemer swineherd of numerous fairy tales with the Prodigal Son swineherd of the parable. He relates them both to the archetypal redeemer in alchemy "who delivers the evil spirit from the divine punishment meted out to him." See C. G. Jung, *The Archetype and the Collective Unconscious*, in *Collected Works*, (Princeton, N.J.: Princeton University Press, 1959), 9: 249.
13. G. B. Shaw, *Major Barbara*, Act 1, p. 211, in *English Drama in Transition*, ed. Henry F. Solerno (New York: Pegasus, 1968).
14. Ibid., pp. 209 and 255.
15. For a full discussion of this play as a drama of internalized maternal imagos, see Alan Roland's "Pinter's *Homecoming*: Imagos in Dramatic Action," *The Psychoanalytic Review* 61 (Fall 1974): 415–27.
16. Quoted from an interview with Ed Bullins in *Ebony* (September 1968) by Stanley Clayes and David Spencer, eds., in their *Contemporary Drama: Thirteen Plays* (New York: Scribners, 1970), p. 495.
17. Ed Bullins, *A Son, Come Home*, in Clayes and Spencer, eds., p. 496.
18. Ibid., p. 501.
19. In Rainer Maria Rilke, *The Notebooks of Malte Laurids Brigge*, trans. M. D. Herter Norton (New York: W. W. Norton, 1949). The Prodigal Son episode occurs in the concluding seven pages of the book, pp. 210–16.
20. Ibid., p. 213.
21. Ibid., p. 212.
22. Ibid., p. 211.
23. Ibid.
24. Ibid. Compare Gide's walled garden and fountain as a stifling, but less threatening architectural image of personal ego boundaries.
25. Ibid., p. 212.
26. Ibid., pp. 30–31.
27. Ibid., p. 31.
28. Ibid., p. 210. Albert Rothenberg in his "Process of Janusian Thinking in Creativity,"

Archives of General Psychiatry 24 (1971), characterizes the ability of poets to conceptualize such multidirectional action, and to form metaphors to represent them, "Janusian thinking," and a function of secondary rather than primary-process thinking, even though it might have similarities even to autistic and psychotic states of mentation. However, in Rilke's case the process seems to be more one of anti-disintegration than the integrative activity of the "healthier" writers Rothenberg had in mind.

29. Rilke, *The Notebooks*, p. 211.
30. Ibid., p. 212.
31. Ibid.
32. Ibid., p. 213.
33. A full account of all my reasons for diagnosing Rilke as a borderline personality, or worse still, possibly as an ambulatory schizophrenic, would carry me beyond my present purpose. However, I refer the reader to authors like Otto Kernberg, whose description of splitting mechanisms as well as of other defensive maneuvers like primitive idealization and omnipotence, fit many of the experiences recorded by Rilke in *The Notebooks*, in the letters, and in the poems. Many of these mental events obviously indicate, as Kernberg says, "generalized fragmentation of intrapsychic experiences and interpersonal relations" that protect the borderline "from total loss of ego-boundaries and dreaded fusion experiences with others...." (*Borderline Conditions and Pathological Narcissism*, [New York; Aronson, 1975], p. 179).

Donald Burnham's way of characterizing the schizophrenic's overvaluation of the effect of physical objects in the surroundings are strongly suggestive of Rilke's poetic style:

The incidental flight of a passing bird, or the shape of a twig in the gutter, may become powerful omens that the person perceives as controlling his feelings and impulses. "Varieties of Reality Restructuring in Schizophrenia," in *The Schizophrenic Reactions*, ed. Robert Cancro (New York: Brunner/Mazel, 1970), p. 200.

Even though one may argue that such intensification of imagery is characteristic also of many "healthy" poets, Rilke's tone always indicates that he relies on it to solve a crisis of sanity. A good example of this in *The Notebooks* is his speculation about the form and movement of the lid of a cannister dropped by the never-seen medical student in the apartment next door:

Now, that is the whole story: a tin object of the kind fell in the next room, rolled, lay still, and, in between, at certain intervals, stamping could be heard. Like all noises that impose themselves by repetition, this also had its internal organization; it ran its whole gamut, never exactly the same. But it was just this precisely which spoke for its lawfulness. It could be violent or mild or melancholy....(p. 154)

Gradually he identifies the sound with a "failure of will" on the part of the student—an obvious projection of his own state. Erich Simenauer's psychological study of Rilke published in 1953, *Rainer Maria Rilke, Legende und Mythos*, diagnosed him as a "compulsive neurotic with aspects of paranoia and hypochondria" (quoted in Frank Wood, *The Ring of Forms*, [New York: Octagon, 1958], p. 91). I would agree with the description of symptoms, but since they serve to ward off disintegration rather than preserve repression, I can not term them "neurotic."

34. Ibid., p. 218.
35. Ibid., p. 215.
36. In 1911, only one year after the publication of *The Notebooks,* Rilke wrote in despair

to Lou Andreas-Salome that he didn't know

> whether he [Malte], who is in part compounded of my own dangers, perishes in order to keep me, as it were, from perishing; or whether I have only now, with these notes, really got into the current that will sweep me away and dash me to pieces. Can you understand that this book has left me stranded like a survivor, my soul in a maze, with no occupation, never to be occupied again? The nearer I approached the end the more strongly did I feel that it would mean an indescribable cleavage, a high watershed, as I always told myself; but now it is clear that all water has flowed towards the old side and that I am going down into a parched land that grows no different. (Quoted in Frank Wood, *Rainer Maria Rilke: The Ring of Forms* [New York: Octagon, 1958], p. 97.)

37. For a good summary of Margaret Mahler's view, upon which my own précis is based, see Gertrude and Rubin Blanck, *Ego Psychology: Theory and Practice* (New York: Columbia University Press, 1974), chap. 4.
38. Rilke, *The Notebooks*, p. 210.
39. Ibid., p. 212.
40. Ibid., p. 215.
41. Otto Fenichel, in his classic work *The Psychoanalytic Theory of Neurosis* (New York: Norton, 1945), cites a poem by Rilke in which the poet develops a similar self-restorative fantasy about God. He himself feels "weak, helpless, and nothing," but by making God a "powerful partner," he reverses the dependency and causes God's self-actualization to be dependent upon himself. "Whereas one is actually dependent on the partner," says Fenichel, "the partner in turn is thought to be magically dependent upon oneself" (pp. 353–54).

    Although Fenichel diagnoses the mental state that prompts this attitude as a "neurosis of extreme sexual submissiveness," it is obvious from the work of later object-relations theorists that this is a symbiotic disturbance centered in problems of fusion and separation.
42. Compare the use of hand imagery in *David and Lisa* and in *The Happiness of Us Alone*, as discussed in chap. 6.

    In *Brother Son, Sister Moon*, feet imagery is almost as important as the imagistic use of hands. The close-ups of Francis's bare feet in the snow as he reconstructs the church and moves over hard rocks are in startling contrast to the sight of the elegant slippers of the Pope (Alec Guinness) moving down the enormous Byzantine stairs at the Vatican.
43. See chap. 3 above.
44. Christopher Lasch was essentially correct for taking Morris Dickstein to task for supposing the youthful rebellions of the sixties to be mainly oedipal rather than "narcissistic" and therefore *pre*-oedipal. See his review of *The Gates of Eden* in *The New York Review of Books*, October 12, 1979, pp. 31–32.

Appendix A: Images of the Mind in Theater and Film

1. See Heinz Kohut, *The Restoration of the Self* (New York: International Universities Press, 1977), pp. 252–61.
2. Christopher Lasch, *The Culture of Narcissism* (New York: W. W. Norton, 1979).
3. Sigmund Freud, "Some Character-Types," p. 171.
4. Joseph Blumenthal, "*Macbeth* into *Throne of Blood*," in *Film and the Liberal Arts*, ed. T. J. Ross (New York: Holt, Rinehart and Winston, 1970), pp. 107–12.

Appendix B: The "Complexes" of Art

1. Leland E. Hinsie and Robert J. Campbell, eds., *Psychiatric Dictionary*, 4th ed. (New York: Oxford University Press, 1970), p. 144, col. 1.
2. Ibid., p. 146, col. 1
3. Freud, "The Theme of the Three Caskets," *Character and Culture*, p. 77.
4. See Rudolf Kausen, "Laius Complex and Mother-Child Symbiosis," *Journal of Individual Psychology* 28 (1972): 33–37. See also Kausen's follow-up discussion, "More on the Laius Complex," *Journal of Individual Psychology* 29 (1973): 88–91. Still another enlightening commentary on this complex is contained in T. S. Vernon, "The Laius Complex," *Humanist* 32 (1972): 27–28. The first discussion of the Laius Complex seems to have occurred in G. H. Graber's "The Son-Complex of the Father," *Der Psychologe* 4 (1952).
5. *Psychiatric Dictionary*, p. 144, col. 1.
6. Ibid., p. 145, col. 2. See also N. N. Dracoulides, "The Genealogies of the Sons of Atreus and the Orestes Myth: Introduction to the Study of the Orestes Complex," *Psyché-Paris* 7 (1952): 805–17.
7. Ibid., p. 143, col. 2. Ernest Jones believes that this situation is so strongly charged with affect because it revives the father's earlier felt Oedipus Complex, in which another love object was also lost.
8. Arpad Pauncz, "Psychopathology of Shakespeare's *King Lear*: Exemplification of the Lear Complex," *American Imago* 9 (1952): 57–78. Other important discussions of this complex are to be found in Pauncz's "The Lear Complex in World Literature," *American Imago* 11 (1954): 51–83; in Richard J. Jaarsma, "The 'Lear Complex' in *Two Gentlemen of Verona*," *Literature and Psychology* 22 (1972): 199–202; and in F. L. Lucas, *Literature and Psychology* (Ann Arbor: University of Michigan Press, 1957), pp. 63–66.
9. Nevertheless, the Medea Complex still survives in clinical descriptions and often includes more of the basic part of the myth: the hatred of the husband by the wife and her aversion to having children. The syndrome of symptoms stemming from the Medea Complex has been elaborated upon by E. S. Stern: "Pain in sexual intercourse (out of fear of pregnancy), prevention or interruption of pregnancy, unwillingness to breast-feed, and general, unfocused signs of marital discord" ("The Medea Complex," *Journal of Medical Science* [1948], p. 321). In reality this version of the Medea Complex harks back to the pre-Oedipal, for it is obvious from the syndrome that the wife is unconsciously acting out a form of sibling rivalry for oral supplies that are in too limited supply from the detested husband.
10. N. D. C. Lewis, "The Psychology of the Castration Reaction," *Psychoanalytic Review* 15 (1928): 174.
11. *Psychiatric Dictionary*, p. 143, col. 1.
12. Fenichel, *The Psychoanalytic Theory of Neurosis*, p. 347.
13. Sigmund Freud, "The Taboo of Virginity" (1918), *Collected Papers* (New York: Basic Books, 1959), 4: 217–35.
14. Karl Gumpertz, "The Judith Complex: Attempt at an Analysis of Hebbel's *Judith* and Flaubert's *Salammbo*," *Zeitschrift fur Sexualwissenschaft* 14 (1927): 289–301.
15. Sigmund Freud, "The Group and the Primal Horde," *Group Psychology,* pp. 122–29.
16. *Psychiatric Dictionary*, p. 143, col. 1.
17. In some societies, a woman's marriage to an in-law, especially to a brother-in-law, would be considered incest, even though there would be no blood ties involved. This was the case in England, for example, until very recently. Hamlet's objection to his

mother's marrying his father's brother, Claudius, is in part an incest-horror based on this concept.

18. *Psychiatric Dictionary*, p. 142, col. 2.
19. Lucas, *Literature and Psychology*, p. 76.
20. Argus Campbell, "The Cory Complex," *Psychology Today* (August 1976), pp. 72–76.
21. Fenichel, *Psychoanalytic Theory*, p. 221.
22. Leo Katz, "The Rumpelstiltskin Complex," *Contemporary Psychoanalysis* 10 (January 1974): 117–24.
23. See Sandor Ferenczi, *Further Contributions to the Theory and Technique of Psycho-Analysis* (London: The Institute of Psycho-Analysis, 1926), and Maryse Choisy, *The Ring of Polycrates* (Paris: L'Arche, n.d.).
24. Lewis Feuer, "Karl Marx and the Promethean Complex," *Encounter* 31 (December 1968): 15–32.
25. See H. A. Murray, "American Icarus," in *Clinical Studies in Personality*, ed. A. Burton and R. E. Harris New York: Harper, 1955), 2: 615–41. Of further interest are Daniel M. Ogilvie's "The Icarus Complex," *Psychology Today* 2 (December 1968): 31 ff., and Michael Sperber's "Camus' *The Fall*: The Icarus Complex," *American Imago* 26 (1969): 269–80.
26. Sigmund Freud, "The Acquisition of Power Over Fire" (1932), *Character and Culture*, p. 299.
27. *Psychiatric Dictionary*, p. 143, col. 1. My own observations on Oedipus's clever use and mastery of oratory to compensate for his lameness are relevant to this complex ("Adler, Oedipus, and the Tyranny of Weakness," *Psychoanalytic Review* 60 [Summer 1973]: 277–95).
28. *Psychiatric Dictionary*, p. 146, col. 1.
29. Sigmund Freud, "Some Character-Types Met With in Psychoanalytic Work" (1916), *Character and Culture*, pp. 158–62.
30. Louis Birner, "The Horatio Complex," unpublished manuscript.
31. Peter A. Martin, "A Psychoanalytic Study of the Marschallin Theme from *Der Rosenkavalier*," *Journal of the American Psychoanalytic Association* 14 (1966): 760–74.
32. Russell Trainer, *The Lolita Complex* (New York: Citadel Press, 1966), p. 61.
33. Sigmund Freud, *The Ego and the Id* (1923), in *Standard Edition*, 19: 48–59.
34. Maryse Choisy, "Le Complex de Phaeton," *Psyché-Paris* 5 (1950): 770–76.
35. Fenichel, *Psychoanalytic Theory*, pp. 399–400.
36. Peter Castelnuovo-Tedesco, "Stealing, Revenge, and the Monte Cristo Complex," *International Journal of Psychoanalysis* 55 (1974), pt. 2: 169–81.
37. *Psychiatric Dictionary*, p. 637, col. 1.
38. D. McClelland, "The Harlequin Complex," in *The Study of Lives*, ed. Robert White (New York: Atherton Press, 1963), pp. 94–119.

Bibliography

PRIMARY SOURCES

Fiction

Chekhov, Anton. "Misery" (1895) and "Rothschild's Fiddle" (1893). In *The Modern Tradition*. 2d ed. Edited by D. F. Howard. Boston: Little, Brown, 1972.

Gide, André. "The Return of the Prodigal Son." In *The André Gide Reader*. Edited by David Littlejohn. New York: Alfred Knopf, 1971.

Grimm, Jacob, and Grimm, Ludwig. *Grimms' Fairy Tales*. New York: Pantheon Books, 1944.

Hall, Richard. *Couplings*. San Francisco: Grey Fox Press, 1981.

James, Henry. *Selected Short Stories of Henry James*. New York: Viking, 1957.

Knowles, John. *Peace Breaks Out*. New York: Holt, Rinehart, and Winston, 1981.

_____. *Phineas*: *Six Stories*. New York: Random House, 1953.

_____. *A Separate Peace*. New York: Bantam, 1972.

Lawrence, D. H. "The Prussian Officer." *In Modern Tradition*. 2d ed. Edited by D. F. Howard. Boston: Little, Brown, 1972.

Parables of the Lost Sheep, the Lost Coin, and the Prodigal Son. Luke 15: 3–32. *The Holy Bible*. Revised Standard Edition. New York: Meridian Books, 1962.

Rilke, Rainer Maria. *The Notebooks of Malte Laurids Brigge*. Translated by M. D. Herter. Norton. New York: W. W. Norton, 1949.

Rubin, Theodor Isaac. *Jordi/Lisa and David*. New York: Ballantine Books, 1962.

Stevenson, Robert Louis. *The Master of Ballantrae*. New York: E. P. Dutton, 1932.

Plays

Bullins, Ed. *A Son, Come Home*. In *Contemporary Drama*: *Thirteen Plays*. Edited by Stanley Clayes and David Spencer. New York: Scribners, 1970.

Hankin, St. John. *The Return of the Prodigal*. In *Edwardian Plays*. Edited by Gerald Weales. New York: Hill and Wang, 1962.

Osborne, John. *Look Back in Anger*. London: Faber and Faber, 1957.

_____. *The World of Paul Slickey*. London: Faber and Faber, 1959.

Pinter, Harold. *The Homecoming*. New York: Grove Press, 1965.

Shaw, George Bernard. *Major Barbara*. In *English Drama in Transition*. Edited by Henry F. Salerno. New York: Pegasus, 1968.

Sophocles. *The Oedipus Plays of Sophocles*. Translated and edited by Paul Roche. New York: New American Library, 1958.

_____. *Oedipus the King*. Translated by Thomas Gould. Englewood Cliffs, N.J.: Prentice-Hall, 1970.

_____. *Oedipus Rex*. Translated by Albert Cook. In *Oedipus Rex: A Mirror for Greek Drama*. Edited by Albert Cook. Belmont, Calif.: Wadsworth, 1963.

Williams, Tennessee. *Kirche, Kutchen, und Kinder*. Performed by the Jean Cocteau Repertory Company at the Bouwerie Lane Theatre in New York City from September 1979 through January 1980.

Films

Brother Sun, Sister Moon (Italy, 1973). Directed by Franco Zeffirelli. Co-written by Lina Wertmuller. Starring Alec Guinness, Graham Faulkner, Judi Bowker, and Valentina Cortese.

David and Lisa (United States, 1962). Produced by Paul M. Heller. Directed by Frank Perry. Written by Eleanor Perry. Starring Janet Margolin, Keir Dullea, and Howard Da Silva.

Each Other (Israel, 1979). Directed and written by Michal Bat-Adam. Produced by Moshe Misrahi. In Hebrew and French.

The Happiness of Us Alone (Japan, 1961). Written and directed by Zenzo Matsuyama. Starring Hideko Takamine, Keiju Kobayashi, and Yuzo Kayama.

Maid and Mistress (see *Servante et maîtresse*).

A Separate Peace (United States, 1972). Directed by Larry Peerce. Starring Parker Stevenson, John Heyl, and William Roerick.

Servante et maîtresse (*Maid and Mistress*) (France, 1977). Directed by Bruno Gantillon. Starring Victor Lanoux add Andrea Fereol. Based on Henri Raynal's 1957 novel *Aux pieds d' Omphale*.

Throne of Blood (Japan, 1957). Directed by Akira Kurosawa. Starring Toshiro Mifune and Isuzu Yamada.

SECONDARY SOURCES

Adler, Alfred. *The Individual Psychology of Alfred Adler*. Edited by Hans L. and Rowena R. Ansbacher. New York: Harper and Row, 1964.

Arnold, Matthew. *The Portable Matthew Arnold*. New York: Viking, 1949.

Atkins, Frances. "The Social Meaning of the Oedipus Myth." *Journal of Individual Psychology* 23 (1966): 173–84.

Bergler, Edmund. *The Basic Neurosis*. New York: Grune and Stratton, 1949.

————. *Homosexuality*: *Disease or Way of Life*? New York: Hill and Wang, 1956.

————. *1000 Homosexuals*. Paterson, N.J.: Pageant Books, 1959.

Bettelheim, Bruno. *The Uses of Enchantment*: *The Meaning and Importance of Fairy Tales*. New York: Alfred A. Knopf, 1976.

Birner, Louis. "The Horatio Complex." Unpublished paper.

Blos, Peter. "The Genealogy of the Ego Ideal." *The Psychoanalytic Study of the Child* 20 (1965): 119–27.

————. *On Adolescence*. New York: The Free Press, 1962.

Blumenthal, Joseph. "*Macbeth* into *Throne of Blood*." In *Film and the Liberal Arts*. Edited by T. J. Ross. New York: Holt, Rinehart, and Winston, 1970.

Burnham, Donald. "Varieties of Reality Structuring in Schizophrenias" In *The Schizophrenic Reactions*. New York: Brunner/Mazel, 1970.

Campbell, Angus. "The Cory Complex." *Psychology Today*, (August 1976), pp. 72–76.

Castelnuovo-Tedesco, Peter. "Stealing, Revenge, and the Monte Cristo Complex." *International Journal of Psychoanalysis* 55 (1974), pt. 2: 169–81.

Choisy, Maryse. "Le Complex de Phaeton." *Psyché-Paris* 5 (1950): 770–76.

————. *The Ring of Polycrates*. Paris: L'Arche, n.d.

Cordle, Thomas. *André Gide*. New York: Twayne, 1969.

Crossett, J. "The Oedipus Rex." In *Oedipus Rex*: *A Mirror for Greek Drama*. Edited by Albert Cook. Belmont, Calif.: Wadsworth, 1963.

Dracoulides, N. N. "The Genealogies of the Sons of the Atreus and Orestes Myth: Introduction to the Study of the Orestes Complex." *Psyché-Paris* 7 (1952): 805–17.

Eliot, T. S. "Hamlet and His Problems." *Selected Essays*. New York: Harcourt, Brace and Company, 1950.

Erikson, Erik H. *Childhood and Society*. New York: W. W. Norton, 1950.

Fenichel, Otto. *The Psychoanalytic Theory of Neurosis*. New York: W. W. Norton, 1945.

Ferenczi, Sandor. "The Sons of the 'Tailor'" (1923). *Further contributions to the Theory and Technique of Psycho-Analysis*. New York: Basic Books, 1952.

Fergusson, Francis. *The Idea of a Theatre*. New York: Anchor Books, 1953.

Feuer, Lewis. "Karl Marx and the Promethean Complex." *Encounter* 31 (December 1968): 15–32.

Freud, Anna. *The Ego and the Mechanisms of Defense*. New York: International Universities Press, 1966.

————. *Normality and Pathology in Childhood*: *Assessments of Development*. New York: International Universities Press, 1966.

Freud, Sigmund. "The Acquisition of Power Over Fire" (1932). *Character and Culture*. Edited by Philip Rieff. New York: Collier Books, 1963.

_____. "A Child Is Being Beaten" (1919). *Standard Edition of the Works of Sigmund Freud*. 24 vols. Translated and edited by James Strachey. vol. 17. London: The Hogarth Press, 1955.

_____. "A Childhood Memory from *Dichtung und Wahrheit*" (1917). *Character and Culture*. Edited by Philip Rieff. New York: Collier Books, 1963.

_____. "Family Romances" (1908). *The Sexual Enlightenment of Children*. Edited by Philip Rieff. New York: Collier, 1963.

_____. *Group Psychology and the Analysis of the Ego* (1921). *Standard Edition*. Edited and translated by James Strachey. vol. 18. London: The Hogarth Press, 1955.

_____. "The Interest of Psycho-Analysis from the Point of View of the Science of Aesthetics" (1913). *Standard Edition*. Edited and translated by James Strachey. vol. 13. London: The Hogarth Press, 1955.

_____. *The Interpretation of Dreams* (1900). Edited by James Strachey. New York: Basic Books, 1955.

_____. *Leonardo da Vinci and a Memory of His Childhood* (1910). *Standard Edition*. Edited and translated by James Strachey. vol. 11. London: The Hogarth Press, 1957.

_____. Letter 1 to Wilhelm Fliess on the universality of the Oedipus Complex (1897). *Standard Edition*. Edited and translated by James Strachey. vol. 1. London: The Hogarth Press, 1966.

_____. "The Moses of Michelangelo." (1914). *Character and Culture*. Edited by Philip Rieff. New York: Collier Books, 1963.

_____. "Mourning and Melancholia" (1917). *Standard Edition*. Edited and translated by James Strachey. vol. 14. London: The Hogarth Press, 1957.

_____. "Psychopathic Characters on the Stage" (1905–1906). *Standard Edition*. Edited and translated by James Strachey. Vol. 7. London: The Hogarth Press, 1953.

_____. "The Relation of the Poet to Daydreaming" (1908). *Character and Culture*. Edited by Philip Rieff. New York: Collier Books, 1963.

_____. "The Taboo of Virginity" (1918). *Collected Papers*. vol. 4. New York: Basic Books, 1959.

_____. "The Theme of the Three Caskets" (1913). *Character and Culture*. Edited by Philip Rieff. New York: Collier Books, 1963.

Friedman, Norman. "Psychology and Literary Form: Toward a Unified Approach." *Psychocultural Review* 2 (Spring 1978): 75–95.

Fromm, Erich. *The Forgotten Language*. New York: Grove Press, 1951.

Frye, Northrop. *A Natural Perspective: The Development of Shakespearean Comedy and Romance*. London: Methuen, 1965.

Glick, I. *The First Year of Bereavement*. New York: Wiley, 1974.

Golden, Lester. "Freud's Oedipus: Its Mytho-Dramatic Basis." *American Imago* 24 (1967): 271–82.

Goldsmith, Barbara. "*A Separate Peace*" (film review). *Harper's Bazaar* 105 (October 1972): 141.

Graber, G. H. "The Son-Complex of the Father." *Der Psychologe* 4 (1952): 10–13.

Graves, Robert. *Greek Myths*. 2 vols. Baltimore: Penguin Books, 1955.

Gumpertz, Karl. "The Judith Complex: Attempt at an Analysis of Hebbel's *Judith* and Flaubert's *Salammbo*." *Zeitschrift für Sexualwissenschaft* 14 (1927): 289–301.

Hall, Edward. *The Hidden Dimension*. New York: Anchor Books, 1969.

Helgerson, Richard. *The Elizabethan Prodigals*. Berkeley: University of California Press, 1976.

Hinsie, Leland E., and Campbell, Robert J., eds. *Psychiatric Dictionary*. 4th ed. New York: Oxford University Press, 1970.

Holland, Norman N. *The Dynamics of Literary Response*. New York: Oxford University Press, 1968.

_____. *Poems in Persons: An Introduction to the Psychoanalysis of Literature*. New York: W. W. Norton, 1973.

Horwitz, B. D. "The Sense of Desolation in Henry James." *Psychocultural Review* 1 (Fall 1977): 466–92.

Huss, Roy; Roland, Alan; et al., eds. *Identity, Identification, and Self-Image*. New York: National Psychological Association for Psychoanalysis, 1972.

_____, and Silverstein, Norman. *The Film Experience*. New York: Harper and Row, 1968.

_____, ed. *New Directions in Psychoculture*. A special issue of *Psychocultural Review* 2 (Spring 1978).

Jaarsma, Richard J. "The 'Lear Complex' in *Two Gentlemen of Verona*." *Literature and Psychology* 22 (1972): 199–202.

Jacobson, Edith. "On Normal and Pathological Moods." *The Psychoanalytic Study of the Child* 12 (1957): 86–92.

James, Henry. *The Art of the Novel*. New York: Scribners, 1934.

Jekels, Ludwig. "The Riddle of Shakespeare's Macbeth." *The Psychoanalytic Review* 30 (1943): 51.

Jones, Ernest. *Hamlet and Oedipus*. Garden City, N.Y.: Doubleday Anchor, 1949.

Jung, C. G. *The Archetype and the Collective Unconscious. Collected Works*, vol. 9. Princeton, N.J.: Princeton University Press, 1959.

Katz, Leo. "The Rumpelstiltskin Complex." *Contemporary Psychoanalysis* 10 (January 1974): 117–24.

Kauffmann, Stanley. "On the Spirit of Dance in Film." *The New Republic*, January 4, 1960, p. 7.

Kausen, Rudolf. "Laius Complex and Mother-Child Symbiosis." *Journal of Individual Psychology* 28 (1972): 33–37.

_____. "More on the Laius Complex." *Journal of Individual Psychology* 29 (1973): 88–91.

Kernberg, Otto. *Borderline Conditions and Pathological Narcissism.* New York: Jason Aronson, 1975.

Knox, Bernard. *Oedipus at Thebes.* New Haven, Conn.: Yale University Press, 1957.

Kohut, Heinz. *The Restoration of the Self.* New York: International Universities Press, 1977.

Kracauer, Sigfried. *Theory of Film.* New York: Oxford University Press, 1965.

Laing, R. D. *The Divided Self.* Harmondsworth: Penguin Books, 1965.

Lasch, Christopher. *The Culture of Narcissism.* New York: W. W. Norton, 1979.

_____. Review of Morris Dickstein's *The Gates of Eden. New York Review of Books*, October 12, 1979, pp. 31–32.

Lattimore, Richmond. "The Poetry of Greek Tragedy." In *Oedipus Rex: A Mirror for Greek Drama.* Edited by Albert Cook. Belmont, Calif.: Wadsworth, 1963.

Lewis, N. D. C. "The Psychology of the Castration Reaction." *The Psychoanalytic Review* 15 (1928): 169–78.

Lucas, F. L. *Literature and Psychology.* Ann Arbor: University of Michigan Press, 1957.

McClelland, D. "The Harlequin Complex." In *The Study of Lives.* Edited by Robert White. New York: Atherton Press, 1963. Pp. 94–119.

Mahler, Margaret S. *On Human Symbiosis and the Vicissitudes of Individuation.* New York: International Universities Press, 1968.

Markle, Durwood, Jr. "Freud, Leonardo and the Lamb." *The Psychoanalytic Review* 57 (1970): 285–88.

Martin, Peter. "A Psychoanalytic Study of the Marschallin Theme From *Der Rosenkavalier." Journal of the American Psychoanalytic Association* 14 (1966): 760–74.

Mullahy, Patrick. *Oedipus: Myth and Complex.* New York: Grove Press, 1955.

Murray, H. A. "American Icarus." In *Clinical Studies in Personality.* Edited by A. Burton and R. E. Harris. New York: Harper, 1955), 2: 615–41.

Noy, Pinchas. "Form Creation in Art: An Ego-Psychological Approach to Creativity." *Psychoanalytic Quarterly* 48 (1979): 229–56.

Oates, Joyce Carol. Letter to Roy Huss, June 22, 1973.

Ogilvie, Daniel M. "The Icarus Complex." *Psychology Today* 2 (December 1968): 31–37, 108.

Osborne, John. *A Better Class of Person.* New York: E. P. Dutton, 1981.

Panken, Shirley. *The Joy of Suffering.* New York: Jason Aronson, 1973.

Panofsky, Erwin. "On Movies." In *Film and the Liberal Arts*. Edited by T. J. Ross. New York: Holt, Rinehart, and Winston, 1970.

Paunz, Arpad. "Psychopathology of Shakespeare's *King Lear*: Exemplification of the Lear Complex." *American Imago* 11 (1954): 51–83.

Peake, Arthur S., ed. *A Commentary on the Bible*. London: Thomas Nelson and Sons, 1937.

Pollack, George. "Mourning and Adaptation." *International Journal of Psycho-Analysis* 42 (1961): 341–46.

Rank, Otto. *The Myth of the Birth of the Hero*. New York; Vintage Books, 1959.

Roland, Alan. "Pinter's *Homecoming*: Images in Dramatic Action." *The Psychoanalytic Review* 61 (Fall 1974): 415–27.

Rose, Gilbert. *The Power of Form*. New York: International Universities Press, 1980.

Rothenberg, Albert. "Process of Janusian Thinking in Creativity." *Archives of General Psychiatry* 24 (1971): 168–75.

Schafer, Roy. *A New Language for Psychoanalysis*. New Haven, Conn.: Yale University Press, 1977.

Smith, Joseph. "On the Work of Mourning." In *Bereavement, Its Psychosocial Aspects*. Edited by B. Schoenberg. New York: Columbia University Press, 1975.

Sperber, Michael. "Camus' *The Fall*: The Icarus Complex." *American Imago* 26 (1969): 269–80.

Stern, E. S. "The Medea Complex." *Journal of Medical Science* (1948), pp. 320–24.

Vernon, T. S. "The Laius Complex." *Humanist* 32 (1972): 27–28.

Way, Lewis. *Adler's Place in Psychology*. New York: Collier Books, 1962.

Weiss, Samuel A. "Osborne's Angry Young Play." *Educational Theatre Journal* 12 (1960): 285.

Withim, Philip. "The Psychodynamics of Literature." *The Psychoanalytic Review* 56 (1969-70): 556–85.

Wolfenstein, Martha. "How Is Mourning Possible?" *The Psychoanalytic Study of the Child* 21 (1966): 91–97.

Wood, Frank. *The Ring of Forms*. New York: Octagon, 1958.

Wordsworth, William. *Wordsworth's Literary Criticism*. Edited by Nowell C. Smith. London: Humphrey Milford, 1925.

Wyatt, David. *Prodigal Sons: A Study of Authorship and Authority*. Baltimore, Md.: Johns Hopkins University Press, 1980.

Yarmolinsky, Avram, ed. Introduction to *The Portable Chekhov*. New York: Viking, 1968.

Zablotny, Elaine. "Vampire and Madonna in the Early Tales of Henry James." *Psychocultural Review* 3 (Summer/Fall 1979): 203–24.

Index

221

Index

Index 223